CARIBBEAN NEW WAVE
Contemporary Short Stories

Selected by Stewart Brown

HEINEMANN

Heinemann International Literature & Textbooks
a division of Heinemann Educational Books Ltd
Halley Court, Jordan Hill, Oxford OX2 8EJ

Heinemann Educational Books Inc
361 Hanover St, Portsmouth, New Hampshire, 03801, USA

Heinemann Educational Books (Nigeria) Ltd
PMB 5205, Ibadan
Heinemann Kenya Ltd
Kijabe Street, PO Box 45314, Nairobi
Heinemann Educational Boleswa
PO Box 10103, Village Post Office, Gaborone, Botswana
Heinemann Publishers (Caribbean) Ltd
175-9 Mountain View Avenue, Kingston 6, Jamaica

OXFORD   LONDON   EDINBURGH
MADRID   PARIS   ATHENS   BOLOGNA
MELBOURNE   SYDNEY   AUCKLAND   SINGAPORE
TOKYO   HARARE   PORTSMOUTH (NH)

Series editor Adewale Maja-Pearce

British Library Cataloguing in Publication Data

New Wave
1. Short stories in English. Caribbean Writers, 1945–
Anthologies
I. Brown, Stewart, 1951–   II. Series
823′ .01′0891821 [FS]

ISBN 0–435–98814–X

Photoset by Wilmaset, Birkenhead, Wirral
Printed and bound in Great Britain by
Cox and Wyman Ltd, Reading, Berkshire

90 91 92 93 94 10 9 8 7 6 5 4 3 2

CONTENTS

ACKNOWLEDGEMENTS

F B André for *Bienvenue au Canada*; James Berry and Dieter Klein Associates, London, for *Miss Dorcas*; Neil Bissoondath, André Deutch Ltd, London and Macmillan, Canada, for *Insecurity* © 1984 from 'Digging Up The Mountains' (Penguin, 1986); Wayne Brown for *Independence Day* © Wayne Brown 1990; Faustin Charles for *Signpost of the Phoenix*; Curtis Brown and John Farquharson, London and Earl Lovelace, for *Shoemaker Arnold* from 'A Brief Conversion' (Heinemann 1988); Cyril Dabydeen for *Mammita's Garden Cove* from 'Still Close to the Island' (Commoners' Publishing, Ottawa, 1980); Zoila Ellis and Cubola Productions, Belize, for *White Christmas an' Pink Jungle* from 'On Heroes, Lizards and Passions' (Cubola Productions, 1988); Farrar, Straus & Giroux, Inc, New York, and Pan Books Ltd, London, for *My Mother* from 'At the Bottom of the River' by Jamaica Kincaid. Copyright © 1983 by Jamaica Kincaid. Reprinted by permission of Farrar, Straus & Giroux, Inc; Hansib Publishing Ltd for *The Stickfighter*, © Willi Chen 1988, first published in 'King of the Carnival and Other Stories' in 1988 by Hansib Publishing Ltd, Tower House, 139–149 Fonthill Road, London, N4 3HF; Clyde Hosein for *The Man at the Gate of the House of Refuge* (The Literary Magazine of Barbados); Amryl Johnson for *Yardstick* © Amryl Johnson 1990; Kelsey Street Press, Berkeley and Collins, London, for *Duppy Get Her* from 'Bake-Face and Other Guava Stories' by Palmer Adisa (Kelsey St. Press, 1986); John Robert Lee for *The Coming of Org* © John Robert Lee, first published in 'The New Voices', Diego Martin, Trinidad & Tobago, 1983; Longman Group Ltd, Harlow, for *Bella Makes Life* by Lorna Goodison from 'Baby Mother and the King of Swords' (Longman Caribbean Writers Series – to be published 1990), and *The Two Grandmothers* by Olive Senior from 'Arrival of the Snake Woman and Other Stories' (Longman Caribbean Writers Series 1989); Ian McDonald for *The Duel in Mercy Ward*; Earl McKenzie for *Fear of the Sea* © Earl McKenzie 1990; Peepal Tree Press, Leeds, for *The Maid in Bel Air* by Jan Shinebourne from 'Wasafiri', and for *Bahadar* by Rooplall Monar from 'Backdam People' (Peepal Tree Press, 1985); Savacou Publications Ltd, Jamaica, for *The Thursday Wife* from 'Woman's Tongue' by Hazel D Campbell (Savacou Publications Ltd, 1985); Lawrence Scott and Chelsea, New York, for *King Sailor One J'Ouvert Morning* © Lawrence Scott 1990, first published in 1987; The Women's Press for *My Mother* from 'Considering Women' by Velma Pollard, published by The Women's Press, London, 1989.

INTRODUCTION

Most of the writers represented in this anthology were unknown ten years ago and even those who have made international reputations – James Berry, Jamaica Kincaid, Earl Lovelace, Olive Senior – have essentially done so in the last decade. This collection of stories provides the reader with a sampler of the energy, commitment and style of a whole new wave of Caribbean writing. The authors represented here have built on the achievements of the writers of the 1950s and 60s but have found that the short story provides the ideal 'way of saying' for their particular concerns and enables them to reach an audience that neither the novel nor the poem can address.

All these stories are grounded in the lived experience of the contemporary Caribbean. Many of them first appeared in regional newspapers or magazines, while others are taken from locally published collections hardly distributed outside the region. Another group of stories are, as it were, messages 'sent back' from writers based overseas, mostly Canada these days, serving both a West Indian and an 'exile' community. But primarily all these authors are writing to be read in the Caribbean, where they were born, where all these stories are set; they assume an audience and a cultural domain that permits them to *intervene* – in all the subtle and complex ways that only literature can – in the ongoing process of shaping the mores and values of Caribbean societies. That earlier generation of writers, for all the quality of their writing and the depth of their commitment to the Caribbean, were never really able to achieve that status *within* the West Indies.

That is not to imply, though, that the themes which dominate the work of contemporary West Indian writers are essentially very much different from those of their predecessors: in this anthology there are stories that deal with race and the legacies of history, with issues of identity and culture, with economic poverty and the cruelties it breeds, and with the tensions between country and city, between young and old, between men and women – the heartland concerns of Caribbean literature. But reading through it again for this Introduction, really for the first time as a collection, I discern that three aspects of contemporary experience seem to me to dominate the selection and distinguish it from earlier anthologies of West Indian short stories: the emergence of women as both author and subject of so many of these stories; the 'creolisation' of a distinctive Indo-Caribbean consciousness; and what we might call the Caribbean version of the North American dream.

More than a third of the stories in this collection are written by women, still short of a 'democratic' representation but, when compared with Andrew Salkey's two major and comprehensive story anthologies of the 60s and 70s in which no women writers appear, that representation suggests the impact that women have had in changing the focus and *voice* of West Indian writing in recent years. And it's remarkable that the nine women's stories in this selection cover such a diversity of the roles that are 'a woman's lot': daughter, granddaughter, friend, lover, wife, mother, grandmother, widow, mistress, servant, higgler, hustler, whether pregnant, menopausal, child-worn or child-free-and-independent . . . Few of the female characters in these stories are in any sense 'victims' – what characterises them, indeed, is their quest to find ways of being (inside, or by escaping from, their society) that acknowledge their dignity and their potential for self-fulfilment. That shift from perseverance and relative passivity (which, for all the respect with which she was treated, is arguably the 'traditional' view of woman in Caribbean fiction) to ambition and self-assertion is evident in the portraits of women that occur in many of the other stories in the collection too. The disgruntled Zelda in Amryl Johnson's story *Yardstick*, who is so disillusioned by the drudgery of her domestic routine that she abandons her family for a dream of escape in America, is representative of that change of attitude.

The Indo-Caribbean experience has, of course, long been a theme for writers with roots in that distinctive culture – most famously in the work of the Naipauls, Sam Selvon and Ismith Khan. But what their work seems to emphasise is the 'strangeness' of that community in a West Indian context, the exotic 'otherness' of the latecomers to the essentially Afro-European societies that made up the 'English' Caribbean. By contrast, most of the stories that emerge from that experience in this collection suggest the extent to which the Indo-Caribbean dimension is being creolised – or is creolising – as it were, into concerns that span the ethnic divides. Indeed, in a story like Neil Bissoondath's *Insecurity* that process of acculturation is taken one stage further and its inevitability is, perhaps, the point of the story. Even a piece set both in the past and almost entirely among an East Indian community, like Rooplall Monar's *Bahadur*, suggests, in its form, that process of cultural creolisation: Bahadur is a classic Anansi figure, 'cunning and cool', a metaphor retained from West African word-culture and now, perhaps, part of the common stock of Caribbean mythology. The tragic figure of Zakir, in Clyde Hosein's moving story *The Man at the Gate of the House of Refuge*, a man released from a long prison sentence into a world he cannot recognise because those 'traditional' divisions have been so eroded, perhaps best illuminates that shift of perspective.

It is possible to see that blurring of cultural divisions as a measure of the extent to which all the people of the Caribbean have been – more or less subtly – recolonised by America. The Caribbean version of the American dream seems to operate at two levels: on the one hand a concern with the ways that American culture has infiltrated and undermined traditional West Indian ways and values and on the other with the idea/prospect/ambition of escape that the USA and more particularly Canada seems to offer to so many of the characters in these stories. Olive Senior's wry tale *The Two Grandmothers* catches the insidious drift towards the Americanisation of values very effectively. In several other stories the prospect – or just the possibility – of escape from the economic struggles of contemporary Caribbean life to a materially more comfortable existence in North America hypnotises and distorts the values of otherwise conventional characters. Lorna Goodison's Bella 'Makes Life', but at what a price; in F. B. André's story *Bienvenue au Canada* the disgruntled wife of the idealistic young doctor, enduring the discomforts of Guyana, 'always compared how we were living with how we could be living in Canada'. At either level, it seems, the Caribbean version of the North American dream breeds discontent and envy.

Stylistically the collection is surprising, perhaps, for its apparent conservatism, for the continuing dominance of a kind of naturalistic social realism. There are interesting exceptions: Jamaica Kincaid is represented by a very inward magic-realist kind of tale; F. B. André's story is told between the two related narratives of characters on different continents; Faustin Charles brilliantly evokes a carnival psychology through the device of Blake's internal monologue in *Signpost of the Phoenix*. Those few stories apart, I'd suggest that one major reason for the writers' determination to make their stories conventionally 'accessible' is the ambition that I mentioned in my opening paragraph: to address a broad West Indian audience and contribute directly to the wider 'extra-literary' socio-political debates over values, attitudes and ways of life.

Inevitably, in a short collection such as this, authors whose work I admire and would like to have included have had to be omitted. At one end of the time-range there is a group of fine short story writers, including for example Barbadians Austin Clarke, Timothy Callender and John Wickham, who made their reputations in the 70s rather than the 80s and so got squeezed out of this selection; at the other end there are young writers like the Trinidadian Jennifer Rahim, the Barbadian Tony Kellman and the Guyanese Ras Michael Jeune whose best work, one feels, will emerge in the next few years and so, when push came to shove in the squabble for available pages, they also got squeezed out of the selection. It's a brutal job being an anthologist! The stories that survived that winnowing, then, while inevitably a partial and personal selection, make up a collection which, I hope and believe, catches the vigour and spirit of the contemporary Caribbean short story.

STEWART BROWN
Centre of West African Studies,
University of Birmingham.

OPAL PALMER ADISA

Duppy Get Her

Duppy nuh wan yuh drop
  yuh picknie deh, guh home
Duppy nuh wan yuh drop
  yuh picknie deh, guh home
Duppy nuh wan yuh drop
  yuh picknie deh, guh home, gal
tie yuh belly, gal, guh home.

Evening falls like dewdrops on oleander petals glistening under the sun. Oshun, goddess of love, is present, her orange-yellow skirt swaying coquettishly. Mosquitoes are like kiskode petals on skin, blown off by the lax odour whispering mischief in the air. Cane fields rustle in frolic; answered by the evening breeze, they dance the merenge, twirling to giddiness. What are the cane fields saying? What is uttered by the leaves? Listen! Listen – with wide eyes.

Suddenly the murmur of the cane fields – almost hypnotic – forces everyone to look in their direction. Swirling, they sing:

Steal away, steal away;
  duppy gwana get yuh, gal, steal away.
Steal away, steal away;
  duppy a come get yuh, gal, steal away.

The labyrishers – gossipers – do not hear; they don't hear, save one – Lilly.

Lilly cleans house, cooks food, washes clothes, irons and does other domestic chores for her living. She has been since she was sixteen; she is eighteen, now, and with child due any day. She sits with Beatrice, her cousin, also a domestic; with Richard, her baby's father and a pot-boiler at the sugar estate; and with Basil and Errol, two other factory hands. They are gathered together, feeling contented at being their own bosses for at least the next twelve hours.

1

The evening is rare in its simple grace. The sun, sinking beyond the cane fields, dominates the sky. All the land kneels in homage to this god of energy and sustainer of life – fully orange, gigantic and mystic, surrounded by black-purple haze. The clouds stand back, way off in respect. The sun, heedful of his power, gyrates and snarls. Lilly glances at him just as he flaps his ears, emitting fire from his nostrils; she checks her laughter. So awed is she by the sun's fire she scarcely breathes. After some moments, Lilly mumbles: 'Lawd, de sun mitey tonite, sah. Look, im on im way home nuh.' Suddenly, the turning of the child in her belly elicits a laugh that escapes deep from her womb.

Beatrice, seated by her, places her hand on Lilly's stomach, feeling the baby's position. 'Dis a definite boy picknie yuh a guh ave. See how yuh belly pointed and de sonofabitch won gi yuh nuh peace.'

'Im mus tek afta im fada.'

Richard turns away in vexation; he chups, kissing his teeth: 'Is me yuh ave mout fah, nuh? Ooman neba satisfy. Wen dem nuh ave nutten else fi seh, dem chat stupidness.' He moves to leave, but changes his mind; he chups again: 'Nuh boda me backside dis evenin yah, gal, nuh boda me backside.'

The breeze whistles by. The dogs cover their ears in embarrassment, while the frogs exchange glances which ask, 'What's troubling him this nice evening, eh? What's troubling him?' A green lizard in response, croaks; its bulging eyes are lit by the sun. There is silence amidst the gathering of two women and three men – maids, pot-boiler and factory-hands.

Silence dominates but in the undercurrent there is anger mingled with amusement and foreboding. Again, the swishing of the cane fields seems to grab everyone's attention. Lilly is rocking. Suddenly noticing a flock of birds in the sky, she points like an excited child. Again, silence. The sun is almost gone. Lilly sees a star, and thinking it must be the very first one in the sky this evening, she quickly makes a wish, anxious for its fulfilment. She resumes her rocking, forgetting what it was she wished for. A rooster cackles near the barbed wire fence separating them from the canal and the cane field beyond. Two dogs are stuck, one in the other.

Richard picks up a stone, throws it at them; he swears under his breath: 'Damn dog – dem nuh ave nuh shame. Look how much bush bout de place, yet dem a fi come rite inna de open.'

Beatrice snickers. Lilly retorts, 'Nuh eberybode wait till nite fi cova dem act inna de darkness like yuh.'

2

'Ooman, me nuh tell yuh nuh boda me soul-case. If yuh nuh ave nutten fi seh, shet yuh backside.'

Beatrice comments, 'Some people hot tonite, Lawd. Mus all dat boilin molasses. De sweetness keep de heat inna de body.' Again silence. Beatrice fidgets in the chair, which is too small for her large behind. Suddenly, she starts singing, a mischievous smile on her face. Her voice is full and melodious, and her song is aimed at Richard, whom she always provokes to anger:

> *Gentle Jesas, meek an mile,*
> *look upon a trouble man.*
> *Ease im soul an let im rest,*
> *for im is a soul distress.*

Lilly bursts out in loud belly-laughter and Errol and Basil sputter. Richard's colour is rising like the pink of a cat's tongue. Anger is clearly written on his face. A sudden wind blows dirt into Beatrice's eye, putting an end to her song.

Richard keenly observes the little gathering and feels excluded. He looks at the dark bodies, envying them. He is the 'red nega' among them. All during his school days, the boys teased him, saying his mother had slept with a sailor. And even though he knew it wasn't true (although he was the fairest one in his family), he was still always hurt; he didn't care if his great-great-grandfather had married an Irish settler whom he resembled. He wanted to be purple-dark like the rest of them so his face wouldn't turn red like the colour of sorrel fruit whenever he got angry. Staying out in the sun didn't help either; it only made his skin tomato. Lean and muscular, he stood out like a guinep among star-apples.

Lately, however (that is, ever since meeting Lilly not yet twelve months ago), Richard has been relaxed. Lilly, lusted after by all the men, the gentlemen of the community included, chose him. Although every once in a while she teases him about his complexion and stings his hand to see her fingerprints revealed, he knows she cares for him.

Richard doesn't feel like being anyone's beating stick tonight, however. He looks from Lilly, sitting with a smile crowning her face, to Errol and Basil, with mischief twinkling in their eyes, to Beatrice, playing her usual pious role. Richard wants to remind Beatrice of the nightly utterances of her mattress and bedsprings, but he holds his tongue as he isn't sure whether it is Errol or Basil or both who pray to the Lord between her thighs at night. He chuckles, stomping the balls of his feet, and then chups, kissing his teeth, before turning to fidget with his bicycle. 'One of des days oonuh gwane wan fi serious and kyan,' he warns.

Richard catches a glimpse of the sun just before it disappears, and it whispers to him: 'Steal away, steal away – duppy gwane box yuh, duppy nuh like yuh, steal away . . .' He looks over his shoulder to see if anyone else heard. No one did; the group is already on to something else.

The cane fields whimper, swishing to and fro. The evening is alive. All the creatures stop to say their piece. Sparkling fireflies called penewales dart in and out of the darkness; crickets are in argument. Even the water in the canal tastes the omen. It rumbles like a vexed child who is sent to sweep up the dirt and gather leaves; the task adds to the child's vexation when the twirling leaves blind his eyes while playing rounders with the breeze. So is the evening sweet yet wicked – as even the nicest woman can be.

The rustling of the cane fields is louder. Beatrice shivers. Blossoms from the ackee tree fall and the wind takes them, blowing them everywhere. Lilly tries to catch the blossoms, but the movement in her belly stops her. She relaxes and pats her stomach.

Beatrice feels her head growing big; it is a ton of bricks on her body. She rubs her arms, feeling the cold-bumps. Something is going to happen. She looks around at Richard, who is still angry, and Basil and Errol, who are sharing some private joke. Beatrice reaches over and rubs Lilly's belly, feeling the child inside kicking. She is certain it's a boy. Again, the murmur of the cane fields. Beatrice quickly blows into her cupped palms and throws the air over her left shoulder. It is her way of telling the duppies to step back. She cannot see the ghosts, but she senses their presence near. Again she cups her palms, blows, and throws her cupped hands over her right shoulder, cursing a bad-word with the motion before mumbling, 'De Lawd is me Shepherd, Ah fear nuh evil . . .' Still she senses an outside force. Lilly is smiling to herself and rocking, one hand patting her stomach.

Beatrice's head swells; she feels it's much larger than her body, much larger than the veranda where they are sitting, much larger than the evening. She hugs her bosom and rocks, trying to put aside the fear that has crept upon her without invitation.

After her mother died when she was six and her father wandered to another town and another woman, Beatrice was taken in by Lilly's mother, who was her aunt. She was two years older than Lilly, so their lives followed similar paths until at fifteen Beatrice's was partially ruined by her Sunday school teacher. Fear made her keep her mouth shut; prayer made the child born dead. Soon thereafter she left, getting

4

several jobs as domestic help before settling in this quiet community. Eight years ago, Beatrice and Lilly both attended their grandparents' funerals, three months apart. They were always close, so over the years, they kept in touch. When Lilly complained of being restless and wanting to leave the overprotective shield of her mother two years ago, Beatrice found her a job with her own employer Mrs Edwards. That was how they came to be together again.

Before Beatrice lost her child, she had promised the Lord that she would spread his name if he killed the life that was growing in her womb. When the child was born strangled, she kept her word, but it was already too late, because she had discovered the joy which lay buried between her legs. As she wasn't pretty, it was easy to have several men without ruining her reputation. No one wanted to boast of sleeping with the coarse, big-busted, no ass, Jesus-crazy maid. This way she had it her way all the time, not really trusting any man in the first place.

Putting aside her reflections, Beatrice leans her head to hear what Basil is saying.

'Oonuh look like oonuh inna anoda world.'

Richard is still fidgeting with his bicycle; Errol has gone to help him. Lilly, rocking on the seatless cane rocker, is hypnotised by the rustling cane field beyond. Beatrice and Basil notice her staring at what to them appears to be nothing. They feel her strangeness like silence between them. Pausing to take it in, they resume their conversation. An ackee blossom falls, disquieting Richard, and he curses: 'See yah, Lawd, yuh nuh test me fait tuh dis yah nite.'

A man and woman have crept out of the cane field. They stand right at the edge on the bank of the canal. To look at the woman is to see an older Lilly. The man is all grey. The woman wears a plaid dress gathered at the waist, and her feet are without shoes. Her husband wears rubber shoes and stained khaki pants turned up at the ankles. His faded shirt is partially unbuttoned, his arm is around his wife's waist. They exude a gentleness like the petals of roses. The woman uses her index finger to beckon to Lilly. Jumping as if pulled from her seat, Lilly bounds towards the man and woman by the cane field beyond the canal and beyond the barbed wire fence. She scrambles over Beatrice's feet.

Beatrice yells, 'Lilly, Lilly, weh yuh a guh? Lilly! Is mad? Yuh mad? Min yuh fall down hurt yuhself. Lilly! Gal, weh yuh a guh!'

Richard runs after Lilly.

Beatrice repeats, 'Lilly, gal, wha get inna yuh?'

Lilly: 'Yuh rass-cloth, leabe me alone. Yuh nuh ear me granny a call me?' She points to what appears to be the canal.

They all stare, seeing no one, hearing nothing. Lilly is close to the fence, running, tearing off her clothes. Fearing that she is going to dive in, Richard reaches for her, but she clutches and attempts the barbed wire fence; Richard pulls at her. She boxes and derides him till he releases her. She tries scrambling through. Richard takes firm hold of her and pulls her safely from the fence. Beatrice is by their side; she helps with Lilly. Errol stands transfixed by the bicycle, while Basil cranes his neck from the veranda. Richard and Beatrice struggle with Lilly, pulling her away from the fence; they are breathless, but luckily, Lilly settles down for a moment.

The woman in the cane field beckons to Lilly, cajoling: 'Lilly, me picknie, come kiss yuh granny and granpa; yuh nuh long fi see we?'

Lilly, strident, gesticulates wildly like a man cheated out of his paycheque. She calls, 'Yes, Granny, me a come, me long fi see yuh.'

Beatrice and Richard struggle with Lilly. Their fright and confusion are as loud as Lilly's screams. Richard tries to rough her up but she merely bucks him off. Beatrice's jaws work, sweat forms on her forehead, and her fleshy arms flail about, comical.

Again, she tries to reason with Lilly: 'Lilly, gal, memba me and you did help dress Granny fah er funeral? Memba, memba, Lilly, how we did cry til we eye swell big? Granny dead. She nuh call yuh.'

'Granny nuh dead; see, she stan deh wid Granpa. Oonuh leh me guh.' At this, Lilly spits at Beatrice and Richard and frees herself from their hold.

She rushes towards the cane field like a man afire in search of water. Richard seizes her, but she now has the strength of many persons; he hollers for Errol and Basil. Lilly rips off her blouse and brassière, and her ample breasts flap about. Richard remembers the taste of her milk, only last night. More hands take hold of her; she bites, scratches and kicks. Miss Maud from next door, hearing the commotion, runs to her fence to learn all about it.

'Leh me guh, leh me guh! Yuh nuh see me granny a call me? Leh me guh.'

Richard: 'Lilly, shet yuh mout. Min Miss Edward ear yuh an yuh loose yuh wuk. Nuhbody nuh call yuh.'

'Miss Edward bumbu-hole – Miss Edward rass-cloth. Oonuh leabe me alone mek me guh tuh me granny and granpa.'

Beatrice scolds: 'Lilly, gal, shet yuh mout. How yuh can speak suh bout Miss Edward? Gal, shet yuh mout for yuh loose yuh wuk.'

'Oonuh rass-cloth, oonuh bumbu-hole, oonuh leabe me alone – mek me guh to me granny.'

The four find it difficult to hold Lilly. She kicks, bucks and tears at her remaining clothes. The evening sings:

Steal away, steal away, duppy get yuh.
Steal away . . . duppy get yuh . . .

From across the fence, Miss Maud offers: 'Lawd, God, duppy done mad me picknie, Lawd God. Jesas! Rub er up wid some frankincense and white rum; rub er up quick come.' Before anyone can respond, she is climbing through the barbed wire fence which separates her yard from theirs, opening a bottle. In her haste, her dress catches on the fence, but she pulls it, ripping the hem. The pungent smell from the bottle vapours into the air.

Miss Maud rubs Lilly's hands, face and neck with the potion, then makes the sign of the cross in the air. Now she sprinkles some of the substance on the ground, muttering: 'Steal away, duppy, steal away. De deed well done; steal away . . .' She looks about her, pats her head and turns to Beatrice. 'Fin piece a red rag, tie er head. Duppy fraid red, fraid red. Our Fada who in heaven, duppy fraid red. Dy kingdom come, tie er head. Dy will be done, tie her head. Ave mercy, Pupa Jesas.'

Lilly breathes heavily; Richard, Errol and Basil hold her firmly.

Says Beatrice, 'She kyan stay ere; dem nuh wan er stay ere.'

Maud explains, 'Dem just wan er home. No arm will be done. Lawd have mercy.'

Richard stares at Lilly: 'Who obeah me sweet Lilly? Who?'

Beatrice explodes: 'Shet yuh mout, Richard, nuhbody nuh set nuh spell pan Lilly, nuhbody obeah er.'

Steal away, chile, steal away.
Duppy nuh wan yuh ere, chile,
*   duppy nuh wan yuh ere.*
Dem nuh wan yuh ere.

It is generally agreed that Lilly must be returned to her place of birth – that for whatever reason, her dead grandparents don't want her where she is. Mrs Edwards is consulted and a car is summoned. Kicking and frothing at the mouth, Lilly is forced into the back of the car. Richard to her right and Basil to her left. Beatrice sits up front with the driver armed with Miss Maud's flask of potion. The car pulls off, leaving a trail of dust.

Mrs Edwards returns to her house; she fumbles inside her medicine cabinet and comes up with a brown vial, the contents of which she sprinkles at each doorway and window and in all four corners of every room. Then she goes back to her rocking chair, her hands folded in her lap, her eyes searching the grey sky.

Miss Maud, the community myalist – healer – returns to her backyard. Her lips are pouted and her eyes intent, as if seeking a shiny shilling in the road; she shakes her head from side to side.

Suddenly she is possessed; she twirls around her yard, her wide skirt billowing out, her hands lifted to the sky, her feet marching time to an invisible drum. Her voice, deep bass, echoes like a man's throughout the entire community:

> *Duppy nuh wan yuh drop*
> *yuh picknie deh, guh home*
> *Duppy nuh wan yuh drop*
> *yuh picknie deh, guh home*
> *Duppy nuh wan yuh drop*
> *yuh picknie deh, guh home, gal,*
> *tie yuh belly, gal, guh home.*
> *Yuh muma seh she neba raise*
> *nuh picknie fi guh lego*
> *Yuh muma seh she neba raise*
> *nuh picknie fi guh lego*
> *Yuh muma seh she neba raise*
> *nuh picknie fi guh lego*
> *tie yuh belly, guh home.*
> *Duppy nuh wan yuh drop*
> *yuh picknie deh*
> *tie yuh belly, guh home.*
> *Guh home.*

Mrs Edwards feels cold-bumps covering her arms as she watches Miss Maud twirling and singing in her yard. The swishing of the cane fields has stopped and suddenly, a sense of desolation – abandonment – takes over. The sky turns a deep mauve, a lone donkey somewhere in the distance brays, brays, brays and the night is on so fully all creep to the safety of their homes and pull the covers tightly over their heads. Only Mrs Edwards sits for a long time on her veranda in the dark, rocking and rocking away the fear and doubt.

Upon returning from taking Lilly home, Beatrice reports that Lilly calmed gradually as she approached her place of birth. In fact, by the time she got home, she was reasonable enough to request from her mother a cup of water sweetened with condensed milk. After drinking the milk, Lilly hugged her mother and they both cried; no one had to restrain her thereafter. Nothing needed to be explained to Lilly's mother, who had been expecting them all day. It appeared she had had a dream from her dead mother the night before.

Prior to this incident, Lilly always claimed that she saw duppies in Mrs Edwards's house and around the estate in general. Since no one else professed such powers, there was no way to verify her claim. Many came to her when they wanted to ask for protection from those in the other world. Often, when they were in Lilly's presence, they asserted that they felt their heads rise and swell to twice their size, but again, since this was only a feeling and nothing visible, nothing could be proven. There were others who wanted to be able to see duppies like Lilly and asked her how they could obtain such powers. Lilly's recommendations were the following: 'Rub dog matta inna yuh eye or visit a graveyard wen de clock strike twelve midnite. Once dere, put yuh head between yuh legs, spit, then get up an walk, not lookin back. Afta dat, yuh will see duppy all de time.'

It is not known if anyone ever followed Lilly's advice, although two women who went to see Lilly had taken to visiting the graveyard daily and were now in the habit of talking to themselves.

◇

Lilly returns to Mrs Edwards's employment exactly ten weeks after the incident, healthy and as sane as before, with her bubbling, carefree manner. She gave birth to a seven-and-a-half pound boy, the spitting image of Richard, the day after her departure. The child was left behind with her mother, who christened him Sam, after his deceased grandfather.

Now when Lilly looks into the cane field, nothing bursts forth and no dead are brought back to life, but every time people see her looking, they remember that evening and somehow, the cane field starts rustling and a voice much like Lilly's rings throughout the entire community, stopping people at their chores:

Leh me guh, leh me guh, oonuh rass-cloth!
Leh me huh – me granny a call me, oonuh leh me guh.
Mrs Edwards bumbu-hole; leh me guh.

No one referred to Mrs Edwards, a highly respected member of her community, in such a manner before, and no one has after Lilly. Lilly, of course, apologised to Mrs Edwards, who graciously forgave her as she was not in possession of herself at the time. And although Mrs Edwards was committed to taking Lilly back in her employment after she gave birth, whenever Mrs Edwards was around her, she was always full of trepidation.

Lilly goes off one other time since the cane field incident. Several years have passed; Lilly is getting married to Richard. This is the big day. She is dressed, waiting to be taken to the church. Her grandmother appears again, but this time alone. Lilly rips her bridal dress to shreds and runs naked to the river, cursing everyone she meets, while Richard waits by the altar. For nine days she has to be tied down with ropes. For nine days, the breeze sings:

> *Steal away, steal away.*
> *Duppy seh nuh, duppy seh nuh.*
> *Steal away . . .*

Lilly's face is a dimpled cake pan. Her body is pleasing like a mango tree laden with fruits. She has eight children, now, six for her husband and two for Richard, the first two. Richard stole away after duppy boxed him the second time. The last that was heard of him, it was reported that he was seen walking and talking to himself, his hair matty and his skin black from dirt. Lilly now has a maid to help her with her many chores; her husband owns a fleet of trucks.

Beatrice has opened up a storefront church in another community far from where the main part of this story took place. Her congregation is said to be ninety-two per cent sturdy black men. Basil is still working as a pot-boiler at the sugar factory. Errol went abroad to England, it could be Canada or America as well, where he is said to have married an East Indian girl, so now he eats with his fingers.

After Lilly left Mrs Edwards' employment, Mrs Edwards swore confidentially to Mrs Salmon, her best friend, that she would never again hire a maid from Agusta valley – that was the district from which Lilly came. Mrs Edwards's, of course, did not admit to a belief in local superstitions.

At least once a year, Miss Maud can still be heard singing at the top of her voice:

> *Duppy nuh wan yuh drop*
> *yuh picknie deh, guh home*
> *Duppy nuh wan yuh drop*
> *yuh picknie deh, guh home*
> *Duppy nuh wan yuh drop*
> *yuh picknie deh, guh home, gal,*
> *tie yuh belly, guh home.*

F. B. ANDRÉ

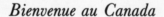

Bienvenue au Canada

Arrêt.

I am at the airport.

Access interdict. Arrivées.

The International Airport.

I park my car somewhere deep in the tangled colon of the Parkade, under a sign that says: REMEMBER YOUR LEVEL. (Good advice is everywhere.)

This is what I like and hate about airports: the magic way doors open and close without you touching them and once inside the instant-coffee dissolve to nervous and expectant. Why do they call these places terminals when they are a communist swirl of anonymity, modular plastic, and rootless plants growing in sunless confusion?

Arrivals is the set stage for a thousand reunions as credits scroll by on the overhead monitors. Disembodied voices have displaced most staff on the Arrivals Level, only car rental and lottery ticket sellers remain, stuck in brittle plastic booths like fruit in yoghurt cups.

The Departures Level is different: ticket-taking clerks are puffed up in importance to Reservation Counter Attendants with an overbearing air of superiority left over from when air travel was all mystique and adventure, Howard Hughes and Lindbergh.

Friends and relatives no longer stay to witness the actual takeoff, now by convention the beginning of a flight has been extended to the boarding gate. The last sight of a loved one is under scrutiny, being scoped and probed in a fluorescent parody of East German border rituals.

The locus of my nervousness is in my jacket pocket, over my heart, in my wallet: a letter from Lily. Flight Number, Date and Time of Arrival, in her neat handwriting. I have scowled over this cryptogram for two weeks and I have decoded nothing. Now the numbers are up and I'm at the airport waiting to meet her.

PLEASE FASTEN SEATBELTS.

OBEY NO SMOKING SIGNS.

We're about to begin our final descent.

I never liked this flight, this connection, Georgetown to Port of Spain to Toronto. I hate the stopover, those Trinidadians know how to make you suffer. If you're flying in from Guyana they treat you like a cockroach, they want to mash you to the ground and then twist their foot on your back.

And God help you if you are a woman travelling alone. And you end up seated next to a Trini man. His wife could be in the very next seat and still he will feel obligated to offer you his sexual services. Only one thing is worse . . . the Trini woman. They all act as if they have a licence to probe and inspect the intimate apparel of your life.

It is my misfortune to be seated next to not one but two. A mother and her daughter. The flight nearly over and this is the first bit of peace and quiet for me. Mother, with daughter in tow, went off to the washroom. Daughter is going up to Toronto to start university. Mother is along to see her 'business fixup good good', to make sure that 'my girlchild don't end up living in no nastiness'.

My God, the scared eager look on that girl's face brought back so many memories. I started to tell daughter what it was like for me when I first went up to university in Canada. Mother gave me one cuteye, a sharp sceptical look as if to say: Who is you?

12

A very good question.

I am Lily Seecharan-Carew, the first married woman in Georgetown to almost keep her maiden name. Even for this hyphenated compromise I had to fight Johnny. He couldn't stand for his wife, couldn't stand for the public to see that he had a wife with a mind of her own. Johnny preached liberation when we were at York. 'Up country people won't – can't understand.' He quickly reconverted once we got back home.

A huge crowd is waiting for Lily's flight. Greeks, Italians and the Portuguese have this in common with West Indians: they all have a thing for airport reunions. Everybody shows up: babies barely outside the womb, old people with one foot in the grave, friends and neighbours who migrated years ago and only vaguely remember the new arrival still come to bear witness.

I have not seen Lily in almost six years. Not since she finished her practicum. She went straight back to Guyana. And got married.

Lily is a widow now.

Aldwin Poon, one of the few people I keep up with from university days, was the one who called and told me about Johnny See. 'Andrew? You hear, boy? You hear about Johnny See? Johnny See get mashup.'

He had read about it in the alumni magazine. Johnny See got a feature obit. That is how I heard about Johnny Seecharan's death. That is how I always and ever heard about Johnny See, after the fact. He was always a rogue planet (revise that to meteorite), pulling things out of orbit.

We came straight from school in Canada, got married right away, and went up country. Johnny had to work off his scholarship. Two years. Johnny had me pre-sold on his idyllic vision of the school teacher and the doctor: it clashed with the dried and whitened cow dung on the ajoupa floor.

When I told him how uncomfortable living up country made me feel, Johnny laughed. He said I had spent too much of my time at York 'reading Romantic poets, too much Plato and not enough Hobbes'.

After the first two years, Johnny extended his contract for one more year. I begged, he promised, and we compromised: we would stay but only until the rains came. When the next dry season came and met us still up country, I refused. No more for me. I went back to Georgetown.

Georgetown was even worse than up country; as a city it betrays so many promises, 'outages', 'interruptions' and 'shortages' made the brief patches when things worked the way they should seem miraculous. Our marriage followed a similar pattern. I complained bitterly and always compared how we were living with how we could be living up in Canada.

Johnny said he was building a base up country, he said he had political ambitions, but most of that was rumshop talk. We bought 'a big house in a good area', just outside Georgetown. And I became The Doctor's Wife.

I got a teaching position at the same Girls' Catholic School that I had attended. My other job was to keep the big house running smooth smooth. And to entertain important and rising political stars lavishly, on my teacher's salary, on the weekends when Johnny came to town.

Johnny See thrived up country, where incidents and accidents are quickly converted into legends and myths. Go to Georgetown today, and go anywhere up country from there – people are still talking about the night Johnny See crashed.

He foretold his own death of course: in joking conversations eerily recalled. In a string of rumshops black men who drank only Scotch talked about the young Indian doctor with 'iron belly and fire in his eyes'. Indians mourned the loss of one of their own with puncheon rum, bitters and salt.

His wake lasted for three days. No glass was ever empty. Fire one, fire one more for Johnny See. Fire down at 31 in a car crash.

The rainy season turns everything to muck so quickly, up country.

I first heard about Johnny See from my parents long before I ever met him. My parents were both Presbyterian teachers; they had made a career of carrying a little learning and the Good Word into remote places. I was born in Gambia, on their first posting, one of my sisters in China, the other in Guyana.

We lived in Guyana the longest. The first time for five years. Then my parents were recalled, the political climate in Guyana was unsettled. And there was also some political infighting going on in the Presbyterian Overseas Outreach Programme. The wife of the couple sent to replace my parents couldn't cope. After a year and a bit she contracted what my parents called 'a topical disease'. My parents were sent back to Guyana to finish up the contract. I stayed behind in Canada to finish up my school year.

When I got back to Guyana, Johnny See had been and gone. He came

14

from up country to Georgetown to take his A-Levels; he went up to Canada on a full scholarship to study medicine. My parents said he was the best and brightest student they had ever taught.

That second stint in Guyana was when I met Lily, she was Lily Carew then.

That summer, after our A-Level exams, waiting for results, we did a lot of walking and hand-holding. Whenever the conversation between us slowed, Lily would ask a lot of questions about Canada. The two years I'd already spent away in school made me an expert. We made plans and dreams for Canada. My parents had me put my name in for a bursary through our church; I got it under the condition that I attend Laurentian, in Sudbury. Lily went to York.

We wrote. We both skipped lunches to pay for long-distance calls. That first year I took the bus down to Toronto to see her three times. Lily came up to Sudbury once.

It was during the week after Christmas, from Boxing Day to New Year's Eve. We got into something then. It was freezing cold in Sudbury. Sometimes I have allowed myself to think that Lily loved me, then. But I have long since rationalised it as us being young, the cold weather, her first Christmas away, and us having the handy privacy of my room.

I saw her only once more, that winter. On the weekend I picked to come down from Sudbury there was a Caribbean Students' Association dance. Lily had the flu but insisted on going. We were having a so-so time at the dance and I was ready to leave at any time but Lily wanted to stay a little longer.

It was well past midnight when Johnny See showed up, high as a kite, with an entourage of loud and proud drinkers.

We were introduced. 'Hey Johnny See, you long streak of misery, come and meet a fellow Guyanese, meet a man who is a Guyanese by proxy.'

Johnny See had the talent, the ability to remain lucid while drunk. He said he knew my parents well, he even called them by their first names. No one under fifty ever dared to call my parents by their first names.

Johnny asked, he whisked a suddenly eager Lily off to dance. When she returned her face was flushed and her eyes were bright and shining.

I continued to write and phone. As soon as school finished Lily went home to Guyana for the summer. I stayed in Sudbury to work for my tuition and a transfer to York.

I got to York in September. Way too late.

Lily and I spent a year avoiding each other. Things changed when she started living with Johnny See, and I stopped hanging out exclusively with West Indians and made some Canadian friends. I realised that I had no 'back home' to return to, Canada was it. By third year it was okay for us to have coffee together again. When in my fourth year I had a crisis of doubt about becoming a teacher, it was Lily who talked me through.

I learned to like Johnny See. I admired his intelligence and I envied his verve. I think he liked me, he accepted me as Lily's friend. I don't think he ever saw me as a threat, and I never fooled myself into thinking that I was or could be.

About one Sunday a month Lily would invite me over. After supper Lily would pick a topic to initiate our 'discussions'. Johnny See looked forward to these discussions that nearly always dissolved into heated arguments. We all did. Women's Lib and Guyanese politics were big favourites, but we ranged far and everything was fair game. Johnny had absolutely no qualms about employing any and all rhetorical weapons. He would make personal attacks on your character if he felt that would give him an edge. When he wanted to be dismissive he would call me a 'neo-colonial hybrid'. He could reduce Lily to tears with the same skill he possessed as a surgeon. Sometimes he would cut too deep and bring out a side of her that was always a shock to me. Lily could curse and swear with the best.

On one of those Sundays, we got on to the topic of love. Johnny See said, 'Love alone is not enough.' It was the first and only time that we all three agreed, but I don't think any of us were talking about the same thing.

It never stopped raining once. Until five minutes before Johnny's funeral.

They came from far off: up country girls, young and thin like cane in arrow, cotton dresses damp with handprints, red eyes in not-so-innocent faces showed where Johnny See passed . . . The bent and the mended, all those who 'got a patchup from the Doc', talked of the deep scar of his passing. The Boys' Presbyterian School let out early for Johnny See; nurses from the hospital still in uniform scattered kerchiefs in the crowd; Johnny's friends from high school days, from university, some in government, and those out of favour with whom he hatched plot and counterplot; a wide circle of young immortals suddenly old, gathered close in black shirt-jacks and shades, under a weak tea sky, sharing the same mirrored look.

And, Johnny's family.

The men I never saw, a wolf pack, scattered to lick its collective wound and choose a new leader. The women filled my house with strange smells from my kitchen, packed up his clothes, and his books, photographs taken down . . . wrapped me in a sari, took a hold of my elbow, steered me to the edge, and handed me a clump to cast and deflect off the polished mahogany casket with the window, for Johnny See . . .

I started missing Lily months before they left to go back to Guyana.

One day after teaching class I asked Lily out for coffee. After the coffee we went walking in what felt like the worst winter weather in the history of the world. I had to tell her how I felt, it was eating me up inside.

'Lily I'm sorry,' I said, 'but I can't stop myself . . . everywhere I look I see you pass. Mornings I'm sure it's you in the pack on the bus. In the grocery I know it's you down at the end of the aisle. I'm going to give myself whiplash. I can't stand the thought of never seeing you again. But in a way, I wish you were gone already.'

Lily took my hand and we walked some more. I thought Lily started to laugh, then I felt Lily starting to cry. We stopped. I didn't know what more to say, so I kissed her. She hesitated, but then she kissed me back.

And we kissed. Clouds of kisses . . . until the winter air was blue about our faces. After that Sunday we both took care. We were never alone together again.

I continued to live in the big house with the sweet scent of roses, with a new role: The Doctor's Widow. Johnny See would have laughed at the irony. During the week when Johnny was away, I had to fend off the most brazen advances from his friends; on his death they abandoned all of their lechery and innuendo, they elected me keeper of his shrine. I felt buried alive with a pharaoh. Covered in guilt. (If only . . . if I had only stayed with him up country, Johnny wouldn't have been rushing back and forth from work to rumshop to Georgetown on weekends.)

The cards and letters kept coming. Long after the fact, the news would boomerang back to the mailbox in envelopes of disbelief from far places in the hearts that Johnny touched: staff in the hospital where he did his residency; the landlord of the basement suite where we lived in

Toronto; classmates and professors wrote of their sadness at the loss of so much potential.

Andrew wrote.

A short sweet tentative note. He told me to have courage, in that halting awkward way of his. His letter made me think of winter, of Canada, the bracing cold, the anonymous order. I put off writing him back. He wrote again. He gave me his telephone number and said, if I ever felt like it to call, collect. I sent him a card at Christmas. He cabled me on my birthday and he managed to get fresh flowers delivered to me.

I like Andrew, I like his decency. I know he loves me. I care, but I don't love him. I could never love him . . . not with all of my heart.

A flashing relay on the overhead monitor says that Lily's flight has just landed. The crowd of greeters surges towards the glass sliding doors. There is movement behind, of officials, and a false start of expectancy as a maintenance crew emerges.

I am with my back secure against a pillar and eyes front. I continue to review the long division of the past six years, the deep root of my feeling for Lily is still irrational. All my expectations are trained on those doors that open by magic.

Johnny's family sent a delegation to insist I come and go up country for a visit. I went for a weekend to star in a comedy of errors. They, in all their up country pragmatism, had made a match for me with one of Johnny's cousins, a young lawyer. They made it clear that he was quite a catch for an ageing widow like me.

Johnny, you always said, 'We only make the choices that we can live with.' Why couldn't I settle back into the lurching insolvency of Guyana like you? With you. Canada was a red flag that I waved between us, at our marriage. For that I feel guilt, for that, Johnny See, I am sorry. But of all the things I have felt in my life, regret is the worst.

That Sunday night as soon as I got back to Georgetown I sat down and wrote Andrew a letter. I told him I was coming up to Toronto for a visit. And I asked if he could meet me at the airport.

Mesdames et Messieurs.

We have just landed.

Bienvenue au Canada.

JAMES BERRY

◁ ———————————◇——————————— ▷

Miss Dorcas

Like all other property owners on the island, Mr William Brooker lived on a hill. His home was named The Haven. High above the main road it looked down haughtily, dazzling the eyes with its whiteness in the sun, far from the clatterings of the village. In clear view, only half a mile away, the sea stretched wide and blue to the skyline. When the sea gave a breeze, the gaily striped awnings heaved around the veranda and the neat bougainvillaea arbours waved a bloom of bright red in front of The Haven. Here, in the distant past, Miss Dorcas had lived for eleven years. Now that Mr Brooker had heard that she had been buried he told his gardener he wanted the carpenters to demolish her cottage straight away.

The gardener understood: nothing of Miss Dorcas's memory should be left visible. The gardener galloped off on the big bay horse towards the district. The road divided Mr Bill's vast acres of coconut palms, pimento, logwood, lime trees and his grassland cattle. At the extreme end of the property the gardener pulled up the powerful horse and dismounted. He held the reins and climbed up on to the road banking and stood on clean-trodden ground.

Children and adults alike had always stood here at the fence to have a peep at the strange Miss Dorcas. Fenced round inside the property, on its hand-sized area of land, her two-roomed and box-like cottage was almost hidden. Overgrown hibiscus and crotons thickly knotted practically concealed the little place that cows, horses, mules, donkeys grazed round. And because she kept her gate barricaded, even food supplies – delivered by a village grocer, paid for by Mr Bill – had to be left over the fence.

Peeping through the foliage, the gardener saw, as he well knew, that the resident lady was not there. The place still had its plaited weeds. Its dug stones or stones merely collected were still there, arranged into their many sculpture-like heaps. The many wreaths of leaves were there laid at the roots of shrubs and at the custard apple and soursop trees. She had sometimes grown vegetables to their full maturity; other times she had pulled them up and replanted them constantly. It was believed also that sometimes her little home had been chaotic with everything scattered everywhere; other times it had been spotless and completely orderly. In the same pattern, sometimes she would be seen in dirty rags; other times she would be fully dressed in her best clothes, with her hair styled and all her beauty aids on. Dressed up like that, she used to sit outside in the wickerwork chair, rocking, stroking her cat, singing:

> Mr Bill, Mr Bill, Mr Bill
> I wish your colour would change
> Mr Bill, Mr Bill, Mr Bill
> I wish your colour would change
> From a backra boy to a darky boy
> I wish your colour would change . . .

The gardener remembered standing right here watching Miss Dorcas rock and sing her song over and over till darkness covered her. And each time he had left her there still singing.

The gardener turned, leapt directly on to the horse's back, shook the reins and galloped away fiercely. Coming towards the village, he turned off the main road. The sweating horse blasted loose stones behind it along the rough uphill road until it was pulled up on level ground at the cemetery.

Miss Dorcas's grave was by the roadside. The gardener took off his cap. He sat there on the horse staring at the heap of freshly turned-over red dirt that had given space to Miss Dorcas in the ground. He imagined the tallish white-haired lady nailed up in the wooden box, cold and silent. From his early childhood Miss Dorcas had been a legend to his village people. When he started at The Haven, though there was no need for it, she herself had given him his first meal in the kitchen. Within a few months she had left, had to leave. He had only known her kind, approachable. The gardener turned the horse round and thundered away as ferociously as before, this time going on Mr Bill's errand.

When he came back to The Haven with the carpenter's reply he saw that Mr Bill was uneasy. He was pacing up and down the red-tiled veranda. The gardener hid behind the arbour. Between the clustered bougainvillaea he fixed his eyes on Mr Bill: a hairy and tropic-tanned arm was fastened in the pocket of his khaki shorts while the other clutched his pipe to his mouth. He was obviously distressed. The gardener's eyes gleamed between the small leaves. This man has every right to suffer, he thought. Let his conscience eat him up like ants feeding on the heart of a tree gone bad. He wouldn't disturb him. The gardener looked behind him and edged away under the eaves of the house and went to the backyard. He sat down on the grass he had mowed two hours before under the branches of the spreading flame tree.

Miss Dorcas's death had stirred the gardener to an unexpected rage beyond his grief. Her death seemed to challenge him with a new and reckless kind of responsibility. He felt pressed there was something for him to do about it. He wiped his hairless brown face with his damp cap. He could taste old sweat mixed with the new, knowing his forehead would soon be damp again. Thoughtfully he raised his head and looked out towards the hill covered with rows of coconut trees. A wide field of hot air shimmered like the ripples of a stream. Cows lazily chewed their cud while the faint breeze stirred a ghostly shadow of coconut leaves over them in the afternoon sun.

The gardener clasped his thigh. Some burrs caught in the frazzled ends of his short trousers had pricked him. He began picking out the burrs with new anger. Mr Bill had given him these cast-off trousers. They were too large, in waist, buttocks and thigh. Mr Bill was like that: he didn't give you anything new or good. He tossed people away when they'd given him their best. Poor Miss Dorcas was caught with that.

Everybody in the district knew Miss Dorcas was the best looking among all other girls. All the men of his father's time said so. Knowing how to be warm and modest, rounded and curved in all the right places, she was the most appealing from Negril to Morant Point, they all said. Her deep brown eyes, her voice, her smiles and slim legs carried her like a princess. Though living alone with her poor granny, she was kept and shaped with a certain kind of pride, everybody said.

Miss Dorcas could have married Mr Felix King, the Parochial Board representative, a man who these days owned lands from mountain to sea and took truckfuls of coconuts and bananas to market, but her granny threw him out. She could have married Mr Walter Hoffman the tax collector but her granny threw him out. The Reverend's son had eyes on Miss Dorcas but her granny put him off. All the other men who hung around with their favours and gifts practically came to blows with Granny. Then Granny got Miss Dorcas a place at the backra-house, saying: she wants her only person in the world to do things nicely, to learn to be respectable and be respected, to get away from all no-good man-hawks.

Miss Dorcas had been quick to learn and Mr Bill had been quick to notice her. He watched her in the garden, about the house and about his meal table. Miss Dorcas began to have supper with him and he began to go to her separate quarters at night. Mr Bill gave Miss Dorcas a room in

The Haven. She took on management of the servants and everything and became the mistress of the household.

Then Mr Bill wanted to marry a backra girl. The man arranged with friends in town to take Miss Dorcas among their servants. When he broke the news to her Miss Dorcas leapt on the backra man like a wild cat. Next day, a dramatically changed person, she was taken to hospital. And Miss Dorcas never recovered from her derangement. After months in hospital she came out with every hair on her head gone white.

Only a black cat Miss Dorcas asked to have from The Haven; and it would seem only a fortnight or so before her death the last of its descendants died.

Uncannily, Miss Charlotte came into the gardener's head. He remembered the time Miss Charlotte had called him to saddle her horse without any previous warning. He didn't see how it was connected to Miss Dorcas and abandoned the thought. In fact there was a connection.

Mrs Brooker had been sitting on the veranda of The Haven. She had read through the day's newspaper and other newspapers and magazines from England. It was before lunch, not time for an afternoon nap. Her finger- and toenails had been reddened and her fair hair washed. The sun poured down wonderfully over the well-kept lawn and garden, over the tops of trees down to the sea. Mr Brooker was out on the property somewhere. In her white playsuit she felt immaculate and lovely but bored. An irritation suddenly seized her and then a drive for adventure, for mischief, for anything. It struck her: for all the six years she had lived at The Haven she'd never seen Dorcas. She called the gardener and told him to saddle her pony.

On her own, Mrs Brooker rode a short way along the drive of royal palms then turned right through the gate and came into the property.

She rode slowly through animals and the shadows of coconut palms, down the hill, and came to Miss Dorcas's cottage fence. She dismounted, tethered the horse and stayed outside the wild hedge and called, 'Dorcas! . . . Dorcas! . . . Dorcas! . . .'

Miss Dorcas came slowly along a track under the tall shrubs and stopped, staring at Mrs Brooker, the strange fair-haired lady dressed in white.

'How are you, Dorcas? . . . Managing? . . . I am the lady at The Haven these days . . .' Mrs Brooker became engrossed, absorbing the strange figure and presence. Barefooted, Miss Dorcas was dressed in a long robe-like dress, made of dry leaves. Her hat was also made of leaves. 'So, you are Dorcas!' Mrs Brooker said to herself. 'Wish we could talk.'

Voluntarily, Miss Dorcas came closer slowly till she held the wire fence. Both women faced each other closely. Steady and strangely calm-looking, Miss Dorcas's eyes were as clear as a child's. Intense, the blue eyes were busy, trying to assess the confronted oddity. 'Dorcas. As woman to woman, I want to ask you something . . . Is it – is it true you had three miscarriages – fathered by Mr Bill? . . . Is it true? . . .' It seemed Miss Dorcas searched herself. She slowly looked away and down. 'Is it true? Try and remember . . . You'd know who told me. Someone who's become a friend. But nobody at the house will say . . . You see, knowing could help me. I want to have children and used to think the fault was his. Will you try and remember, Dorcas? Will you? And tell me? . . .'

Miss Dorcas slowly lifted her head, stared at Mrs Brooker and turned away, towards the open sunlight round her cottage door.

Mrs Brooker remounted the horse. She cantered away over the hill and said nothing to Mr Brooker about her visit.

The gardener groaned a sigh. Village people believed Miss Dorcas was not yet forty years old. It was odd too that nobody pushed their way in to assist her. He remembered that Miss Dorcas had really belonged to Mr Bill and Mr Bill was not part of the village. He remembered that his own father secretly took fruits and vegetables and left them over the fence for Miss Dorcas and sometimes she did not touch them. Suddenly apprehension seized the gardener: suppose it wasn't Miss Dorcas that worried and bothered Mr Bill! Suppose the man didn't have any conscience at all!

Presently Mr Bill's great voice came bellowing over the backyard. Because the gardener had not reported back to him from the carpenter he was wild. Then the gardener's face showed so much pleasure that it irritated and added more to Mr Bill's fury. Mr Bill roared at him, wanting to know how soon the carpenters would smash down the building and have the fence and overgrowth cleared. They would come in the morning, the gardener told him. Mr Bill puffed his pipe and walked away.

The gardener caught hold of the lawnmower and gave it a great push. He whistled a joyful hymn as the mower ripped through the grass.

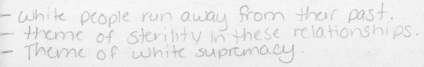

— White people run away from their past.
— theme of sterility in these relationships.
— Theme of white supremacy.

NEIL BISSOONDATH

Insecurity

'We're very insecure in this place, you know.' Alistair Ramgoolam crossed his fat legs and smiled beatifically, his plump cheeks, gouged by bad childhood acne, quivering at the effect his words had had. 'You fly down here, you look around, you see a beautiful island, sun, coconut trees, beaches. But I live here and I see a different reality. I see the university students parading Marx and Castro on the campus, I see more policemen with guns, I see people rioting downtown, I see my friends running away to Vancouver and Miami. So you can see, we are very insecure down here. That is why I want you to put the money your company owes me into my Toronto bank account. It is my own private insurance. The bank will notify me the money has been deposited and the government here won't notice a thing.'

Their business concluded, the visitor pocketed Mr Ramgoolam's account number and stood ready to leave. He asked to use the phone. 'I'd like to call a taxi. My flight leaves early in the morning.'

'No, no.' Mr Ramgoolam gestured impatiently with his plump arm. 'Vijay will drive you into town. You're staying at the Hilton, not so?'

The visitor nodded.

'Vijay! Vijay!' Mr Ramgoolam's silver hair – stirred, the visitor noticed, by the slightest movement – jumped as if alive.

Vijay's voice rattled like a falling can as it came in irritated response from the bowels of the house. 'Coming, Pa, coming.'

The tick-tock of Vijay's table-tennis game continued and Mr Ramgoolam, chest heaving, bellowed, 'Vijay!'

Still smiling beatifically, Mr Ramgoolam turned to his visitor and said, 'So when you'll be coming back to the islands again?'

The visitor shrugged and smiled. 'That depends on the company. Not for a long time probably.'

'You like Yonge Street too much to leave it again soon, eh?' Mr Ramgoolam chuckled. The visitor smiled politely.

Vijay, rake thin and wild-eyed, shuffled into the living room.

Mr Ramgoolam saw the visitor to Vijay's sports car, the latest model on the road. 'You won't forget to get the letter to my son, eh? Remember, it's Markham Street, the house number and phone number on the envelope. You won't forget, eh?'

'I won't forget,' the visitor said. They shook hands.

Mr Ramgoolam was back in his house before the gravel spat up by the tyres of the car had settled. He followed the tail-lights through a heavily burglar-proofed window – Vijay was speeding again, probably showing off; he'd need another talking to. Nodding ponderously, he muttered, 'We're very insecure in this place, yes, very insecure.'

Alistair Ramgoolam was a self-made man who thought back with pride to his poor childhood. He credited this poverty with preventing in him the aloofness he often detected in his friends: a detachment from the island, a sneering view of its history. He had, he felt, a fine grasp on the island, on its history and its politics, its people and its culture. He had developed a set of 'views' and anecdotes which he used to liven up parties. It distressed him that his views and anecdotes rarely had the desired effect, arousing instead only a deadpan sarcasm. He had written them down and had them privately published in a thin volume. Except for those he'd given away as gifts, all five hundred copies were collecting dust in cardboard boxes under the table-tennis board.

Mr Ramgoolam had seen the British when they were the colonial masters and he had attended the farewell ball for the last British governor. He had seen the Americans arrive with the Second World War, setting up their bases on large tracts of the best agricultural land; and he had seen the last of them leave, the Stars and Stripes tucked securely under the commander's arm, more than twenty years after the end of the war. He had seen the British, no longer masters and barely respected, leave the island in a state of independence. And he had seen that euphoric state quickly degenerate into a carnival of radicals and madmen.

His life at the fringe of events, he felt, had given him a certain authority over and comprehension of the past. But the present, with its confusion and corruption, eluded him. The sense of drift nurtured unease in Mr Ramgoolam.

He would always remember one particular day in late August, 1969. He had popped out of his air-conditioned downtown office to visit the chief customs officer at the docks. As an importer of foreign foods and wines, Mr Ramgoolam made it his business to keep the various officials who controlled the various entry stamps happy and content. On that day, he was walking hurriedly past the downtown square when a black

25

youth, hair twisted into worm-like pigtails, thrust a pink leaflet into his unwilling hands. It was a socialist tract, full of new words and bombast. Mr Ramgoolam had glanced irritatedly at it, noticed several spelling mistakes, crumpled it up, and thrown it on the sidewalk. Then he remembered he was a member of the Chamber of Commerce Keep-Our-City-Clean Committee and he picked it up. Later that evening he found it in his pants pocket. He smoothed it out, read it, and decided it was nothing less than subversion and treason. At the next party he attended, he expounded his views on socialism. He was told to stop boring everyone.

Not long after the party, riots and demonstrations – dubbed 'Black Power' by the television and the newspaper – occurred in the streets. Mr Ramgoolam's store lost a window pane and the walls were scribbled with 'Socialism' and 'Black Communism'. The words bedevilled the last of Mr Ramgoolam's black hairs into the mass of silver.

As he watched the last black stripe blend in, Mr Ramgoolam realised that, with an ineffectual government and a growing military, one night could bring the country a change so cataclysmic that the only issue would be rapid flight. And failing that, poverty, at best.

He had no desire to return to the moneyless nobility of his childhood: pride was one thing, stupidity quite another, and Alistair Ramgoolam was acutely aware of the difference.

He began looking for ways of smuggling money out of the island to an illegal foreign bank account. A resourceful man, he soon found several undetectable methods: buying travellers' cheques and bank drafts off friends, having money owed him by foreign companies paid into the illegal account, buying foreign currency from travellers at generous rates of exchange. His eldest son was attending university in Toronto, so it was through him that Mr Ramgoolam established his account.

The sum grew quickly. Mr Ramgoolam became an exporter of island foods and crafts, deflating the prices he reported to the island's government and inflating those he charged the foreign companies. The difference was put into the Toronto account. Every cent not spent on his somewhat lavish lifestyle was poured into his purchases of bank drafts and travellers' cheques.

The official mail service, untrustworthy and growing more expensive by the day, was not entrusted with Mr Ramgoolam's correspondence with his son. Visitors to or from Toronto, friend or stranger, were asked to perform favours.

Over the years, with a steadily developing business and ever-increasing foreign dealings, Mr Ramgoolam's account grew larger and larger, to more than forty thousand dollars.

He contemplated his bankbooks with great satisfaction. Should flight be necessary – and the more time passed, the more Mr Ramgoolam became convinced it would – there would be something to run to beyond bare refuge.

The more insecure he saw his island becoming, the more secure he himself felt. From this secure insecurity a new attitude, one of which he had never before been aware, arose in him. The island of his birth, on which he had grown up and where he had made his fortune, was transformed by a process of mind into a kind of temporary home. Its history ceased to be important, its present turned into a fluid holding pattern which would eventually give way. The confusion had been prepared for, and all that was left was the enjoyment that could be squeezed out of the island between now and then. He could hope for death here but his grandchildren, maybe even his children, would continue the emigration which his grandfather had started in India, and during which the island had proved, in the end, to be nothing more than a stopover.

When the Toronto account reached fifty thousand dollars, Mr Ramgoolam received a letter from his eldest son. He reminded his father that Vijay would be coming to Toronto to study and that the fifty thousand dollars was lying fallow in the account, collecting interest, yes, but slowly. Wouldn't it be better to invest in a house? This would mean that Vijay – Mr Ramgoolam noticed his eldest son had discreetly left himself out – would not have to pay rent and, with the rapidly escalating property prices in Toronto, a modest fifty-thousand-dollar house could be resold later at a great profit.

His first reading of the letter brought a chuckle to Mr Ramgoolam's throat. His independent-minded son, it seemed, was looking for a way of not paying rent. But then he felt a ripple of quiet rage run through him: his son had always made an issue of being independent, of making it on his own. Paying for the privilege, Mr Ramgoolam thought, was the first requisite of independence. He put the suggestion out of his mind.

Later that night, just before bed, he read the letter aloud to his wife. This had long been their custom. She complained continually of 'weakness' in the eyes. As he lay in bed afterwards, the words 'great profit' stayed with him.

His wife said, 'You going to buy it?'

He said, 'Is not such a bad idea. I have to think.'

When he awoke at four the next morning for his usual Hindu

devotions, Mr Ramgoolam's mind was made up. He walked around the garden picking the dew-smothered flowers with which he would garland the deities in his private prayer room and, breathing in the cool, fresh air of the young dawn's semi-light, he became convinced that the decision was already blessed by the beauty of the morning.

After a cold shower, Mr Ramgoolam draped his fine cotton *dhoti* around his waist and prayed before his gods, calling their blessings on to himself, his wife, his sons, and the new house soon to be bought, cash, in Toronto. It was his contention that blessed business dealings were safer than unblessed ones.

He spent the rest of the morning writing a letter to his son, giving instructions that before any deals were made he was to be consulted. He didn't want any crooked real estate agent fooling his son, Toronto sophisticate or not. He also warned that the place should be close enough to Vijay's school that he wouldn't have to travel too far: a short ride on public transportation was acceptable but his son should always remember that it was below the station of a Ramgoolam to depend on buses and trains.

That was an important point, Mr Ramgoolam thought. It might force his independent son to raise his sights a little. He probably used public transportation quite regularly in Toronto, whereas here on the island he would not have heard of sitting in a bus next to some sweaty farmer. The letter, Mr Ramgoolam hoped, would remind his eldest son of the standards expected of a member of his family.

The letter was dispatched that evening with the friend of a friend of a friend who just happened to be leaving for Toronto.

A week passed and Mr Ramgoolam heard nothing from his son. He began to worry: if *he* were buying a house, you could be sure *he'd* have found a place and signed the deal by now. That son of his just had no business sense: didn't he know that time was money? A week could mean the difference of a thousand dollars! Mr Ramgoolam said to his wife, 'I just wish he'd learn to be independent on somebody else's money.'

He was walking in the garden worrying about his money and kicking at the grass when Vijay shouted from the house, 'Pa, Pa! Toronto calling.'

Mr Ramgoolam hurried in, his cheeks jiggling. 'Hello.' It was the real estate agent calling.

The operator said, 'Will you accept the charges?'

Accept the charges? Mr Ramgoolam was momentarily unsettled. 'No.' He slammed the phone down. He glared at Vijay sitting at the dining table. 'What kind of businessman he is anyway? Calling collect. He's getting my money and he expects me to pay for his business call? He crazy or what, eh?' Incensed, he ran out into the garden. Every few minutes, Vijay could hear him muttering about 'cheapness'.

The telephone rang again half an hour later.

This call was from his son and, luckily, not collect. The first thing Mr Ramgoolam said was, 'Get rid of that cheap agent. I don't trust him. Get somebody else.'

The son agreed. Then he asked whether his father would be willing to go above fifty thousand, to, say, sixty or sixty-five. Only such a sum would assure a good house in a proper location. Less would mean a good house, yes, but a long way on public transportation for Vijay.

Mr Ramgoolam pictured Vijay riding on some rickety bus with a smelly fish vendor for company. He broke out in a cold sweat. 'Now wait up a minute . . . awright, awright, sixty or sixty-five. But not a cent more. And close the deal quickly. Time is money, you know.'

Time dragged by. Nothing was heard from Toronto for a week. Mr Ramgoolam began to worry. What was that no-good son of his up to now? Wasting time as usual, probably running off somewhere being independent.

Another week went by and Mr Ramgoolam began brooding over the house in Toronto. He couldn't get his mind off it. He stopped going to the office. Not even prayer seemed to ease his growing doubts. Wasn't it better to have the cash safely in the bank, slowly but surely collecting its interest? And what about Vijay? The money for his schooling was to have come from that account: now he'd have to take money with him, and Mr Ramgoolam hadn't counted on that. Above all, the house was going to cost ten to fifteen thousand more than the Toronto account contained; that was a lot of money to smuggle out. Would it mean a mortgage? He hated mortgages and credit. He hated owing. Buy only when you could pay: it was another of his convictions.

After three more days and a sleepless night, Mr Ramgoolam eased himself out of bed at 3.30 am. He might as well pray. It always helped, eased the mind however little.

There was very little light that morning and the flowers he collected were wilted and soggy. He stubbed his toe on a stone and cursed, softly, in Hindi. The cold shower felt not so much refreshing as merely cold.

He prayed, his *dhoti* falling in careless folds, his gods sad with their colourless flowers.

When he finished he wrote a quick letter to his son, ordering him to leave all the money in the bank and to forget about buying a house. He couldn't afford it at the present time, he said.

He signed it and sealed it. He wondered briefly whether he should telephone or telegram but decided they were both too expensive. The next problem was to find someone who was going to Toronto. That was easy: the representative of his biggest Toronto client, the one staying at the Hilton, would be coming to the house this evening to finalise a deal and to get the Toronto account number. He could take the letter.

Five days passed and Mr Ramgoolam heard nothing from his eldest son. Once more he began to worry. Couldn't the fool call to say he'd got the letter and the money was safe? He spent the morning in bed nursing his burning ulcer.

On the morning of the sixth day the call came.

'Hello, Pa?' His son's voice was sharp and clear, as if he were calling from across the street. 'You're now the proud owner of a house in Toronto. The deal went through yesterday. It's all finalised.'

Mr Ramgoolam's jaw fell open. His cheeks quivered. 'What? You didn't get my letter?'

'You mean the one the company rep brought up? Not yet. He just called me last night. I'm going to collect the letter this evening, before the ballet.'

'Be-be-be-fore the ballet?' Mr Ramgoolam ran his pudgy fingers down the length of his perspiring face. He could feel his heart thumping heavily against the fat in his chest.

'Yes, I'm going to the ballet tonight. Good news about the house, eh? I did exactly as you told me, Pa. I did it as quickly as possible. Time is money, as you always say.'

'Yes-yes,' said Mr Ramgoolam. 'Time is money, son, time is money. We're very insecure in this place, you know.'

His son said, 'What?'

'Nothing.' Mr Ramgoolam ran his hand, trembling, through his hair. 'Goodbye.' He replaced the receiver. The wooden floor seemed to dance beneath him and, for a moment, he had a sense of slippage, of life turned to running liquid. He saw his son sitting in the living room of the Toronto house – sitting, smiling, in a room Mr Ramgoolam knew to be there, but the hardened outlines of which he could not distinguish – and he suddenly understood how far his son had gone. Just as his father had grown distant from India; just as he himself had grown even further from the life that, in memory, his father had represented and then, later

30

in life, from that which he himself had known on the island, so too had his eldest son gone beyond. Mr Ramgoolam had been able to picture the money sitting in the bank, piles of bills; but this house, and his son sitting there with ballet tickets in his hand: this was something softer, hazier, less graspable. He now saw himself as being left behind, caught between the shades of his father and, unexpectedly, of his son. And he knew that his insecurity, until then always in the land around him, in the details of life daily lived, was now within him. It was as if his legs had suddenly gone hollow, two shells of utter fragility.

There was only one thing left, one thing to hold on to. He hurried to his room and, brushing his wife aside, dressed quickly. Then he swallowed two hefty gulps of his stomach medicine and called out to Vijay to drive him to the office.

WAYNE BROWN

Independence Day

He was 85, old as the century, and as he overheard the Independence Day celebrations on the radio – the sonorous nonsense, the folk songs, the ingenuous child's prize-winning essay, piously, drawlingly rendered by a press-ganged dee-jay, and the military parades, the cymbals clashing without resonance in the sultry air – he wasn't so much as tempted by the illusion that all of it had anything to do with him. The year of his birth was a kind of pivot: 62 years earlier the island's slaves had been freed, and the same number of years later their descendants had been granted independence; but though the latter date had a private meaning for him (he had retired that year from his career-long accountant's post with a large and enigmatic shipping firm, and had felt the coursing river of his life abruptly, alarmingly slacken, and strange debris begin breaking surface in its drifting) he had let the passing parade go all but unnoticed, in the corner of an eye already clouding with cataract.

31

All it meant, he had irritably told Clare, who at 60 could still exhibit the mischievous bright curiosity of a girl, and who that night had dragged him down to the Square and was happily remarking the mob's excitement: 'Isn't it fun?' – all it meant, he told her, was that in place of the pompous white fools who had ruled till then, pompous black fools now would; and nothing that had happened in the 23 years since (so far as he had noticed) had tempted him to lift this self-exculpating sentence. He was an old man, irascible, stubborn, and more lonely than he knew since Clare's death from cancer four years ago; he lived in the cramped but vivid world of the suburban house they had occupied for so long that its chain-link fence had come to delineate the landscape of his mind; and, as the inhabitants of a drear coast learn simultaneously to register and ignore the sound of the sea, since Clare had gone he had mastered the art of simultaneously acknowledging and disavowing that other world, upon whose authenticity the radio was heraldically, absurdly insisting.

So now, when he looked up from the letter he was laboriously writing (arthritic fingers bunched round the pen's throat, cataract-cleansed eyes held well back from the page, so that he seemed to be looking down his nose at what he was writing) it was not to ponder the many blessings the President was opining (in that sibylline, butter-smooth voice) that the Republic had a right to be thankful for, but because he thought he had heard a faint crash in the kitchen.

He lifted his gaze abstractedly, as drinking cattle do; but no secondary tumult came, the image of the bare-footed girl, the new girl, materialised only as far as a swart neck and pair of convex eyes before changing its mind and fading away again; and after a further, absent-minded pause, he resumed writing. He had written:

'Shadow is feeling his years. It's as much as he can manage now to negotiate the steps, one by one, and slouch out, and lie in the sun, twitching his ears and sighing heavily from time to time. Which is what he mostly does these days. A while ago he sniffed around where a butterfly (whose name you'd probably know, it was black and blue but not an Emperor, it had white spots) was dancing on the air before him, but his snap at it was pure ritual, a slow-motion snap if I ever saw one. He still misses you; wanders into the bedroom sometimes and stands dejected at the foot of your bed, eyes front but sort of listening, or at least waiting; but nothing happens of course, and after a while like that he wanders back out.

'I am well but for the usual pains and pills. The giddiness is no worse than when you were here, but no less of a nuisance either. Eyesight holding out . . .'

In the beginning he had questioned these monthly newsletters to Clare. He believed in none of the usual things, ghosts, God, life-after-death, and at first, writing to Clare, he had felt like a fool. But he had talked to her for most of his life, since her death there had been no one to talk to; and so, leaving his judgement as to the point or inanity of these letters unresolved, in the end he had gone on writing them. It was something he did on the last day of each month, that was all; yet, writing them, he felt himself like one half of an arch, unbuttressed by her bright ripostes, having to hold itself upright by its own tension. Truth is, they were a strain, these letters; they imprisoned him, not so much in the past as in his solitary strength. And yet he wrote them, for the orderliness and finality with which they wrapped up each otherwise unstructured month, and as an antidote to many other things (that gibberish on the radio, for example). He wrote:

'I am teaching the new girl chess, or trying to. Did I tell you about the new girl? She's a child; Guyanese for sure, though she won't admit it (these people never cease to amaze me with what fools they take us to be). You know I hate strange people about the house, but she came to the gate and it was raining and she looked thoroughly scared. And as you know the maid's room is empty. That was three weeks ago. Her name, she says, is Maude.

'She's a terrible cook and a worse cleaner, and about once every three days I have to roar at her to turn down the blasted instrument which apparently does all her thinking and singing and speechifying for her. But I keep her on, for the moment; not sure why.

'Maude's private world, I should tell you, is full of sweatiness; sweatiness of fear, sweatiness of sex. As to the first, I think she thinks the immigration people are looking for her (well, of course they aren't); as to the second, some nights a black shadow slips in through the gate and disappears into her room, and the next morning she is all surliness and sleepiness. I make a point of not interfering. Not my business. But you should see her trying to play chess . . .'

He sat back, seeing before him Maude's shiny intent face, her sprawled and planted elbow, one fist pushing up the smooth skin of her cheek and tugging her mouth half open, her habitual pout giving way, whenever it was her turn to play, to a predator's grim grin, and her shining eyes (in the startling white of the moist round eyeballs), all defiance and anger when, sooner or later, he muttered the soft threat, 'Check!'

33

Maude playing chess was a joke. After ten lessons she was still not averse, in a tight spot, to leapfrogging her pent-up king draughtswise out of trouble; or swerving a threatened knight clean off the board ('One-two-one!' she would say triumphantly, the last emphatic right-angled 'one' landing the piece with a clack on the polished mahogany table); or even, in a tantrum, rising and imperiously sweeping the pieces off the board ('Look!' he would bellow, angrier than he had been in years, and they would glare at each other, old man and girl, sudden murder standing in the air between them) . . .

He sat back. There were other things he had meant to tell Clare – that their only son John has passed through last week en route to some conference in Caracas; that the philodendron had caught itself in the corner; that Julius Sumairsingh had died – but suddenly he didn't feel like going on.

Besides, it was five to five. He waited, folding the unfinished letter (and then, absently, folding it smaller and smaller) and, a few minutes later, the barefooted girl came in with his cocoa and the chessboard, saying 'Afternoon' without looking at him; smoothing the skirt along her bottom with both hands; dropping into the opposite chair. Girlishly, gratuitously, she smoothed the open board once or twice, before applying the appropriate pieces to it; finished, she looked up at him at last, her forehead shining, saying shyly, defiantly, 'Ready, sah.'

He felt the whole house, his life, focus on the board between them. He felt the concentrated presence of her, his unknowable opposition. For the first time that day he heard the radio clearly, a nasal female voice: '. . . and the slaves, throwing off their chains . . .' And he rose, baring his teeth slightly against the usual volley of pain, and switched the radio off.

'Okay,' he said, returning, with a grim glance at her, to turn the board around (shakily restoring the white queen that, in the process, he'd knocked down): 'I'm white. You're black. Now pay attention.' Already concentrating hard himself, a crustily frowning old man, unaware of the fleeting womanly smile she allowed herself as she, too, bent over the board.

HAZEL D. CAMPBELL

◁ ■■■■■■■ ◇ ■■■■■■■ ▷

The Thursday Wife

Shortly after Bertie and Mary got married, things started to get very bad.

Bertie had been a waiter working the hotels in Montego Bay but he had been laid off soon after the wedding and they decided to move to Kingston.

They had enough money to pay the first month's rent for their one room and to buy food for a while. But as the days passed and Bertie could get no work at all, starvation began to stare them in the face.

Still Bertie insisted that his young wife could not go out to work. She was so pretty, he thought, with her light colour skin and brown curly hair, anywhere she went to work the men would want to touch her, and that would cause him to kill. So when somebody told her that she could get a job as a store clerk in one of the Syrian stores downtown, he forbade her even to think about it.

Things went from bad to worse for them. The final blow came when Bertie got food poisoning from the can of sardines they shared over a two-day period. The young wife didn't know that she shouldn't leave the sardines in the can overnight and on the second day made a sandwich for her husband with it. The left-overs weren't enough to share so she pretended that she had already eaten when he came home weary and hungry after another futile day looking for work.

That night as she held the chamber pot for his vomit and watched him writhing in pain, the thought that he might die and leave her penniless in the big, hostile city filled her with great fear. So the next day when he was better but still too weak to contradict her too violently, she suggested that it might be better if she went back to her country, the country from which he had taken her a mere six months before. She could stay with her sister. They would give up the room and he could move in with his cousin until he found a job. Then, when things got better she would come back and they would start again.

They parted reluctantly because they really liked each other and the young love was still burning hotly in their veins, but it couldn't be helped.

For six months Mary fretted in her sister's house. They were all very kind to her and she made herself useful in the house and the shop, but it was not the same. She longed for her husband and her own home once more. And he didn't write. Much later she would find out that he was barely literate and that it wouldn't occur to him to write her a letter. And although she thought about him constantly, she didn't even know his cousin's address to write to him.

One Sunday morning as she was washing her hair in the basin under the pear tree in the back yard, her sister came to tell her, mysteriously, that she had a 'gentleman visitor'. Mary didn't want to see anyone. Of late, some of the country gentlemen aware of her lonely status had been trying to 'talk her up'. She wasn't interested in any of them. So she took her time drying and combing her hair and when she went upstairs she nearly died of shock, because there, sitting on the veranda talking to her sister, was her husband Bertie.

He had come for her. Things had improved. He had found a job, rented another room and got a few things together. So once again Mary left her country home and went with her husband to start a new life in Kingston.

There was only one thing about the new life that Mary did not like. Bertie had a live-in job. He worked for some white people up on top of a hill and had to stay on the premises for he was chauffeur, babysitter, watchman and waiter for their numerous parties – whatever they might ask him to do. He worked hard all week and was only allowed a half-day on Thursdays and that was all the time he had to be at home with Mary. For most of the rest of the week, she saw him only in snatches. Whenever he could, he would sneak away while on some errand with the car and drop in for a quick visit. But on Thursday evening Bertie came home to spend the night, free until six o'clock the next morning.

And on Thursday evenings Mary bloomed. Early Thursday morning she would wash her hair and plait it, twisting it around her head, the way Bertie liked it. She would thoroughly clean their room and the little veranda which served as kitchen and dining room on occasion. She would also make sure that the vase on the bureau was ready, for he always brought her some flowers from the white people's garden. Then she would cook his favourite meal, stewed peas and rice. When everything was ready, she would wash herself carefully and change all her clothes and rest a while so that by two o'clock when he came home she was as fresh as a new bride.

Her heart would lift in anticipation as she heard him whistling as he entered the yard. He would stop and greet anybody who happened to be about, then he would step loudly on to the little veranda, then rap – pam pa pam pam on their door. And, pretending that she didn't know it was he, she would call, 'Who's that?' and he would answer, 'Who you expecting?' Then she would open the door and he would haul her into his arms and on to their bed and ravish her in the most rewarding ways. Later he would say, as if they were just meeting, 'So how you do?' and she would answer shyly, 'All right you know.'

Then they would eat and dress and he would take her to a movie or to visit his cousin or they would go downtown after the shops had closed and walk through the quiet streets and stop for a while at the seaside at the bottom of King Street laughing at the antics of the little boys diving in and out of the water as naked as the day they were born.

Afterwards they would stop at a little parlour and buy patties and ice-cream and then they would go home for another bout of lovemaking, falling asleep in each other's arms until the clock alarmed at five o'clock next morning and he jumped up to race to catch the first bus so that he wouldn't be late for work – until the next Thursday.

And so it went on month after month. One year passed, two, three, four years. Their love continued bright and shining, fanned into flame on Thursday and smouldering during the rest of the week. No children came to spoil their duet, but Mary was not unhappy.

During this time she had learned how to cope with her loneliness. For one thing there was the church, nearly all day Sunday, two nights during the week with an extra night once a month for women's meeting.

Also she was a visiting sister which meant that many mornings she spent the time visiting the sick and the shut-ins, encouraging them spiritually and doing what she could to help their physical needs.

Since all her husband's domestic chores were taken care of at his work place, she had a lot of time on her hands. She washed and cooked and kept house only for herself, and as Bertie gave her generously from his pay, small though it was, she could always manage to find a little something to take for those poorer than herself and earned a name as an Angel of Mercy. Mary was well satisfied with her life.

The lustfulness of her husband and his liking for the movie house and a drink or two bothered her Christian principles from time to time. But he was so good to her, she felt that she owed it to him to do whatever he wanted on the one day of the week when he could be with her. In fact she took almost sinful pleasure in breaking the church rules without having a guilty conscience. Wasn't she merely being submissive to her husband as the Bible taught?

Then one Sunday morning, just as she was getting ready for church, without any warning, Bertie descended on her in a taxi carrying all his clothes and belongings. Bertie had come home. He had left the job in the white people's mansion and had got a better-paying one working as a waiter in a restaurant in a hotel uptown. Now he would be with her every day of the week and not just Thursdays any more.

'Isn't it wonderful?' he asked her, enthusiastically. He had kept it as a surprise for her.

Mary agreed that it was wonderful but it was with regret that she stopped dressing for church for they had a visiting evangelist who was hot with the Holy Ghost and made the church walls shake with his message and the strong amens it brought forth.

However, her husband had come home, so she helped him to settle in and set about preparing Sunday dinner, a thing she rarely did, since she had nobody to cook for but herself. And she was happy, as she thought that for the first time since she was married she would truly have her husband by her side. She might even get him to go to church with her.

A couple of weeks passed before Mary began to admit that she was uneasy. At first she couldn't think why. The first time she thought that it might be because Bertie was around so much, she pushed the thought aside. How ungrateful to think such a thing!

But her life had been drastically changed by his continuous presence.

First, there was the problem of accommodating him and his possessions. She had to squeeze up her good clothes in the wardrobe and make room for his clothes in one of the bureau drawers. She had to find place for his shoes and personal things like shaving set and cologne – he was quite a sweet man, she thought. The room looked quite crowded now and was more difficult to keep clean and tidy, but he insisted on tidiness at all times so that it seemed she was always dusting and straightening or putting things away.

He was miserable about his clothes, she found herself complaining to a church sister. He had even threatened to box her because she hadn't ironed his merinos. She didn't iron these because they stretched out so easily that she had folded them neatly and put them in his drawer. But he had taken them all out and thrown them about the room shouting and calling her a lazy woman. She had been so ashamed, for the neighbours could hear every word he said.

He was miserable about his food too, but fortunately he was allowed to eat at the restaurant, so she didn't have to cook for him too often.

Then she had to curtail many of her activities. The first Tuesday night after he came home, she had dressed herself as usual to go to prayer meeting but when she was putting on her hat, he came into the room and asked her where she thought she was going. Now that he was home, he said, she didn't have to worry with all them church foolishness any more. Mary was so upset she couldn't speak and after that she could only go out on the nights when he was on the late evening shift because if he came home before her he would always quarrel.

When she tried to explain to the parson why she was no longer as diligent in her church duties as before, he was very unsympathetic and thundered at her.

'Sister Mary, God first! Everything else comes after.'

Bertie laughed at her friends.

'Where you know all them meek and mild pious woman from?' he would tease her. 'Them walk like them can't mash ants, but I bet you everyone of them is as sinful as Satan.'

One day he embarrassed her beyond words by ordering them to be quiet in his house. She hadn't been feeling well and three sisters had come to visit her, but when they raised a hymn he had shut them up so violently that they had hastened away without even praying for her.

'Can't stand that damn croaking and wailing,' he told Mary irritably, when she tried to protest.

Yet he expected her to be nice to his friends. Every now and then some of his friends who Mary was meeting for the first time would drop by and she would have to fetch ice and fix drinks while they chatted and laughed.

That was the men.

One evening a woman came to see him. A woman whom he hugged affectionately and brought in to sit on the good chair in their room.

Mary was wary of her from the beginning. But he explained the association innocently enough. She was the house-girl where he used to work and she had washed and cooked for him.

Mary and Bertie sat on the bed while Bertie and the woman reminisced and laughed.

'You remember the day when Miss Levy couldn't find her brown wig to go to the party and how we search down the whole place till we finally find it outside and all the dog them playing with it?' the woman said – Corrine was her name.

'And how them used to leave salt fish for we dinner when them wasn't eating in, but we used to tek out steak and cook it,' Bertie added his story.

'Remember, the day we was going on outing to Ocho Rios and we cook and tek away so much things Miss Levy couldn't help but notice.

39

But we swear it wasn't we but must be her beg beg sister who did come up and tek them.'

Bertie didn't laugh so heartily at this. In fact he glanced a little nervously at the very quiet Mary who had started to wonder what else Corrine had done for him besides washing and cooking.

The way they laughed and joked together made Mary feel like an outsider, that she didn't know her husband.

Corrine, it seemed, was tired of working for the white people and Bertie had promised to get her a job at the hotel so she had come to find out what was happening.

Mary couldn't help but notice how Corrine's eyes darted around the room as if she was taking notes about how they lived. Mary decided that she didn't like her.

When she was ready to leave Bertie offered to walk her to the bus stop and Mary made up her mind to ask him point-blank about her suspicions. But Bertie didn't return and Mary seized the opportunity to sneak away to her church service. When she returned, Bertie was in bed, but strangely he didn't ask her where she had been nor did he fuss about not finding her at home when he got back.

Shortly after that, Bertie began to stay away from home one night in a week or a fortnight, then one night per week regularly, then two and three nights every week. He told Mary that the hotel restaurant at which he worked had started closing very late especially on weekends and that they had set aside two rooms for the staff to sleep rather than have them travel home in the wee morning hours.

Mary said nothing. Not even after the night when she suddenly became ill and on the way to the hospital in a taxi, she begged the neighbour who was accompanying her to stop at the hotel to tell Bertie.

The neighbour was told that Bertie had left for home long ago as the restaurant closed at ten o'clock.

She never asked him about this.

Gradually Mary found that life had returned to its old pattern of regular church-going as Bertie was either not at home or showed no interest in her comings and goings.

Things were like this for some time before it finally dawned on Mary that he was now coming home only once or twice each week. And that since he wasn't wearing the clothes he had there, she had little washing and ironing to do and she didn't have to be constantly cleaning and straightening the house. In fact she was a Thursday wife once more – almost.

And still she didn't say anything, for hadn't the parson insisted – 'God first and all things after'? If this was God's way of giving her the time to serve Him, then she would accept it without murmur or complaint.

When Bertie began to make excuses for not paying the rent or for not giving her any money, she used her savings to buy a sewing machine and went to the Singer classes to refresh her memory. A long time ago she used to sew when she was in the country.

Mary started taking in sewing. She spoiled a few dresses but slowly got the hang of it, and soon enough between the church sisters and others she had more work than she could handle. So between serving the Lord and earning a living she had little time to be lonely and was often surprised when she returned from church to find Bertie in bed on the nights he chose to come to her.

He rarely attempted to make love to her any longer and she was glad because for both of them it was now a joyless exercise.

This pattern continued. Mary didn't know what he did with his time, and she didn't ask him any questions. But one afternoon when she returned home after being out most of the day on a mission of mercy, her neighbour told her that a woman with two small children had been looking for her and had waited some hours hoping to see her. When she asked what the woman looked like, she realised that it was Corrine, who had visited them some years before. Corrine who used to wash and cook for Bertie. Instinctively she knew that this was the reason why he had all but left her. She wondered what Corrine wanted from her. Why she had visited her.

Mary brooded on this for some days so that the next time Bertie came to visit her, she broke her vow of silence and told him about the woman's visit.

She could not quite understand Bertie's reaction. At first he seemed frightened, then angry, then embarrassed and when Mary said, 'I wonder what she want?' he shrugged his shoulders and said, 'I tired. I going to bed.'

Mary sat in the best chair, worn now and faded like her marriage. She sighed. He wasn't even interested enough for them to have a quarrel. Since he was there she couldn't use the machine so what could she do to pass the time? It was too early to go to bed, she thought.

She sighed again and got up to fetch her sewing. At least she could do some handwork.

She sighed another time as she sat down and looked across the room at him lying on the bed in his underwear.

He wasn't even handsome any longer, she thought. Middle age was creeping up on him. Then she acknowledged with surprise that she

41

didn't have any feelings for him any longer. She didn't love him. She didn't even like him. It wasn't that he was no longer physically attractive, for she too had put on weight and her stomach had started its middle-age swell. It was more the fact that he was a stranger to her. As if she had never ever been truly married to him. She didn't know him.

She wondered when he would make up his mind to leave her altogether. She didn't know why he bothered to keep up the pretence.

She could not know that Bertie was not asleep. That he lay there wondering how he had got himself into so much confusion. That most of all he was wondering how he had left this good woman to get involved first with Corrine and now with the devil who was out to mash up his life.

He thought of Corrine and her two children and how lately she had started nagging him, and how the children were getting on his nerves as they always seemed to be crying.

And he thought of Mary, patient Mary, who through all the years had never even questioned him when many other women would have made a stink. He thought how she always welcomed him, never turned him away even though she had more than good reason to do so.

He thought also of the other woman who had recently begun to pursue him. He had met her at the restaurant. She was a customer. She had invited him out after work and he had accepted. At first it was exciting to be with this superior, polished lady, but lately the things she wanted him to do in bed made him feel rebellious.

Corrine, he thought, had come to see Mary because she was wondering why he was staying out so often.

What a mess! he thought. The best thing to do, perhaps, was to come back to his wife Mary. He was getting tired of those other demanding women.

'Cho! Mary,' he said, turning around suddenly and startling her. 'Turn off the light now, and come to bed.'

Mary, dutiful as ever, sighed. She hoped he had no amorous thoughts. That night more than ever she would not be able to accommodate him.

Perhaps she wouldn't ever be able to accommodate him again.

FAUSTIN CHARLES

◁ ■■■■■■■■■■■■■■■ ◇ ■■■■■■■■■■■■■■■ ▷

Signpost of the Phoenix

As a carpenter and sign-painter, Blake gets a lot of work for the two days of Carnival: painting flags, decorating brass and copper, building wooden structures, bending wire and designing costumes for the many band-leaders and others who sought his services and advice. Carnival time was his supreme triumph; he always felt outside himself and bigger than himself, a king, king of the world. The few weeks preceding the two-day festival, he would sit alone in his room in the city, thinking and planning about the bands, the masqueraders and the spectacle; the unforgettable beauty of past Carnival bands, and the greater glory of the things to come.

O God Ah seein dem comin down de road like fire burnin up de place de sun happy forever in meh life Papa an Mama dat is mas in yuh mas an dont name me but Ah higher dan a kite yuh never see action like dat movin in yuh face an outa yuh face creation killin dem wid handiwork an footwork an bodywork over an under ontop an below yonder an beyond anyting yuh ever dream of in dis world an de nex musicman in yuh born days steelban is yuh sweetest saviour pan makin an shakin yuh ways wid de free spirit yuh eyeball comin outa yuh head an yuh soul takin a flight to de ends of a rainbow all a dem should win firs prize wid dey heart turnin inside out for love an rejoicin O lord for de two days Ah is King Ah bigger dan anyting on dis side of de eart Ah provin mehself better dan mehself in so many ways for everybody to see an put a crown on meh head so many time Ah tellin people dat Ah is de greatest inventor wen it come to make an remakin costume jus look at dat history ban call Carib Warriors & Hunters man some wounded men lookin like dey really really hurt in battle Papa sailor ban will always be popular cause dey does make every dem people danein like dey real for true look at dem rhinestone glitterin an dem beadwork flatterin in de sun look how dem frill cuttin de light an shapin up ripples in de sky to make yuh eye pop out dey mus win someting if not firs prize dey mus make some kinda impression on everybody min an soul look at de jumpup in sagating everybody watchin dat dazzlin yellow an crimson slicin nice nice allyuh move let dem pass nice great an keep rememberin dem for de

43

twodays let de whole town open up for dem cause mas like dat will never dead clap dem shout bravo an lose yuhself wid happiness cause today Mondaymas dey ridin high an dey comin back tomorrow Tuesday for de breakaway watch dem good keep dem at de top of yuh list cause King Carnival say dis is mas of clas We Papa de city jumpin up as King Carnival start de ball a rollin for two solid days of fete Man woman an chile in Jour Ouvert dress up ringin roun de streets wid de road march tamin a dragon who get away from dey wildest dreams look bacchanal wen dey meet de snakeman an de midnight robber nice movement pardner nice let yuh mas see my mas an all a we boun for glory man Ah happy for so dat Ah come to live in de city dis town can make yuh or break yuh an dat is if yuh stupid not me Ah make someting of mehself Carnival is a tonic for meh betterment look at dat Moko Jumbie watchin me an twistin up e waist in magic sweetpan tunin de Jab Molassi an Dame Lorraine eyein we wid a mysterious eyebeam hear dem singin Netty Netty give meh de ting dat yuh have in yuh belly hear dem shoutin Is de moustache we want Hitler some of dem drunk like a fish hear some leaders comin up an down de road wid another refrain In a Calabash sweet an on target shack shack an bottle an spoon too de shouter ban swingin thru de crowd chantin ole mas come to stay steel ringin in meh head an Ah seein another ban Ah work for Spanish Sailors & Soldiers dey movin so proud Ah like de blue an silver goldbraid silverwettin corners velvetlinin hip an shoulder meh fingertouch here an dere is outa dis world all a dem so sure of deyself wid de look on dey face an how dey carryin dey costume an dey positions in de ban dey look so powerful an mighty Ah sure dey goin to win either firs secon or tird prize dey really doin someting to everybody all a dem head high up like dey braver dan de sun an moon put together dat is de great work of many months an years an some nights widout sleep an yuh wakeup plannin an tinkin an retinkin an replannin an den de paintin bendin buildin reworkin wirebendin redoin an undoin hammerin out copper tin steel cardboard wood an stone an brass an silver seein an reseein silver an steel singin an dancin yellow brown red fringin inside an outside de peacock feather sequin shapin rhinestone bead an glass on wire an iron an wood in red flashin crimson spikes yuh seein fire an wirenettin catchin crepepaper in trimmins of orange an vermilion on mauve an bronze lightin green waves skyblue sparkles de bells of stars splittin blue flame into de sun explodin into de glitter of rubies an edges of diamond strikin silk an satin an embroidered goldsides seein breastplate ridin de emerald road footstep in pink gem lines in purple lookin up an down an all about everybody ripe wid de sweetness of de everlastin light an de sweetness of

all is golden like a emperor cause today an tomorrow all man an woman
an chile is on de road everybody tune up wid steelban everybody laughin
seein demself in one another mas in yuh mas in a butterflyman an
tangerine woman comin outa yuh face wid powderup smile an ting roun
an roun de tuneboom makin style wid de face of clown givin dem room
de two stickfighter an dem clickin stick an makin trick wid a skeleton
hangin over dey head like a jackindebox set free de pingpong shapin de
glare of de sun on de face of a scarlet bat on skates Ah like how e
sidesteppin de children dress up standin on de pavement dey sharin e
joy an e mas good for so look at de sweat on de furry breath of dat man
playin tiger behin de Devil ban comin in a stream of fire an steel all a
dem swayin an callin for more iron an more liquor catchin dey power in
a mirror full wid sapphire an de imps an dem wid dey pitchforks red
spreadin joy in needlework an dyein yuh face an nan in de paint of yuh
body sing de tune loud an clear Is trouble in Arima Is trouble by de
corner hol on to a woman hugup an kiss she an if yuh cant fin a woman
hugup a man yuh feelin de polkadot beast climbin thru yuh flesh in de
ban capsizin wid a crash in de biggest sailorban yuh ever see comin from
one side a de town an reachin de other side yuh head goin roun like a
windmill O lord listen to sweet sweet pan iron clinkkkkkkkkkkkk
jinglinnnnnnnnnnnn yuh waist make outa sweetness dan-
cinnnnnnnnnnnn yuhself from here to eternity pingponnnnnnnnnnng
comin roun de bridge Papa dat is mas father boss de flag nnnnn dey
name African Tribesmen & Gods dey jumpinnnnnnnnn robus like a
storm openup an let dem go dey fearless wid de tiger lion an snakeskin
an dem spear teethinnnnnnn a mighty chantinnnnnnnn cause dey
comin to change de judges decision like fire runninnnnnnn all about
watch dem pretty step Ah remember dem from a little boy de firs time
Ah ever see mas de chiefs an dem look makin style but gran man dey
puttin someting far far down inside yuh cause rememberin a ban yuh
seeeeeeeeeeeee long long time wen Carnival did firs start outa de way
everybody cause ban like dis yuhll see in every Carnival till yuh dead
look at dem leopardskin framin in two wid de ostrichfeather stickinup on
de hunters head reelin backwards on de throne of dey glory fancy
woodwork spinnnnnnnnnn into circles on dey bodyline drivin out
greennnnnnnnnnnn velvet skies an frilly gold metal workinnnnnnnnn
an blazinnnnnnnn thru dey shoulder an ches dem beadwork necklace
plaitup so great yuh can feel it on yuh O God King Kabaka come to take
all de prizes dey have in de place de tenorpan beatin so
sweeeeeeeeeeeeeeeeeeeeeeeet bringin dem on like thunder diamond tone
sweeeeeeeeeeeeeeeetpin de place wid de winners of all a dem name

45

watchin mas like dis is de only time man feel man is man an life sweeeeeeeeeeeeeeet ripe blood de birdfeathers givin signal to all on de sittin down carryin throne a holy seat carve outa mahogany an polish wid ingrowin varnish to dazzle a star flowerin de lion flowin mane hot on de trail of de skygods an de eart gods steel an silver breakin stone an changin colour in de hot sun again an again dey singin in meh brain Legba Eshu Nyambi Ogun Shango carvinnnnnnn ivory from de souls of de windin elephant de drummers in de backgroun get de han waves from de Oba an dis town can never be de same after seeinnnnnn dis ban comin all over dem after seein dis ban all man feel to play mas any kinda mas so long as dey playin mas for now an till it over people watchin one another in wonder an tellin demself dat dey have to search deep deep down inside dem to fin de true praise for dis hellava ban dat change dey life for as long as dey know wen an how in dis world an de nex comin on always strong liftin dey life to de highest enjoyment yes Carnival isa powerful ting in showin off Bannnnnnnnnnnnnnnnnns clashin into one another reapin de fruits of dey labour for so long an de two days colour temptation devourinnnnnnn de haves of all de happiness in pulpin plumes swinginnnnnnn headpiece risinnnnnnn like a torch leadin de way to de depths of de lookinglass an hallelujah sendin shocks up an down yuh spine forevermore warpaint on de tide turnin caterpillar injectinnnnnnn de leafy patterns in seeds make outa silver an organdie runnin cross de velveteen tantalisin de ban Hindu Worshippers & Keepers of the Temple of Brahma seein Krishna wid de Holy Vedic scripture jumpin up in de splendour of de Taj Mahal shinnin outside is de Pundits prayin O lord deliver us to mas victory today an tomorrow de tipsy sari an dohti stretchin from head to bosom an waist an down to de groun de girls an dem pretty too bad nice craft saffron namin de Sadhu an Sahib from de untouchable skippin in time an line up gentle for de Mogul survivor strikin dey foundation wid every blow from de drums an shake of brass bells unveilin de deity on pink lotus an Kshatriya de line a warriors de gong soundin an de shreds of tulsi leaf sweet taffeta to relax on as de smooth pebbles an sticks of sandalwood invite yuh to join dem in dey canboulay like a dream over dey heads an under dey skin it resemble Husai festival de flagwaver Sirdar tellin de Brahmins to bring up de sections to de front look at how Vishnu an Siva smilin very sure of deyself silk eye silk heartways to dye cotton days in flesh an orion watch de temple headpiece fillin all wid de same question Wholl be de ban of de year but a lotta people ent min cause all de ban an dem good bos mas father crossin over de park a ban a small one callin demself Dutch Seafarers & Discoverers wid lightning in dey tracks dey goin by quick

like dey ent too sure of a place in de prizegivin Ah did de work on dey
small ship an de standardbearer Ah ent tink dey have a chane of winnin
any of de top prizes cause dey too small if dey wus big dey might have
been in someting but otherwise no still dey costume full a surprises de
fleets in dem cannon rollin wood on wheels an de galvanise cracker
boom on dey uniform admiral an all salute de plasterparis cannonball
gun flint an de air full a smoke an joke comin up behin dem is one of de
big bans of de day Ah can see dem now clear de sign readin The
Emperor of France & His Court from head to foot dey in shinnin armour
steel raisin steel helmet plungin sword lances an battleaxe dey watchin
hard an mighty dey puttin new strange light in people eye cause dey
dressup to kill chargin reelin into glory wid de emperor standin taller
dan e longest memory e can remember silver on bronze cuttin up space
like a demon come to rule de twodays wid might an right in dey brain an
in dey body dey watchin elegant controllin deyself wid majesty for a
noble ting in dey ban man it very big look how dey flexin dey muscle wid
horse an carriage wid dem King inside feelin eself de only ting under
heaven dey takin every space wid dey big self an willin to take on anyting
besides dat dey eye searchin every way for any ban dat can beat dis ban
in de lan blue an silver flamin thru nickleplate standup de bravest de
trumpets soun a call for de palaceguards formation marchin on to a
victory dey will never forget spikeout dey fortunes of war an service to
dey radiant king steerin outa goldleaf an fringes of fireglass olive turnin
up de hill China The Ming Dynasty Ah have a special likeness for dis
ban Ah did some work on dey banners an it comin home to me me true
true dey gentle an graceful performin light like a feather de red skirtin
silk so soft into lilac an jade from west to de east livewire feet upon
jasmin an violetgold spinnin stain settin nylon into peacockblue an
turquoise trimmin an de needlework of butterflies treadin de tapestry
engravin gold an indigo stripes into brocade an lace skippin along de
threads of light green buttons twangin totems of ermine into rainbow
clusters on de gran emblem floats an stills wid Confucius an de Emperor
in dignity de sections of de court an palace guards in rows of gold an silk
in deep azure like a fairytale de gowns line wid satin balancin de
spotlight on a curtain of swansdown in pinkpetals of a luckycharm up to
de great wall leadin to a temple of bright yellow wid ultraviolet patterns
showin quilts of silver an lime green engravin of de signs a de zodiac see
de lanterns wavin free home an away fanfare heraldin de Empress in she
dazzlin cape shoulders erect proud thru shotsilk in pompous satin wid
pearl linin de opal smile in de reflection of de dragonbanner passin wid
flutes silverspeckle into periwinkleblue an beamin lame performin in

gracious swerves flamingoribbons on poplin followin yellow skies of chestnut threadin goldleaf an slippers dancin into de military gong an de wiseole a soothsayer tellin de magic carpet ride to step aside meh frien Achong an Bertie Ching playin sagaboy today an tomorrow happy wid everybody dey meetup showin dey embroidery tunic an satin hat streakin in heavy wide eye sleeve delicate onto de chrome bird in a tide a fishermen rowin home in farreachin glaze on robes into sleak tiger linen along de imperial clan loom like porcelain on a section of footsoldiers chargin de barrier man dem pretty too bad sword features over green an blue velveteen showin de way pass de Syrian store an up for de prizegivin nice mandarin man an dem boun to take someting away today waitin on de judges stan one of de bigges ban yuh can see today an people say dey comin back tomorrow for more excitement dey name A History of Imperial England O God dey some thousands strong yuh cant see de end or where dey start from Papa look at St George an de dragon in steel clingin to silver in e han in de dragon mout master columns of horsemen an footsoldiers an de charge of de light brigade look Sir Walter Raleigh in brass gleamin copper hangin on e swordknife Francis Drake makin style wid e head in gold an blue jacket in silver gauze look at de knights in mighty armour Richard de lionheart an Ivanhoe smilin in high collars passin de formation a cannonfire an parade of Queen Victoria Queen Elizabeth in a gran salute for all to see an wonder outa dey min look de horse drawn carriage of gold onto strokes of chrome jewels of fire into velvet adornin de segments of flashin ermine on a cluster of pearls de Royal Artillery in plenty fuss an honour transformin muskets into hammer out sheets of silver an varnish soft wood into de crowns of rubies an crystal onto opal framin gold glass bead work Admiral Nelson an e fleet strike de platform in silver linin breastplate an de beige an brown zinc into plastic ship walk takes a comman echoin de high quality of contruction father in meh han holdin up deyself in leatherstrips an bleedin brocade of Shakespeare jumpin in time wid George de third an King Alfred along side King Arthur beckonin de Knights of de Roun Table wid de Duke of Wellington smilin on Henry de Eight an Mary Queen of Scots an King Charles de firs onto Oliver Cromwell an e Rounheads wid de Archbishop of Canterbury onto a Prince of Wales an some Princes an Princesses an other Dukes and Duchesses wid Hawkins Henry Morgan an dem steppin masterful in de place like up to de Tower of London make outa wood an cardboard an asbestos an roofin strips of tin iron wid brass O God dey movin like a real rivalry an de trumpet an dem trombone jammin sweet like fire in de emblem of red white an blue homage de glitter an clash of steel an silver blendin de session of de Changin of de guards bringin up de factions of de Royal Dragoons de Royal Battalion wid banner of a golden lion on satin thru silver shinnin into steel an blue green plumes outa dey headpiece de shinnin armour swayin wid gunboats cannon fire outside de ship rollin on wheels into de ermine fur like a magic carpet on de groun holdin up de bigges crowd all roun de place dis is like a gran celebration an everybody like dey want to join in an follow dis ban cause dey really pass boss wid dey projection an dem ring an ruff collar roun dey neck so elegant some people even feel to cry wen dey see mas like dis some people want to go home now after seein a ban like dis but dey stayin an feastin dey eye on de ban like dey hypnotise outa dey head an dem Royal Grenadier guards lookin bold like dey ready for action it seem like nuthin can match dem braid on big buckle shoes an white stockin tight fittin in silver silk sparklin breeches onto velvet puffs makin dey shoulders stan out champion man look at de touches of metallic green an amethyst into a blaze of crimson an gold in de neckline some of dem face powderup nice dancin in de Royal court fancy footwork even on de pavement an de plumes set in heavy costume jewellery dey ent big but dey boastin deyself an provokin a clap from everybody dey carryin deyself to de brim an de cape of de king make outa lame line wid rhinestones in silver bead cutouts longer dan de ship wid four pageboys holdin it up de doublets rich wid silver an gold braidin an crowns of cutglass line ring outa gold trim wid large glass bead emerald mas in yuh mas man mas like fire an fire in yuh tail dazzlin yuh eye an dem everytime yuh look back behin in front an yonder anywhere yuh turn yuh body an soul feelin like it strain an yuh brain comin outa yuh head an goin back in better dan it wus before roun de corner comin in darts leaps an kicks is one of de bigges ban yuhll see today an tomorrow dey name wait let meh see de flag good yes Ah seein like all de other ban an dem will have to settle for de secon or de tird prize today an tomorrow dis is really one a de bes history mas Ah see for a long time in all de pas carnival yes man allyuh great allyuh have everything under control wid mas look at dem shield an lance pretty like pretty self in spinnin gold leaf an velvet cord sparklin like a gem Ah hear people already sayin dat one or two of de individual an dem already win a prize for dey costume cuttin nice in every way an dey ent showin off at all cause dey know dey great so dey jus takin it easy an enjoyin deyself wid all dey have cause dey know de ban a de year title in dey bag Ah seein a small group a boys marchin an jumpin in a ban comin by de junction dey playin a Expedition of Henry the Navigator Ah know one or two a dem potagee boy playin in dis ban dey lookin alright but again dey only have bout two hundred playin in de ban even wid dat Ah ent tink dey have a chance of winnin ban a de year dey might win a prize but not de firs prize dey stylish an stately movin like waves comin ashore an dey brigade of cannonguns cutlass sword hawkbells an a row of dem handlin a caravel like if dey really at sea facin high win an high sea drift look how dey controllin dat ship make outa plywood an castiron an zinc on wire paint wid lightgreen an greybrown brace wid thinnin an de flag flyin nice look at dem folds a strippin silver an jackets wid button of steel into polish helmets an blindin breastplate wid leather patchwork fittin to a swordcase watch dat man playin Infante Dom Hanrique de prince wid e hat wid tassels long gold button on e velvet robe an braids a rhinestones ring roun e collar look at de way de yellow an green look at Vasco da Gama an Cabral approachin in painstakin riproarin costume dem floats de Kingdom of Portugal mus get a special prize man dem bead goldin it clear now dey name Sailors Ashore USA Warship Skipjack man dis ban ent care what dey do dey throwin powder on all de women an dem face dey jumpin all over de place officers an men spreadin joy dey ship rigged up good goin on bicycle wheels goin smooth an dem tanks an guns lookin real powerful man dey mean war in de place de sailors in dey white drill an white caps an black ties de officers in dey grey suits an stripes an decoration serious for so Ah feastin meh eye on all dem military cord an dem smart officer hat wid dey fancy medals an dey revolvers roun dey wais smart man look jus look at de jeep an de anti aircraft gun an dem dey fix bayonet an dey nice fittin gabardine an shinnin black shoes man dey ready to defen any body from anyting dey real real ready for any kinda war look how some a dem tumblin in de canal man de fleets in Ah tell yuh get ready an hide yuh girlchile an dem look navyblue to kill or stop anyting dey cuttin very sharp in de hot sun man dey rockin de ship some a dem hug up in a long line swayin to an fro an plenty a dem drunk like hell wid rum an sweet pan brayin in dey head like de town catch afire look de captain inspectin dem dey doin a short drill an dem sailor boy standin at real attention look at dem spotted green khaki outfit sprawlin on de groun wid dey guns creepin up on de enemy wen dey lan ashore look at de SPs and MPs an some wounded men lookin like dey really really hurt in battle Papa sailor ban will always be popular cause dey does make everybody feel so happy de rifles an de drillin an de marchin is someting special dey is a favourite of every man woman an chile cause some people feel dat dey might not be able to afford to play in a big history ban but dey can always play someting in a sailor ban cause it cheap compare to a big history mas an of course yuh can use yuh sailor clothes to wear after

Carnival look at dey saga shuffle an heavy goggles thick gloves an pipe in dey mout dey staggerin an swingin an de girls wid dey fashion ting corbeau lock behin breezin down de street like high spot glamour gals an de rhythm shakin dey wais in fan meh saga boy fan meh an Ah went to donkey city to circumcise meh body an de mule say to de donkey sagaboy dont caray behin meh donkey whoa dont tear up meh junior commando yes is sweetenin de bodyline an look at dem army flashin dey bazooka an han grenade dey breakaway today an wen sailor man get pay e out to burnup de town wid liquor an woman watch dat fireman dance nuh watch King Sailor excellin in fancy bodywork look at dem dazzlin medallions an ribbons yes dem yankee sailors come to take over an comin up by de market some Wild Indians an Chiefs an now move outa de way any jamet look at dem feas yuh eye on dem man red blue black an white Indians dem costume is outa dis world man look at dem red satin fringe skirt an merino wid red dye an dem paint up feather on sequins an rhinestone an wig black fray out hemp rope man jus look at dat headpiece a high crown of wire cover wid red paper ribbon an artificial roses an dem war bonnet make outa fowl feather an peacock feather an dem faces paint wid warpaint in roocoo an dem long beads an dat mirror makin de sun shine outa dey face look at Chief Sittin Bull an Crazy Horse givin de braves de warrior cry de spear an dem look mean Ah tell yuh look at dem cut an paint on red pearl in between dat swansdown ripplin in de breeze dem ostrich feather in every colour yuh can tink of green an blue an velveteen strips an brown on mauve on pink an crimson gold on silver nettin an dey have a canoe make outa cardboard an plywood an dey have wigwam rollin on bicyclewheel goin nice an smooth man look de medicine man jumpin up an makin style look at dat fellar smokin a peacepipe in dem turquoise line on limegreen tinge wid maroon an yellow an lilac overall an de animalskin in leatherette an dem fine extra fine needlework on de wigwam everyting like it lightin in de sun people sayin already dat outa all de ban an dem a prize mus go to either King Philip from de Spanish history ban or Queen Elizabeth from de English history ban or Louis de fourteen from de French history ban or Henry de Navigator from de Portuguese ban or de Emperor from de golden age of China ban an de man playin Lord Krishna from de worshippers an followers of de Hindu ban or de fellar playin de Kabaka from de Africa ban one a dese mus win de prize for de bes individual mas of de year an one outa dese ban an dem boun to take away de ban a de year prize

WILLI CHEN

◁ ━━━━━━━━━━━ ◇ ━━━━━━━━━━━ ▷

The Stickfighter

When I took him down that afternoon amid the black flutter of wings darkening the branches overhead, the sun was almost down, but the heat was still there, trapped in the hollows that encircled the tree of death. There was no time to pause or to find the answers for all those questions that rushed into my brain: the squabbles, the unanswered letters and his long absence. All these answers were lost for ever in the dampness of his brows and quieted by the pallor of death.

I touched his cold arm, turning him around where the noose had bitten sharply at the nape of his neck. I was struck by the blueness of his skin and its tautness, by the morbid puffing out of his eyelids and cheeks that could not contain the protruding tongue – I had seen enough. I eased the tension of the corpse as he swung back under the groan of the rope and our life time's friendship rallied in front of me just before I swung the cutlass, felling him on to soft ground.

Bastahall loomed in the distance, a dusty, arid maze, a scrabble of brown earth trampled by oxen. On my left, the sea of cane ended at the mangroves which receded seawards, where the vegetation was lush and green with the glut of herons, lily white. I had tied the cart at the nearby clumps of blacksage. The beast was still, not even moving to shake the flies off its rump, as if sensing the gravity of the situation, with the stench of death around us.

Rain fell that afternoon and mud clung to my boots in wet chunks. With petite marie sticking to my pants' fold and around my chest, I had difficulty getting the body on to the cart. I tied the hands together, then passed the rope around the body so that the arms remained together. The denim trousers were stiff with mud from the fields where he had worked.

When I first met him he was already in his thirties, gaunt, nothing extraordinary in his walk or speech. There was nothing startling enough to stir him. His was a world of peace and work. He spent his time in the shelter of the pens, caring for the animals and feeding them. He could have been well over six feet, but his lean figure lent him an air of pure grace. I knew he was strong in all his gentleness, but it was in the gayelle where he circled like a hawk on the hot sand, head tied, and the red end cloth of his stick fluttering in the breeze like a signal of death, that I saw in him special quality which made him a champion.

Those were Scottie's heydays, black and powerful, already renowned in the districts as an established stickman, who used to come down from Carolina to play in Couva, his stick pushed straight behind his back at his buttocks as if it were the natural position for keeping his weapon. He limped slightly, bending his right knee a little more quickly than he should, with a slight drag of his foot, almost in a slow crawl. But in the gayelle no one observed his peculiar gait, for when the stick was held poised with both hands, people looked at its whirring speed as it became alive.

Then there was 'Nation', that mulatto who grinned impishly under the barrage of blows, but who always retaliated with a speed and power that could break his opponent's stick in two. He was very swift, but Alphaeus was even more dangerous. He, too, came in search of battle down the mud paths from Chickland, head aloft, tied with the narrow strip of white cloth in fine style.

All the battles were fierce and colourful. Blood dripped on the sand, oozing from the broken heads. They continued long into the night as the kegs of Mountain Dew emptied and the drums boomed louder and louder around the bonfire. On those afternoons of gruelling pace, the strongest survived as they circled the hot sand under the blazing sun that parched their throats and broiled their sweating bodies.

It was strange that no one really knew his real name and no one ever bothered to find out. But everyone called him Bogo, even the smallest child, and they suspected it was only a nickname which he had brought with him when he first came into the village. Perhaps it was his quiet nature that impressed us, his ambling, carefree nonchalance, and the way the smoked-out cigarette butts hung from his half-closed lips, the long ash drooping precariously to the side whilst the smoke rings rose over his head in measured puffs.

Late one afternoon Bogo arrived from Esperanza village where he occupied a single room in the barracks, which stood adjoining others in rabbit-hutch fashion with the bland façade of cheap bricks. He looked happy, the straw hat took on a steep slant and the red parrot feather on it was colourful. He met us drinking beneath Latchun's shop. He knocked the ash off his cigarette and said, 'Boys, ah getting married.'

'Doh make joke, man!' Ramlal said.

'Yes, man, ah going shack up with Indrani.'

'Who you mean? Rajbool daughter-in-law?' I asked.

'Used to be, man. Ah taking over now.' Bogo thumped his stick on the ground as Boyoon downed the glass of Carupano rum and spat, missing the spittoon by a full two feet. I jumped off my stool.

Ramlal poured another drink and said, 'Come man, Bogo. You mean to tell me dat you going take Indrani away from Sonnyboy, and they not even married three months yet?'

Bogo took off his straw hat and patted it, straightening the bright red parrot feather. He replied, 'Dat girl getting real bad treatment and she don't have no family.'

'How you come in this business?' I asked him.

'I come in this business because ah seeing advantage.' He turned the hat around in his hand.

'Is true, Ramlal,' Boyoon said. 'Since dat girl come to live by, is endless horrors for she; licks like peas.'

'What she do so bad?' Ramlal asked.

Boyoon continued, holding the glass of rum in his hand: 'Well, boy. Ah hear is two time she does get licks; in the morning and in the evening, that is before he go to work and when he come back. One time she run away by she sister in Felicity. Dat is the only family she have.'

'And why she don't stay there?' I asked him.

'Well, ah hear the sister and all have de same problem. She does get she share ah licks too. De only difference is she have children and she can't go no way,' Boyoon continued.

'But, Bogo, you don't have no right wid she either and dat is husband and wife business,' Ramlal interjected.

'Dat is true, Ram, but you going to wait till she dead before ah man do something. The man drunk everyday. He father have cattle and land. Dat doh mean he must beat the woman like that,' Bogo said, still turning the hat in his hands as he patted the red feather.

'Do what you want, Bogo, but dis ting will bring trouble and besides Sonnyboy not going to take this lying down. He bad like crab and not only that, he know more badjohns than you.'

Bogo gave the hat one turn with his right hand, balancing its crown at the tip of the index finger of his left hand and raising his head he said, 'Well, boy, anybody could be a badjohn and ah don make up me mind already; the girl coming by me. I have a old cot and she will stay as long as she want.'

Then in one movement he tossed his hat into the air, in a wide arc. As it descended, Bogo shifted lithely, braced himself and then, rocking on the tip of his toes, moved his head as if wanting to dodge it. With arms outstretched for balance, he bent his knees the same way I saw him so many times before in the gayelle. Then he raised his shoulders and the hat fell plump on the crown of his head, with its peak turned backwards. He jumped, pulling his stick over our heads and with the same movement of his arm, swung it around and around until his hand became almost invisible. The stick climbed skywards with its end cloth trailing. For a moment we stood looking at Bogo standing slim and tall like some signpost in the yard. He moved once more. Slowly at first, like a cricketer in the field anticipating the ball in the air, shifting to the right, then to the left and suddenly he raised his right arm in a flash, and the plummeting stick appeared in his hand. Raising it once more he swung the stick, churning the air as it whirled at an astonishing speed. In a minute he was gone leaving us mesmerised by his dexterity.

One week passed and Indrani's move to Bogo's room on the sugar estate was the only incident that warranted any lengthy talk in the rumshops, or in the fields amongst women with their blackened faces where the sway of poignards would stop momentarily and their chatter take on new colour. The people thought about Bogo, a renegade and skulker, the ignoble penman, a labourer who found himself her keeper, her lover. To Sonnyboy, the spoilt son of the prominent village landlord, this state of affairs was a slap in the face; an insult to his prestige, discrediting his manhood.

It was no surprise then that Sonnyboy came up to the barracks one day with some of his friends and demanded that Indrani come home. It was evening time, when the last cane carts were rumbling home and the cane cutters walked behind, swinging their empty calabashes and crocksticks, their clothes blackened from the burnt cane ash.

Standing at the roadside near his Land Rover jeep, Sonnyboy called, 'Indrani, you home? Ah come for you!'

The small group of men with him remained silent. There were three of them, one sitting on the bonnet of the jeep. Hearing no reply, he left the group and came into the yard. He encircled his mouth with his hands and called out in a half-demanding, half-pleading manner. In the darkness he hoped that the men standing around the jeep could not detect the urgent tone of his voice.

'Indrani, make up you mind, ah losing me patience. Indrani, ah not begging,' he said. 'If you don't come, it go be real war and tell Bogo he go be in it too.'

Behind the fragile door, Indrani peeped through the crack and became frightened. She saw him in the yard. She hoped he would not come any closer to the gallery. He continued, 'Indrani, answer or I go break down the door.'

She gathered courage: 'Ah not coming back and if you touch the door, Bogo go do for you.'

'Oh is so? Well is me and you. Go tell Bogo is war. You hear? Is war!'

'Go away now, ah not coming back,' she replied.

'Tell Bogo is fire today and we waiting by the marketplace for he.' He shouted desperately in a louder tone so that his friends could hear him. 'Tell he come with his pouistick. Is blood and sand. It go be licks and we go spread he out like rice on the ground, you hear?' he shouted angrily.

The Land Rover sped off in a cloud of dust.

The next day was market day. The women trekked from Bastahall, Springland and from as far as Indian Trail that went beyond remote Carolina. They came with oiled feet, dressed in their waterwashed tunics, unstarched orhnis, with glinting bangles and nose rings and with baskets under their arms, as they filtered into the marketplace and crowded the vendors who crouched behind stalls and squatted behind shallow trays of Indian sweetmeats and market produce. Colourful clothes were displayed and bright bolts of cloth cascaded from carts. The hawkers peddled their wares with an open voice beneath the papery grace of whirling windmills held shoulder high, colouring the wind.

Far from the hustle and chatter of bartering women was the gayelle, a small grass-fringed patch of earth that shimmered in the sun, the white sand soft and hot. Around its perimeter sat the drummers with busy hands, their naked legs wrapped tightly around the drums. It was here the men gathered to smoke ganja, as the stench of Mountain Dew soured their breaths and clouded their senses in wanton gaiety. It was here too they found action.

Bogo was standing, leaning against the watermelon shed one foot on the crossbar, as if to support the rickety structure. His hat angled and his cigarette dropped, accentuating the smirk on his lips. He waved an arm and soon we were deep in conversation.

'Boy Charlo, I must keep Indrani. I get to like the woman now, but I don't know what will happen.'

'Well, you sure Sonnyboy will take her back?' I asked.

'That I don't know. You mean she have to go back for more licks, better she go back to she uncle,' he said.

He could not disguise the tone of pity in his voice. His moistened eyes betrayed his feelings. With his arm over my shoulders, we walked into the open when the sudden outburst of voices assailed us in a frenzy. The voices were distinct in the crowded stalls.

'Bogo, they looking for you, Scottie and Ranny, and Victory . . . Nation and all. Sonnyboy bring them for you . . . is cut ass dey say.'

'Better turn back,' another voice said. I grabbed Bogo's arm, tugging at it and said, 'We better really do that, Bogo. Is trouble up there. Let us go home, man.'

But he just stood there, suddenly motionless, and the twinkle had gone from the brown of his eyes and in its place came the cold glint of steel. His whole body tensed, and I knew it was useless pleading with him, for the time had come, as Sonnyboy had promised.

The crowd gathered around the gayelle. Tar-chested, Scottie seemed blacker in the sun as he stood against the soft milkiness of clouds with the daubs of violet shadows beneath his brows, his lips and flaring nostrils. He loomed even more terrible in the sunlight, a figure of doom bringing with him expertise and power, as he strutted on the sand, like some overgrown African doll with the strip of yellow around his head. He threw his stick on the ground in challenge, picked up sand in his hand, rubbed his wrists and forearms and flexed his fingers. Then he raised his bois high over his head and shouted in defiance:

'Is Bogo, ah want, that mule-pen man. Where he?'

We stood in the shade; Bogo was silent as he leant on his stick.

'Where' the man wife, lover man?' Scottie bellowed.

I pulled Bogo's shirt sleeve again.

'You can't fight that man, Bogo. He go kill you.'

'Never run from a man yet, Charlo.'

Scottie exposed his mighty chest, reeled around in a circle to the pound of drumbeats, churning up the sand like a rhinoceros preparing to charge.

'Come, Bogo, is blood ah want. You afraid? Either you bring Indrani or play bois with me,' Scottie shouted.

A chuckle rippled through the crowd. I saw Bogo straighten himself and I knew then that he was angry. He walked into the gayelle, stick in hand, a gaunt figure, wiry in his whip-like stance, his old straw hat pulled right over his eyes and the long cigarette drooping from the corner of his lips. He stood like some dry mora yard post with neither colour in his figure nor valour in his presence except for the one red parrot feather in his hat band. Scottie pranced up and down like the champion he had long proven himself to be, gallant, strong, warrior from the Carolina foothills, pride of his villages.

Bogo pulled his hat over his head to hide his eyes, and when he raised his stick, the red end cloth fluttered, the pouistick gleamed and the brass of the ring at the other end sparkled in the sun. Scottie approached him in the squatting position as he shook his weapon over his chest, clasping it with both hands, his massive thighs angled to support his gargantuan frame. The yellow strand of cloth lifted in the breeze behind his head, and someone at the back muttered, 'That is stickman. He from Carolina and I never see his head bust yet.'

'That the man Sonnyboy bring to beat Bogo?' another asked.

'That the killer. Watch how he foot, strong like iron.'

No one saw the first blow, only the scuffle of moving feet as they lifted the sand in the wind, but Scottie had struck the first stroke, following up with four more in rapid succession. Then Bogo, cool, his eyes beneath the dim canopy of his old straw hat, shifted his tall frame to the left and parried the blows with little fuss. The drumming stopped, the crowd gasped. Scottie's face showed surprise and Bogo, standing erect, did nothing but pulled his hat over his head once more and the drummers pounded the goatskins again.

Now Bogo, tall in the sun, raised his head. His right leg trailed with the pants' fold loose on the sand, and he peeped from below that old straw hat once more, his eyes concealed, rolling like marbles within the dark confines, as if to verify the position of the moving target. The strip of yellow cloth swayed in the breeze and his own head bobbed and weaved to the drum beat.

Suddenly he exploded into action. Speed was the keynote of his attack. His slender poui came down with lightning force on Scottie's head, reddening the white sand around his feet as the thronging crowd, hoarse and sweaty, backed away in disbelief, as they saw their champion reel under the battering blows. Six times the limbering stick descended from the blue heavens, digging deeply on the same spot on the crown of his head until the white of Scottie's eyes shone, exuding cold terror and pain. The yellow strip on his head reddened to a deep scarlet.

A gentle wind rustled through the coconut trees but it failed to soothe Scottie's wounds and the drops of his own blood seemed larger and redder than jumbie beads in the sand. He knelt on the ground a pitiful sight, spattered with his own blood and his shirt in tatters. The crowd roared in disbelief. Scottie, the black giant from Carolina, was biting dust. Sonnyboy then turned to Victory.

Victory sprang out from the coconut shade, snarling. There was evidence of skill and experience in this man. A scar ran from the top of his head to his brows, over the eyelids down to his chin on the left of his face; his left eye never blinked. He pranced up and down with his 'bois' raised, smooth, brown and thick. Bogo stationed himself at the other end of the gayelle, still bobbing and weaving to the staccato of drumbeats, eyes still hidden beneath his hat and his pants' fold dragged over the sand. They circled and taunted each other – Bogo forever watchful – Victory, swarthy and muscular, sneaky in his feinting movements. The drummers struck up a note of frenzy. The crowds pushed; the men sang;

> *'Is you moustache we want, Hitler*
> *Oi Oi Oi.*
> *Is you moustache we want Hitler.*
> *Hear what Chamberlain say?'*

Sonnyboy bellowed, 'Take him, Victory. Is he blood we want, not Hitler moustache.'

There was a sudden rush and Victory, stooped so low that his grey stubble touched the ground, lifted himself like some leviathan out of the marsh, with hands upraised, and dug and dug again with his 'bois' into Bogo's head.

Victory was savage in all his assaults. He crouched and bent his whole body from the waist sideways as he levelled his poui before him. Again he charged with terrific speed, coming with both hands clasped on his stick, leaping high into the air, before landing in the arena. His stick whirled and tore into Bogo, who by this time had withdrawn to the left. Bogo drew his bois across his chest and, holding it vertically on the ground, received the full force of his opponent's blows. His stick vibrated under the strain, and one blow caught him on his waist, tearing his shirt.

Victory stepped back once more, both hands clasped his stick whilst he rested on his knees, as if taking stock of the situation, assessing the skill and the craft of this stickman. Who was he and where did he come from? Rising again he tiptoed to another attack, but Bogo advanced slowly, still gazing from beneath the shade of his straw hat, the pants' fold trailing on the sand. They angled again, Bogo moved up, shook his head to the beat of the drums. He paused, now turned to the right, then to the left, stalked his prey, spun his web. Victory turned to the left too, then Bogo jumped. He darted like lightning, the red end-cloth dived to the ground. The spot of brass dazzled, turned in a circle and crashed on Victory's head, tearing into his temple and behind his left ear. Blood splashed on the sand.

The crowd pressed forward, only to scatter when the fighters clashed in mid-air and the rattle of their sticks echoed through the coconut groves. Victory fired four times, one missed its mark. Bogo crouched, blocked twice and ducked from the last stroke. Then he levelled his bois at Victory's head. The crowd moved nearer again seeing only the quick movement of his hands and the brass ring that circled over Victory's head like a bee diving to sting. A new fissure appeared on Victory's right temple and soon his whole head reddened in the sun.

He stumbled on the ground and his blood mixed with that of Scottie's, while Bogo stood like an obelisk, calmly swaying with the music of drumbeat, his eyes peering from beneath the rim of his straw hat. The drummers stopped. Bogo watched, not even acknowledging the chant from the crowd. Despising the lusty clamour for more blood he walked towards Victory, held his hand and lifted him up. He tore a strip out of his own shirt and bandaged the head wound, knotting it tightly at the back of Victory's head. Then putting his stick back in his hand calmly, he walked out of the gayelle.

I saw him pull that old straw hat over his head again as he disappeared into the crowd with the red parrot tail bright as ever. It was then that another challenging voice erupted from the other end of the gayelle as 'Nation', dressed in black silk and a scarf around his neck, jumped into the arena, hoarse from the war cries loud in his throat. But by then, Bogo had already gone.

That was the last I saw of Bogo for some time because I had moved into Charuma at the end of the Carnival season and, for once, avoided the hot black cane stalks for the cool of cacao and coffee. The hiatus proved no remedy for forgetting and the haunting memories of Ramlal and Boyoon, Mountain Dew and rhummy in the almond shade came in flashes before me.

Bogo remained on my mind. He visited me twice, after which he seemed to disappear. I wrote him two letters which were never answered. It was Boyoon's account of his whereabouts that troubled me. I met him at Jerningham Junction on the railway platform, about four months later.

The midday special train left me in Savonetta, a small outpost with a signal cabin, a solitary hut in the middle of peas and bodi beans. I jumped behind my knapsack, leapt over the oil-soaked railway sleepers and I was soon in Esperanza. I was confronted by padlock and crapaud timber scantlings set diagonally across the front door of Bogo's barrack room. Three hens picked spilled rice in the yard; an overturned tub lay beneath a drooping clothes line. Bogo was not there, and there was no sign of Indrani. The neighbours huddled behind closed windows. After two hollers and a mild obscenity I went out of the yard. It was then I met Ramlal.

'Charlo, it is you boy?' he greeted me. 'Boy, plenty take place since you gone,' he spoke excitedly, as he nearly ran into me.

'Well, ah could see that because I don't see Bogo home, house lock up tight, tight, tight and the neighbours and them, the same thing but they peeping out only and not saying anything.'

'Well, boy, them have a right, because Bogo gone on the rampage.'

'How you mean?'

'You didn't hear wha' happen? Boy, is a long story since you leave. You remember after the fight, after Bogo beat Scottie and Victory, well, Sonnyboy couldn't take it and his own father was shamed because he say a penman take away his daughter-in-law and that his own son was useless. Well, Sonnyboy and the old man had a big quarrel. Sonnyboy never thought Bogo could beat them two champion stickman. So you know what happen next? They find Indrani behind the bamboo one night. She throat cut.'

'When that happen?' I asked.

'Last week.'

'Who do it?'

'Is Sonnyboy, everybody saying so because they find he hat in the same bush and the Land Rover tyre mark in the trace.'

'And where Bogo?'

'Bogo gone mad same time boy, and went up the hill. He find Sonnyboy by No. 2 scale and beat him with that same stick until the man dead. Wasn't nice to see, boy, because he push the stick straight through the man mouth and leave it. Then he went by the pen afterwards, somebody say they see him leaving for the hills.'

'When that was?'

'That was two days ago, Charlo.'

Over the mule pens I looked towards the Bastahall hills, stark and grim against a watery sky. I hastened towards the cart standing near the water trough and soon, after a crack with my whip, the animal turned and bounded towards the track leading up to the winding incline. I stood on the cart, holding the reins.

About three miles up the tortuous climb the cart slowed down to a trot, then finally stopped. There the road narrowed and the sugar cane hemmed us in from both sides.

Gazing up to the undulating foothills, I looked for the ominous sign which soon came; a tiny speck, as motionless as a stone. I had to look for a second speck and when I found it, the third and fourth appeared not long afterwards with the same effortless turn in the air, round and round in a circle. The fifth and sixth hovering over a darker mass below confirmed the omen of death, and it was then that I knew I had found him.

CYRIL DABYDEEN

◁ ■■■■■■■■■■■■■■■■■ ◇ ■■■■■■■■■■■■■■■■■ ▷

Mammita's Garden Cove

'Where d'you come from?' Max was used to the question; used to being told no as well. He walked away, feet kicking hard ground, telling himself that he must persevere. More than anything else he knew he must find a job before long. In a way being unemployed made him feel prepared for hell itself even though he knew too that somewhere there was a sweet heaven waiting for him. How couldn't it be? After all he was in Canada. He wanted to laugh all of a sudden.

He continued walking along, thoughts drifting back to the far-gone past. Was it that far-gone? He wasn't sure . . . yet his thoughts kept going back, to the time he was on the island and how he used to dream about being in Canada, of starting an entirely new life. He remembered those dreams clearly now; remembered too thinking of marrying some sweet island-woman with whom he'd share his life, of having children and later buying a house. Maybe someday he'd even own a cottage on the edge of the city. He wasn't too sure where one built a cottage, but there had to be a cottage. He'd then be in the middle class; life would be different from the hand-to-mouth existence he was used to.

His heels pressed into the asphalt, walking on. And slowly he began to sense a revulsion for everything around him. Maybe he was really happy on the island – more than he realised. Once more he thought about a job; if he didn't find one soon he might starve. But as the reality of this dawned on him he began laughing. No! No one starved in Canada; that only happened in such places as India or Africa. But definitely not Canada! A growling in his stomach reminded him of reality. A slight panic. Max stepped quickly, walking, looking around, feeling like a fugitive.

He decided to return home to his room in the ramshackle rooming house. There for a while he'd find solace. He always did, staring at the walls, and thinking.

Christ! Same thing again, day-dreaming. And he remembered his cronies on the island, their faces reappearing, their words clear and fresh in his ears.

'Max, when you get to that cold-cold place, you'd have ice freezin' yuh

62

up yuh insides . . . freezin' yuh, you hear me!' A burst of loud laughter. Max didn't reply. And when they started again he laughed loudly too. West Indian laughter was always contagious – how couldn't it be?

Another, cynically said, 'Put on some weight, Max. You must, man!' More laughter. The voice continued, 'But imagine Max becoming fat though . . .' The laughter rose louder – in Max's head now. He pictured the faces of the fellas on the island, still lazing around while they sat in Mammita's Garden Cove. He remembered how he used to go there, often with a novel in his hand; the others used to call him a 'bookworm'. Max never minded; he'd only smile and think that he wasn't really a bookworm. They'd say to him, 'Hey, bookworm, tell us what yuh readin' about! What's goin through that head o' yours, eh?' Max would merely smile; he loved reading, loved escaping into the world of fantasy. Mammita's turn: she'd look at him, then turn to the others, her body shaking as she'd say, 'At least Max knows where he's goin'! . . . He'll get far . . . far I tell yuh!'

Max wished he'd gotten far: and he thought that Mammita would really be surprised to see him living half-starved in a ramshackle rooming house in downtown Toronto with the last few dollars in his pocket and still wondering whether he'd have enough for the next week's rent. He wished more than anything else that a job would fall into his lap. Oh, how he wished this could happen!

And his thoughts drifted back to the manager of the restaurant asking, 'Where d'you come from?'

Max walked on. He thought of the wonderful time he and Tony had had before when they'd go out drinking together – then he had a job. Now Max felt he and Tony had grown apart – and he felt terribly alone.

Tony had shouted after him, 'The trouble with you West Indians is that you give yourselves away too easily! Man, you've got to be tough . . . you people laugh too easily, too . . .'

Max hurried on, wondering if Tony was right. Life was becoming more complex for him: he couldn't easily sort out the role he should play as Tony's voice echoed in his head.

All of a sudden he didn't feel like going any farther. It was no use entering another restaurant. Besides, he was getting tired. And the solace of the bare walls of his room became an attraction to him.

He closed his eyes trying to obliterate everything. But even with his eyes closed he began to imagine large waves being painted against the wall, mind waves; this had happened before each time he'd closed his eyes. Now he fought against the waves, but he wasn't succeeding – they kept coming back constantly, buffeting him. He closed his eyes tightly – but without avail.

Slowly, inevitably, the island came back. Waves never failed to bring it back. And swishing palm trees. The balmy nights . . . his mind's trumped-up defence mechanism . . .

Back to Mammita's Garden Cove. The fellas were all there playing dominoes on the tables, a few yards away from Mammita's counter stocked with buns and fruit drinks; pine drink in particular, red, red – like blood. He'd often watch her pouring the stuff from the large enamel pail into the bottles for all to see. Mammita knew the tricks of her trade, knew how to entice the fellas into buying her pine drink and buns. But sometimes Slick used to give her hell.

Max imagined Slick in action now – Slick saying to Mammita, 'You should put more of that stuff into my glass . . . make it really full, woman! Don't cheat us like dat, Mammita . . . remember we's your best customers!'

Mammita was ready for Slick too. 'Yuh mouth too damn quick! Why yuh don't shut up and play dominoes, eh? Is what de hell gettin' into yuh? You think is the kiss-me-arse few cents that you spendin' here does keep me opening this place from mawning to night?'

The others laughed; they waited now to hear what Slick would say. 'Mammita,' he began, 'you's one helluva woman. I'd give my life to spend one night wid yuh. Just one night, Mammita!'

An explosion of further laughter. They knew Slick was a mock-lecher when he wanted to be.

Mammita was infuriated now. 'Why yuh don't get outa my place, Slick, instead of stayin' here and *loving* somebody wid dem pieces of wood – always clapping away like de sound of short-lived thunder and bawling out ecstasy like a clarion call from heaven given by one of them Jehovah Witnesses!'

More laughter.

Slick felt his tongue fastened to the roof of his mouth for a while. The other fellas bent with laughter. When they stopped, Slick was still struggling to come up with a smart-alecky answer; they all knew now that Mammita had won that round. But Slick wasn't one to be defeated that easily – another round would soon come up and he'd think of the right words before long; then the laughter would be on her.

Max hadn't forgotten . . . only remembrances . . . like the re-run of an old movie which was stored at the deepest layers of his mind. And he could still hear the waves – his mind paintings on the wall almost. And the laughter. The clap of dominoes next, echoing now throughout Mammita's Garden Cove and then all over his room, in his head, whirring next like the agitated flapping of a thousand pairs of wings.

He opened his eyes and picked up the novel at the side of his bed, looking at the frayed title, feeling the words expanding in his brain; he'd been reading George Lamming's *The Emigrants* over and over again, not sure why; unconsciously perhaps the Barbadian's style, his dialogue, gave him a sense of continuity with his past. And as he read, lipping the words, he thought of his own boyhood, growing up with a grandmother who often reminded him that he hadn't a father, that perhaps he had a dozen fathers scattered all over the island. Sometimes he'd laugh as she'd tell him this; but now he didn't – he merely tried to imagine the face of the one man who had sired him, who perhaps had made his mother happy one long night in the tropics.

Remembrances still.

The landlady knocked on his door.

Max suddenly hated her for disturbing him.

As soon as he opened the door she said, 'You're gonna pay the rent now?' A faint smile on her face; Max wasn't sure what to make of her.

'Next week,' he mechanically replied.

'You're always saying next week. You? Not working still, eh?' Her voice barely sympathetic. Max kept looking at her, assessing her. 'I didn't say that,' he muttered under his breath. Another moment he felt like snapping at her, but then he knew he had no choice. He was looking closely at her face, her eyes, her mouth; she wasn't bad-looking he thought. Why didn't he think about her like this before? Wasn't he interested?

And the more he looked at her, the more she kept smiling. And once more he began wondering if he was imagining all this. He remembered too how often she smiled at him each time she saw him entering the house. A few times she had come up to his room, almost pushing her way in even though he never remembered inviting her in. Sometimes she'd just stand there, waiting, expecting him to do something.

He shook his head a little – he felt too dizzy to think clearly. He merely stood rooted like a tree.

As she walked out this time somehow he continued thinking about her face; her body next – he noticed her firm legs, her shapely behind. He knew she didn't have a husband – maybe she was just lonely. And he remembered too the first time he had knocked on her door looking for a room how she'd smiled invitingly. Immediately he had made up his mind to stay there.

Tony was living in the rooming house then; with a wide grin he had suggested, 'Try putting a paper bag over her head. Maybe she'd like it that way – who knows?'

Max was immediately disgusted at this suggestion.

'You have a sick mind, Tony!'

Tony ignored this; he was still laughing. 'C'mon, man, let's face it; she may even think she's a member of the Ku-Klux Klan. She may even like it . . . like playing the role!'

Max twisted his lips, grimacing in further disgust.

Tony added, 'Just a suggestion, man. You blacks are supposed to be good at it!'

Max didn't bother to reply.

Back to Mammita's Garden Cove. Many of the boys had fantasised making love to Mammita; they'd look at her buxom figure, especially her ample hips, high bust, and imagine themselves the recipients of her favours. But they knew that even at thirty, Mammita was a God-fearin' woman who would have nothing to do with sex out of wedlock.

Slick used to tease her, 'Woman, you're as ripe as a mango. What yuh waitin' for?'

'Mind yuh own business! D'you think I'd be interested in you?'

'I fail to understand, woman.' Slick laughed. So did the others.

Even Mammita found herself laughing this time.

Bertie, Slick's closest friend, used to say,

'Slick, I believe that woman has something in her heart fo' you. Intense feelings, man. I can sense it!'

But Slick would never take the bait.

Bertie would turn to Max and ask, 'Say, Max, you readin' a lot of books, what d'you think eh?'

The others would laugh – they never failed to do this – but they wouldn't wait to hear an answer before clapping dominoes all of a sudden again with the sound of unexpected tropical rain.

Mammita was now having the last word. 'I choosin' m'man carefully when de right time cometh.'

'Is that the one the Lawd is gonna send fo' you?' Slick quickly asked.

'De Lawd's ways are always de best, Slick! No mistakin' dat, you hear me?'

Slick ahemmed and continued playing, knowing that he'd try again a few minutes later.

◇

Next day – once more on the streets, Max's head held high.

'Who're you looking for, sport?'

'The manager . . .'

'I'm the manager, what d'you want?'

He decided to be blunt. 'A job!'

The manager fingered his collar before barking out a short laugh. 'We have enough o' you people around here in this restaurant. Jus' take a peep inside, man. Go on – look! What d'you see? Lots o' coloured people workin' for me, right? Look, I'd really like to hire you, but I don't want my customers thinking I'm running an immigrant show here. I'm in business . . . right? Business is always business!'

Max didn't wait to hear more; he walked on, undaunted. Head still an imaginary pillar to the sky. He passed the next restaurant quickly, this one didn't look as it if had any prospects for him.

He nodded to a fellow he passed along, who looked like a West Indian; maybe he too was looking for work. The fellow didn't return his courtesy. Max wasn't sure why, didn't really care. Fleetingly he thought that perhaps the fellow was scared of familiarity.

After the fifth restaurant he decided that he had had enough. And he thought now of improving his skills, attending night school once again. But he didn't have the money; he was hoping that with a steady job he'd really embark on this.

Later that evening, despondent, he returned to his room. This time the landlady met him at the door.

'Any luck?'

He didn't answer.

She followed him up the stairs.

'Did you have any luck?'

'No.'

She attempted a short laugh. 'I know you're unemployed. You can't fool me you know.'

She followed him as far as his room. 'You could stay here, longer if you like. I mean it . . . just trying to do you a favour you know.'

Max wasn't listening. Mammita's words resounded in his ears suddenly. 'I waitin' for de Lawd to decide on the right one fo' me!'

He sensed her presence closer to him. He slowly opened the door; he couldn't close it in her face.

She put a hand against his shoulder. He turned around and faced her.

'You're not angry with me, eh?' she asked, her voice almost a pleading whisper.

He thought of Tony too at that moment.

Suddenly he wanted her; her body seemed like food to him. He felt a deep, deep yearning, with the intensity of pain. Slowly he put out a hand, deliberately, like a feeler, touching her.

She half-giggled, then muttered, 'I'm not used to this . . . since my husband died . . . that was almost three years ago.' She suddenly wiped her eyes; another tear dropped down her nose.

He was touched. 'How did he die?'

'In a fire,' she said rather quickly, 'caused by his own cigarette . . . he was a drunk . . . a no-good anyway! His company was all that I wanted.' She sniffed, wiping the tear from her nose, and then apologising.

A flood of sympathy went through him. He impulsively leaned forward and kissed her. Immediately she pulled his head close down to her face, and he could feel her fingers begin to dig into the back of his neck and ears. He didn't mind; he kissed her fiercely, more fiercely as she kept pulling him into her almost. His fingers fumbled with her blouse. He was surprised with the ease with which it came off; then he fingered her bra – but he was having difficulty now. She guided him, and he could feel a tremor go through her veins, coursing through her entire body as his passion rose to meet hers.

Mammita was saying, 'You fellas . . . you don't know what it is I'm waiting for! Why eh?'

Slick laughed. 'Don't worry Mammita . . . you will be with us a long time here.'

He was ungallant, Max thought; he buried his head deep in his book, smelling it, touching it almost with his nose. Then he looked up – Mammita was still leaning against the counter looking at him, at them. His eye caught hers after a while; she smiled; he was about to smile too.

She was ready to go. Max watched her as she put on her things, somewhat hurriedly now; he watched her smooth the ruffled collar of her blouse; her actions appeared quick, almost unnatural. 'You could stay on,' she murmured, 'as long as you want.' Her head lowered a little; then, 'When d'you want me to come again?'

He didn't answer; he wasn't even listening to her. In a way he was preoccupied; he wasn't sure if she was offended or not. He moved a little from the room, watching her going down the stairs, watching her walking down next. Once she stopped and looked back at him – looking now as if she was a different person altogether.

'Maybe you'd find a job soon, eh?' she said.

'Maybe,' he muttered, not sure if she heard him or not.

ZOILA ELLIS

◁ ■■■■■■■■■■■■■ ◇ ■■■■■■■■■■■■■ ▷

White Christmas an' Pink Jungle

'Eh, Julia, stop gaze, car will knock you down.'

'What?'

'I say stop gaze. What do you? You got worries or what?'

'Cho! Me? Dat is one thing me don't have pet.'

Julia, walking down New Road, opened her umbrella to shield her face from the glaring midday sun. As she walked, her thoughts were bitter. 'Darn fas'; she well and want find out my business.'

She walked down Douglas Jones Street and then hit Freetown Road. She walked down until she reached the Farmer's Market. Sweat was running down her back and under her armpits, making her clothes stick to her skin. Her head ached as it always did if she stayed in the sun too long especially now that she was just recovering from the flu. A slight breeze fluffed up the dust on the street blowing it into her face and she sneezed twice, feeling her whole body double with the motion. When it was over, she felt slightly dizzy. She crossed the street and entered the market compound, looking for a place to rest. On a weekday like this, there were few shoppers. The stall owners were mostly in the back of their stalls arranging whatever produce they had for the day. Julia spied a fat Spanish man leaning over the counter in his vegetable stall near the entrance of the compound. She did not want to stop but her head was beginning to swing and her legs were feeling as if at any minute she would collapse.

'Mista, I could sit down under ya?' She pointed to a bench set against his stall. 'I don't feel good at all.'

'What happen Miss?' he asked, leaning over to watch her closely as she slumped on the bench, her head propped against the wall of the stall.

'Nottn', nottn' sah.' Her voice was a whisper. 'Jus' please mek me sit down a little bit.'

Julia's head slid down lower and lower as the weakness overtook her body and she fainted. The stall owner watched, amazed as her body slipped in a heap to the ground. Then, jumping up, he rushed out of his stall and banged on the counter of the neighbouring stall. Presently, a stout East Indian woman emerged plaiting her hair. She did not wait to be told anything. Hurriedly she followed his beckoning finger to the spot where Julia lay in a heap on the ground.

'Who dat?' she asked, worriedly.

'Me don't know. She jus' come here to ask me to sit down a little bit like how she nevah feel good and the nex' ting me know is she faint.'

'Cho! How you know she faint? Maybe she dead.'

'She no dead man, she di move she han'.'

'Move let me examine her. Give me some cold watah Mista Max. Yu got alcohol in yu stall?'

'No, but maybe my wife got. Let me mek haste an' go for it.'

He ran off, breathing fast, his fat belly jumping up and down in front of him. Miss Marta, for that was the East Indian woman's name, knelt down by the still form of the girl lying on the ground and put her ear against her chest to hear her heartbeat. Then she took the girl's cold hands between her own warm ones and rubbed them briskly, murmuring gently as she worked.

'Alright pet, let me put some cold watah on yu forehead. Lawd, yu han' dem cold, cold, cold. I wonder what do you? Oh, thank Gawd, Mista Max di come wid the alcohol.'

Mista Max hurried up, puffing and blowing, sweat running down his fat face. He shoved the bottle of alcohol into Miss Marta's waiting hand. She opened it quickly and doused it liberally over the girl's head and face.

'Eh, Miss Marta! Stop pour the alcohol in she head,' he protested, 'she di get up.'

They both peered anxiously into Julia's face as her eyelids fluttered open. She stared uncomprehendingly at the strangers bending over her. For a minute no one spoke. Then a tear slowly trickled out of the corner of Julia's eye and slid down her cheek. Miss Marta moved quickly and put her two fat arms around her consolingly.

'Ah man. Don't bawl dahlin'. Is nothing to bawl for. Hush! Hush dahlin'.'

But Julia couldn't seem to stop the tears from falling. Even when she was squeezed into the taxi between Miss Marta and Mista Max, the tears kept falling as she wept silently. It was not until she was seated inside the outpatient clinic at the Belize City Hospital that she stopped. It was Miss Marta who made the nurse hurry up and attend to her, dramatically explaining how she was so sick that she had fainted out on the street. The whole crowd in the outpatient clinic was silent as Miss Marta told the story to the nurse as loudly as she possibly could. Then when she was finished the crowd looked at Julia from head to foot, clearly speculating as to what had made her pass out.

'Belly,' muttered one woman to another.

'Soun' like heart,' was one old lady's opinion.

'No man,' contradicted a third. 'Dat is definitely pressure.'

'Well,' added a fourth doubtfully, 'could be sugar. Same ting happen to me last year. Drop down in church.'

With all that they made her pass them and she saw the doctor just as soon as the person he was attending to had left.

The doctor stood at the door of the office, looked at the card in his hand and then called out her name. 'Miss Julia Taylor?'

She entered and sat in his office. Her gaze fixed on the floor.

'Well, Miss, what is your problem?' She was silent.

He looked at the card again.

'Ah. Fainting.'

He asked her other questions and this time she answered in monosyllables. Then he examined her. Finally he asked:

'When did you see your last period, Miss?'

She was shocked out of her half-dead state. She stared straight at him and fear flashed like lightning across her face.

'I no memba.'

'You don't remember?'

'No dacta, I no memba . . .'

She did not even remember the details after that. She felt better after he gave her a tablet to swallow but her mind was in a turmoil. When she got home she thought about the test she would have to take the following week and she knew she could be in big trouble. Still, life couldn't stop. There was still work and she still had to go.

'Miss, yu sell black colouring?'

'I no memba.'

'Whe yu mean, yu no memba?'

'Oh. Sorry Miss,' Julia apologised. 'I was thinking 'bout something.'

'Well you betta study yu job. Yu got black colouring?'

'Yes ma'am. Anyting else?'

'Yes, gimme one bottle black colouring. You got eggs?'

'No ma'am. Eggs finish.'

'Finish! An' da jus' 15th? You all mus' be putting them tings up for special people. Don't tell me nottn' 'bout finish. Every year me buy my eggs dem right here fi my black cake and every year me buy my black colouring an' everyting else here. You all di sleep up dis year. What di go on? I is good customah you know. Ask Mista Jones. Every Crismus me buy here.'

'Sorry Miss. Di mennonites truck no coming back till Monday.'

'Lawd! Dah what me will do! Man, me stop buy here if is so you all will treat me. You wait till I see Jonesy.'

The woman grabbed her market bag off the counter and marched out of the shop. Julia hardly noticed. She was trying to think.

'I no memba.'

She did not even hear Dorothy come up behind her until a voice said teasingly:

'Me no memba neither. Julia my child, how you always saying, "I no memba," mind yu di talk to yuself. Dat is the first sign.'

Julia did not smile. Instead she said:

'Dorothy, you would work for me next week Monday? Then I work for you Sattiday.'

Dorothy thought for a moment.

'But if you work for me Saturday den I will no get overtime.'

Julia brushed that aside.

'I will give you the money I mek fi ovahtime.'

Dorothy looked surprised.

'Well is what you have to do so!'

'Don't worry 'bout dat. You will work for me?'

'Alright. But jus' don't mess aroun' wid my money,' Dorothy warned as she moved away to serve two women who had just come in.

'Miss, you got fruits?' one asked. 'I want two pounds raisin, plus some mix fruits. How much fi yu mix fruits? Let me see it. Oh! You have dem bag off already. $5.00 a pound!' The woman gasped, then continued:

'My gawd! These local or imported? Cherrymae, what you doing 'cross there? Look here. Look how much the thiefing Jonesy di sell his mix fruits for, no gyal?'

'Well Lois, is yu worries now. I tell you to buy it when we went to Chetumal las' week.'

72

'Cherrymae! You tell me that Customs would take it away at the border.'

'Me tell you dat? How me would tell you something like dat and I buy mine there? Memba you get confuse with de peso you had. Then you disappear in the market with Maudie. Is mus' Maudie tell yu dat. Well, how much poun' a cake you want mek?'

'Two poun'.'

'Well then, jus' buy half poun' of mix fruits an' half poun' of cherries.' Cherrymae beckoned Julia.

'Miss, you have cherries? How much for it?'

'Seven dollars a poun'.'

The one called Lois exclaimed.

'What!'

'Lois, no use yu bawl. Dat is di price nowadays. Dat is the cheapes' you will get it,' said Cherrymae. 'Buy half poun'.'

'But Cherrymae! I have to buy the ham an' turkey yet! My money will done!'

'Don't worry Lois, you got enough money. When we done from here we could walk over by Baymen Avenue. Them got some small ham and turkey reasonable.'

'But Lawd Cherrymae, that far!' Cherrymae turned and looked straight at her.

'Lois, you want Crismus or not?' She then turned back to the counter where Dorothy stood waiting impatiently.

'Miss, give me half poun' of cherry and half poun' of mix fruit. Is for this lady here,' she said pointing to her companion called Lois.

As it was being wrapped, Lois sighed.

'Ay, Cherrymae, I tell you, only because them children di expec' this black cake an' ham an' turkey, or else I would forget the whole thing.'

Cherrymae laughed.

'Don't mind you, I wonder what Hubert would say 'bout that when he bring them boys home Crismus mawnin'!'

'Say? What he could say?' Lois sucked her teeth. 'He lucky I don't ship he to his woman house Crismus mawnin' mek him eat turkey there.' She picked up her parcel.

'How much Miss?'

'Six dollars,' Dorothy answered and waited for the money.

The money was paid and then the two left carrying between them a hefty straw bag loaded with groceries. Julia and Dorothy watched them leave and then they burst out laughing.

'Them two is kicks,' Julia remarked as she put back the bucket with the mixed fruits.

'You know them?' Dorothy asked, surprised.

'Of course. The breggin' one she live right 'round here by the areas. An' in this Pink Jungle Area me know everybody but not everybody know me. Some of them could only take up themself. That Cherrymae, her son jus' send she a TV from States for Crismus and she make sure everybody hear 'bout it. You see her, she can't afford current in she house. I don't know what she will do with the TV. She mus' will sell it. Three months aback them cut out the light. Couldn't pay. Then she son send TV for she instead of send money to mek them fix up the dog-siddown that his ma live in. Las' Crismus he send a refridge. As to that, that mus' get rusty by now because me see she send buy ice every Sunday.'

Dorothy laughed. 'The other one what name Lois, she look like she got plenty money though.'

Julia sniffed.

'No mus' got! Her gentleman sell weed right 'round here. She an' all.'

'Cho!' Dorothy gasped. 'An' hear how she cry hard time.'

'Is so she always do so people don't talk. But people still talk so me don't know who she think she di fool.'

Dorothy laughed as she went to serve a woman who entered the shop.

'Miss,' the woman asked, 'you sell toys?'

'No ma'am,' she answered.

'Thank you then,' said the woman as she left.

Dorothy turned to Julia saying:

'She mus' come from Hattieville or one of them small village where one shop got everything.'

Julia laughed saying:

'She betta go to them big shop on Albert Street for dat.'

'Cho! You see how she look broke. She just will smell those high price an' she will run. All like she so can't go deh. We poor people go 'cross the border for cheap toys for we pikni. My son tell me this mawnin' that he want one Walkman for Crismus. An' he only four you know.'

'So you tell him 'bout Santa den?' Julia asked.

'Me no tell that little boy nottn'. He sit down front the TV whole day an' when me get home he could tell me 'bout all what he see. He only smart gyal! From yesterday he start tell me 'bout Santa. He tell me he sees one pretty, pretty Santa front of the White House in Washington where the President live. All of that yu know! He done know what is President! Then he tell me how Santa will bring he anything he want if he behave good. So whole week the boy is behave gyal, because he want dis Walkman so bad. My big daughter she want a roller skates and my second son he want a boxing gloves. Me will have to find all those things you know! I pray that my aunty sen' me money from New York. Pikni is expensive gyal! You lucky you only got one baby. How old is he again? Five months?'

'Yes, 24th of this month will mek five months,' Julia answered slowly, then quickly added:

'Look, is four o'clock, time to shut up.'

They quickly shut and bolted the store, then left going their separate ways home.

For the rest of the week business was fast. Julia got home late every day because she had to walk far, all the way to Lake Independence to pick up the baby from her granny's house. She took her time every day because she did not want to have another fainting spell. But somehow, although she felt weak, she never for that week felt as bad as she had done that day when she fainted. She went back to the Farmer's Market to thank Miss Marta for her help. Miss Marta had given her some Billy Webb bark to drink and other bush medicine to strengthen her blood. According to Miss Marta, Julia was 'poor a blood'. Every day, she drank some of the medicine after she put the baby to sleep. She and the baby were alone in the room they rented in the long barracks. It used to be she, the baby and Charles. But now, Charles had gone for good.

Saturday, payday, Julia walked home into the long barracks carrying the baby. It was night, but the heat was on. Everyone else living in the long barracks was out cooling off. The yard had the strong scent of marijuana being smoked. It was brightly lit with light from the nearby street lamp and each room had a naked bulb suspended from the ceiling. Pa Charles sat on a stool in front of his room smoking a cigarette. He called Julia.

'Night Miss Julie. What a heat gyal! You alright?'

'Sure Pa Charles,' she answered. She usually gave him two dollars out of her pay. He only had one leg and could not work because he had asthma. Besides he was over fifty. He was grateful for the help and had made himself her guardian. She was especially grateful for his protection now that Charles was gone. She continued on her way passing the table in the middle of the yard where the boys were banging dominoes.

'Night sweet thing,' one of them called out. She didn't answer. She heard Pa Charles shout out something to the young man but she was not listening. She went inside her room and locked the door.

After the baby was asleep she took her purse and emptied the money on the bed. She counted it twice. It was all there. Three hundred dollars. Her pay and the money from the syndicate that she had joined in order to have the extra money for Christmas. She knew exactly what she would buy with it. A new piece of linoleum and a tablecloth for Granny; some apples, grapes and a ham and turkey for herself; and a toy for the baby. Folding it carefully she tucked the wad of notes into a hole under the flooring.

Sunday, she took the baby to Granny and spent the day. She did not tell Granny about the syndicate money. She wanted to surprise her with the linoleum.

'Granny, what you want Santa bring for you?' she asked jokingly as she washed up the dirty plates in a pan outside the door.

'Child,' Granny did not smile, 'I jus' want one wish. I wish dat you and this baby would have healt' and strength to face the evils of this world.'

'Lawd Granny, don't get so serious. Is Crismus yu know,' Julia protested. 'Me and Junior quite alright. I mean you wouldn't want some pretty piece of linoleum for di parlour and some new curtains for the window then?'

'Well true you know,' Granny said thoughtfully looking around the parlour and examining it as if seeing it for the first time. 'True. If I win a good lottery I would varnish the settee and the rocking chair, paint up di wall little bit and maybe buy a piece of linoleum.'

'What colour you would buy?' questioned Julia eagerly.

'A nice skyblue,' Granny answered without hesitation. 'You know blue is my fav'rite colour.' She burst into song. 'I'll have a blue Crismus without you, I'll be so blue thinking about you. How did the song go again? That used to be yu Grandpa song. Oh yes! That an' "I'm dreamin' of a white Crismus jus' like the ones I used to know". Five years this Crismus since you Grandpa gawn to res' child. You mus' come with me to service Crismus Eve mek us pray for him soul. Reveren' ask for you las' Sunday. I was shame to tell how you stop go to church.' She looked at Julia disapprovingly. Julia avoided her gaze and changed the subject saying:

'Well, Granny, yu never know what life will bring, you know. Maybe you still win the lott'ry after all.'

'Cho! My luck finish for this year pet. Let's hope things get better nex' year.'

'Things will definitely get better, man.' Julia said confidently. 'Since the wutless Charles gone, at leas' now I don't have to hide to give you money when payday. After the Crismus I will look for a better job with more pay so I could save an' try go to States. Las' time Goddy write, she say that if I get there she could definitely find me a job.'

Granny was silent for a moment. Then she said:

'Well, dat soun' good. I hope it works out, jus' don't res' your heart 'pon the States thing. Sometimes them pipple is lone big offer.'

'Not all, though. Las' year Goddy send me plenty pear and grape and apple until I never know what to do with them. Memba you did get?'

'True, I memba. You Goddy is a good woman for true. An' to think she used to empty people night pail for a living.'

Julia laughed:

'I wish I could pay somebody to empty mine for me. Every morning I go to Barracks and I have to leave Junior alone home. I don't like it. Well, by nex' Crismus at leas' I have to move out the long barracks. If I mek enough money I could rent a house with sewerage and bath.'

'Well, maybe you find a nice young man to settle down with and tek care of you!' Granny said as she sat down in the rocking chair and fanned herself. Julia picked up the baby and put him to her breast to suck, sitting down in the settee opposite, before answering.

'That woudn't bad, but that hard to find. Meantime, every mouth mus' be fed.'

Granny rocked silently for a moment. Then she said:

'Well, child, you soun' like the world done harden you. Don't mek that happen. You young yet, so you mus' think 'bout yu future. But, my dear, I jus' hope you don't have to do nottn' that will cause you to hang yu head in shame.'

Julia said nothing, she just looked down at the baby nursing at her breast. She let it nurse for a little while and then tucked her breast inside her dress, getting up from the settee in one swift motion.

'Let me go before it get late, hear,' she said, bustling about as she packed her bag. Granny watched her, sensing that her mood had changed and wondering what was the cause of it. Julia knew that her Granny was curious but she did not want to enter into any discussion, afraid that she would reveal the incident when she fainted. Granny suffered from high blood pressure. She would worry too much. After all, it was nothing, she was just a little 'poor a blood'. That was all.

Tuesday morning she decided to stop worrying. Somehow she would have to work this thing out. It was still early and there was no one in the shop but herself and Dorothy. The radio was blaring out. Julia sang along.

'Santa, when will you come to the ghetto.'

Dorothy looked up from what she was doing.

'Well, you bright this morning. Yesterday I mi think say the Crismus spirit lef' yu.'

Julia laughed.

'Me only like the song gyal.'

'Well, mind you call rain. This cold front we have now jus' nice. We don't want rain 'long with it. Especially Crismus Eve night pet. Me and Robert going to dance at CBA with Rhaburn. You will come? You could bring lovah-bway.'

Julia looked up, surprised.

'Who dat?'

'Charles of course.'

'Me and he finish.'

'Bruck up and you all was sweetah than loving Josie and Betsy syrup! How long?'

'Two months.'

Dorothy looked long and searchingly at Julia.

'Oh! So that's why you want me work in yu place. You want to see doctor.

Julia was astonished.

'How you know!'

Dorothy laughed.

'Honey child, I jus' have to look 'pon a woman an' I could know. Don't get vex. Is nottn' to shame 'bout. You will keep it?'

'I don't know.'

'You want it?'

'No. Yes, I mean, I don't know.'

'Well, you have to make up yu mind what you will do. If you don't want it, I could help you fix yu problem. It will jus' cost yu three hundred, an' you will not land up at hospital. But you have to mek your mind up early, otherwise nottn' doing.'

That night Julia took the money out from under the flooring, counted and recounted it, went to bed and worried.

Wednesday morning dawned bright and early. Today was the day she had planned to go and shop for the linoleum for Granny and to do all her other Christmas shopping. She took the money out again from under the flooring and stared at it. She did not put it back under the flooring but left it scattered on the bed. Midday she came home for dinner, she looked at it and tried to decide what she should do. Still, she could not. Wednesday night she bundled up the baby, put the money in her purse and decided she would go window-shopping. Maybe a decision would come along the way. She returned, tired, her feet aching and the wad of notes still tucked in a pocket of her purse.

Thursday night, Christmas Eve, she did the same thing. Only now she went all the way to Lake Independence, picked up Granny and took her along, hoping that Granny would want something so bad she would feel like she had to spend the money to buy it for her. But Granny could not walk far and soon got tired. The cold weather made her joints ache and the crowd of Christmas shoppers confused her, she said. After barely an hour she and Julia had to take a taxi home.

Later that night, Julia sat with Granny in the crowded church listening to the Christmas Carols being sung by the choir at the Christmas Eve service. At midnight the church bells rang out loud and Granny turned to her and hugged her.

'Merry Crismus, baby.'

'Merry Crismus, Granny,' she answered, tears in her eyes. 'Sorry I couldn't get yu nottn' for Crismus.'

Granny waved that aside.

'Cho!' she laughed. 'You never believe what I tell you. I done get my Crismus gift. Me, you and this baby with healt' an' strength. That is Crismus for me. An' if that is everyday thing then I got Crismus every day.'

There was nothing Julia could say. She just hugged Granny hard. Suddenly she reached into her bra and pulled out the wad of dollars, thrusting it into Granny's hand.

'Granny take this. I don't care what you say. You mus' could buy something you need with it.'

Granny was silent and they both stood still as around them the noise of well-wishers full of Christmas cheer rang out. Then Granny reached up and took Julia's small face between her wrinkled hands saying gently:

'Thank yu dahlin' but I no need it. You need it more. When you eighteen and pregnant, is no joke. You use it. You do whatever yu think right with it. That is my Crismus gift for you.'

LORNA GOODISON

◁ ━━━━━━━◇━━━━━━━ ▷

Bella Makes Life

He was embarrassed when he saw her coming towards him. He wished
he could have just disappeared into the crowd and kept going as far
away from Norman Manley Airport as was possible. Bella returning.
Bella come back from New York after a whole year. Bella dressed in
some clothes which make her look like a chequer cab. What in God's
name was a big forty-odd-year-old woman who was fat when she leave
Jamaica, and get worse fat since she go to America, what was this
woman doing dressed like this? Bella was wearing stretch-to-fit black
pants, over that she had on a big yellow and black checked blouse, on
her feet was a pair of yellow booties, in her hand was a big yellow
handbag and she had on a pair of yellow framed glasses. See ya Jesus!
Bella no done yet, she had dyed her hair with red oxide and Jherry curls
it till it shine like it grease and spray. Oh Bella what happen to you?
Joseph never ever bother take in her anklet and her big bracelets and her
gold chain with a pendant, big as a name plate on a lawyer's office,
marked 'Material Girl'.

Joseph could sense the change in Bella through her letters, when she
just went to New York, she used to write him D.V. every week.

Dear Joe Joe,

How keeping my darling? I hope fine. I miss you and the children so
till I think I want to die. Down in Brooklyn here where I'm living, I
see a lot of Jamaicans, but I don't mix up with them. The lady who
sponsor me say that a lot of the Jamaicans up here is doing wrongs
and I don't want to mix up with those things as you can imagine. You
know that I am only here to work some dollars to help you and me to
make life when I come home. Please don't have any other woman
while I'm gone. I know that a man nature different from a woman, but
please do, try and keep yourself to yourself till we meet and I'm saving
all my love for you.

Your sweet, sweet,

Bella

80

That was one of the first letters that Bella write Joseph, here one of the last letters.

Dear Joseph,

What you saying? I really sorry that my letter take so long to reach you and that the Post Office seem to be robbing people money left, right and centre . . . Man, Jamaica is something else again. I don't write as often as I used to because I working two jobs. My night job is doing waitressing in a night club on Nostrand Avenue, the work is hard but tips is good. I make friends with a girl on the job named Yvonne and sometimes she and I go with some other friends on a picnic or go up to Bear Mountain. I guess that's where Peaches says she saw me. I figure I might as well enjoy myself while I not so old yet.

Your baby

Bella

Enjoy herself? This time Joseph was working so hard to send the two children to school clean and neat, Joseph become mother and father for them, even learn to plait the little girl hair. Enjoy himself? Joseph friend them start to laugh after him because is like him done with woman.

Joseph really try to keep himself to himself. Although the nice, nice woman who live at the corner of the next road. Nice woman you know, always talking so pleasant to him. Joseph make sure that the two of them just remain social friends . . . and Bella inna New York about she gone a Bear Mountain, make blabba mouth Peaches come back from New York and tell everybody inna the yard how she buck up Bella a picnic and how Bella really inna the Yankee life fully.

It was Norman, Joseph's brother, who said that Bella looked like a chequer cab. Norman had driven Joseph and the children to the airport in his van to meet Bella, because she write to say she was coming with a lot of things. When the children saw her they jumped up and down yelling mama come, mama come . . . When Norman saw her (he was famous for his wit), he said, 'Blerd Naught, a Bella dat, whatta way she favour a chequer cab.' When Bella finally cleared her many and huge bags from Customs and come outside, Joseph was very quiet, he didn't know quite how to greet the new Bella. Mark you Bella was always 'nuff' but she really was never as wild as this. She ran up to Joseph and he put his arms around her, part of him felt a great sense of relief, that she was home, that Joseph and Bella and their two children were a family once more.

81

Bella was talking a little too loudly. 'Man I tell you those Customs people really give me a warm time. Oh it's so great to be home though, it was so cold! in New York!!' As she said this she handed her winter coat with its mock fur collar to her daughter who staggered under the weight of it. Norman who was still chuckling to himself over his chequer cab joke said, 'Bwoy, Bella a you broader than Broadway.' Bella said, 'Tell me about it . . .'

They all went home. Joseph kind of kept quiet all the way home and allowed the children to be united with their mother . . . she was still Mama Bella though, asking them about school, if they had received certain parcels she had sent and raising an alarm how she had sent a pair of the latest high top sneakers for the boy and that they had obviously stolen it at the Post Office.

Every now and again she leaned across and kissed Joseph. He was a little embarrassed but pleased . . . ! One time she whispered in his ear, 'I hope you remember I've been saving all my love for you.' This was a new Bella though, the boldness and the forwardness was not the old Bella who used to save all her love for when they were alone together with the bolt on the door.

She would not encourage too much display of affection before the children. That change in Bella pleased Joseph. There were some other changes in Bella that did not please him so much though. Like he thought that all the things in the many suitcases were for their family, no sir, while Bella brought quite a few things for them, she had also brought a lot of things to sell and many evenings when Joe Joe come home from work just wanting a little peace and quiet, to eat him dinner, watch a little TV and go to him bed and hug up his woman, his woman (Bella) was out selling clothes and things. She would go to different offices and apartment buildings and she was always talking about which big important brown girl owed her money . . . Joseph never loved that. He liked the idea of having extra money, they now had a number of thing they could not afford before, but he missed the old Bella who he could just sit down and reason with and talk about certain little things that a one have store up in a one heart . . . Bella said, America teach her that if you want it, you have to go for it. Joe Joe nearly ask her if she want what? The truth is that Joe Joe felt that they were doing quite alright. He owned a taxi which usually did quite well, they lived in a Government Scheme which gave you the shell of a house on a little piece of land under a scheme called 'Start to build up your own home' . . .

. . . and they had built up quite a comfortable little two-bedroom house with a nice living room, kitchen, bathroom and veranda . . . What did Bella mean when she said, 'You have to make it'? As far as Joe Joe was concerned, he had made it. And him was not going to go and kill himself to get to live upon Beverley Hills because anyhow the people up there see all him taxi friend them drive up that way, to visit him, them would call police and set guard dog on them . . . Joe Joe was fairly contented . . . is what happen to Bella?

'Come ya little Bella, siddown, make me ask you something, you no think say that you could just park the buying and selling little make me and you reason bout somethings?'

'Joe Joe you live well yah, I have three girls from the bank coming to fit some dresses and if them buy them then is good breads that.'

After a while, Joe Joe stopped trying to reclaim their friendship. After a month, Bella said she wanted to go back to New York. Joe Joe asked her if she was serious. 'You know that nobody can't love you like me, Joe Joe.'

Joe Joe wondered about that. Sometimes he looked at the lady at the corner of the next road. Their social friendship had been severely curtailed since Bella returned home, but sometimes he found himself missing the little talks they used to have about life and things in general.

She was a very simple woman. He liked her style, she was not fussy. Sometimes he noticed a man coming to her, the man drive a Lada, look like him could work with the Government, but him look married too. You know how some man just look married? Well this man here look like a man who wear a plaid Bermuda shorts with slippers when him relax on a Sunday evening, and that is a married man uniform.

When Joe Joe began to think of life without Bella, the lady at the corner of the next road began to look better and better to him.

'So Bella really gone back a New York?'

'Yes mi dear, she say she got to make it while she can . . .'

'Make what?'

'It!'

'A wha it so?'

'You know . . . Oh forget it.'

And that is what Joe Joe decided to do. The lady, whose name was Miss Blossom, started to send over dinner for Joe Joe not long after Bella went back to New York.

'Be careful of them stew peas and rice you a eat from that lady they you know, mine she want tie you.' Joe Joe said . . . 'True?' and continued eating the dinner that Miss Blossom had sent over for him. He didn't care what Peaches said, her mouth was too big anyway. He just wanted to enjoy eating the 'woman food' somehow, food taste different, taste more nourishing when a woman cook it.

Bella write to say that she was doing fine.

Dear Joe Joe,

I know you're mad with me because you didn't want me to come back to the States, but darling, I'm just trying to make it so that you and me and the children can live a better life and stop having to box feeding outta hog mouth . . .

Now that really hurt Joe Joe. He would never describe their life together as that . . . True sometimes things had been tight but they always had enough to eat and wear . . . 'box feeding outta hog mouth' . . . that was the lowest level of human existence and all these years he thought they were doing fine, that is how Bella saw their life together . . . well sir. Joe Joe was so vex that him never even bother to reply to that letter.

Joe Joe started to take Miss Blossom to pictures and little by little the line of demarcation between social friends and sweetheart just blurred. Joe Joe tell her that the married man better stop come to her and Miss Blossom say, him was only a social friend and Joe Joe say 'yes', just like how him and her was a social friend . . . and she told him he was too jealous and him say yes him was 'but I don't want to see the man in here again', and she said 'Lord Joe Joe.'

Little by little Miss Blossom started to look after the children and look after Joe Joe clothes and meals, is like they choose to forget Bella altogether. Then one Christmas time Bella phone over the grocery shop and tell Mr Lee to tell Joe Joe that she was coming home for Christmas.

Well to tell the truth, Joe Joe never want to hear anything like that. Although Miss Blossom couldn't compare to Bella because Bella was the first woman Joe Joe ever really love . . . Joe Joe was feeling quite contented and he was a simple man, him never really want to take on Bella and her excitement and her 'got to make it'. Anyway, him tell Miss Blossom say Bella coming home and she say to him, 'Well Joe, I think you should tell her that, anything stay too long will serve two masters, or two mistresses as the case might be.'

Joe Joe say '. . . mmmmm . . .' but remember say 'Bella is mi baby mother you know and no matter what is the situation, respect is due.'

Miss Blossom said that 'when Bella a take up herself and gone to New York and leave him, she should know that respect was due to him too.'

Joe Joe say, 'yes' but him is a man who believe that all things must be done decently and in good order, so if him was going to put away Bella him would have to do it in the right and proper way.

Miss Blossom say, she hope that when Bella gone again him don't bother ask her *fi nuttin*. Joe Joe became very depressed.

If Bella looked like a chequer cab the first time, she looked like Miami Vice this time, inna a pants suit that look like it have in every colour flowers in the world and the colour them loud! And Bella broader than ever . . . Oh man. Norman said, 'Bees mus take up Bella inna that clothes dey. Any how she pass Hope Gardens them must water her.'

Bella seemed to be oblivious to the fact that Joe Joe was under great strain . . . She greeted him as if they had parted yesterday . . . 'Joe Joe what you saying sweet pea.' Joe Joe just looked at her and shook his head and said, 'Wha happen Bella?' They went home but Joe Joe felt like he and the children went to meet a stranger at the airport. Bella had become even stranger than before to Joe Joe. When she suggested that he perform a particular act to her while they were making love, he asked her exactly what she was doing in America, if she was sure she was just waitressing at the club . . . Bella said, that he should come forward, because this was the age of women's liberation. Joe Joe told her that she should liberate her backside outta him life because he couldn't take her.

Bella cried and said how much she loved him . . . Then things became really intense and it was like a movie and they had to turn up the radio really high to prevent the children from hearing them . . . Oh well, as Bella always said, 'Nobody can love you like me.'

Joe Joe decided to just bite him tongue while Bella was home. He took to coming home very late all through the Christmas season, because the house was usually full of Bella's posse including 'the Yvonne' of Bear Mountain fame and when they came to visit the house was just full up of loud laughing and talking and all kinds of references that Joe Joe didn't understand. The truth was that he was really dying for Bella to leave. He really didn't much like the woman she had become. First of all everything she gave to him or the children, she tell them how much it cost . . . 'Devon, beg you don't bother to take that Walkman outside, is twenty-nine-ninety-nine I pay for it at Crazy Eddie's', or 'Ann-Marie, just take time with that jagging suit, I pay twenty-three dollars for it in May's Department Store.' Oh Lord.

Bella also came armed with two junior Jherri curls kits and one day Joe Joe come home and find him son and him daughter heads well Jherri curls off.

Joe Joe nearly went mad. 'So you want Devon fi tun pimp or what?'

'Joe, you really so behind time, you should see all the kids on my block.'

'On your block, well me ago black up you eye if you don't find some way fi take that nastiness outta my youth man hair, him look like a cocaine seller . . . Bella what the hell do you, you make America turn you inna idiat? Why you don't just gwan up there and stay then, me tired a you foolishness . . .'

Bella couldn't believe that Joe Joe was saying this to her . . . then she told him that he was a worthless good for nuttin and that him never have no ambition, him just want to stay right inna the little two by four (their house) and no want no better and that she was really looking for a better way and that he clearly did not fit into her plans.

Joe Joe say, him glad she talk what was in her mind because now him realise say that she was really just a use him fi convenience through nobody a New York no want her. Bella said . . . then he said . . . Oh, they said some things to each other!

One thing though Bella catch her fraid and try wash out the Jherri curls outta Devon hair. No amount of washing could bring it round, the barber had was to nearly bald the little boy head and he spent the worse Christmas of his life.

All his friends 'smashed' him as they passed by. As New Year done so, Bella pack up herself and went back to New York.

Joe Joe make a two weeks pass before him make a check by Miss Blossom. The whole Christmas gone him never see her. He figured that she had gone to spend the holidays in the country with her family. When he asked in the yard where she was, they told him they had no idea where she was gone, and that her room was empty. Joe Joe felt like a beaten man. He went home and decided to just look after him two children and just rest within himself. About a month later he was driving home when he saw somebody looking like Miss Blossom standing at the corner of the road. It look like Miss Blossom, but no, it couldn't be, this woman was dressed like a punk . . . in full black, she had on a black socks with a lace frill frothing over the top of her black leather boots. A big woman. He slowed the cab down and said, 'Blossom . . . where you was?' . . . and then he thought quickly, 'No, don't bother answer me . . . you go to New York, right?' 'No,' said Blossom, 'I was in Fort Lawdadale . . . You seem to think only Bella one can go to America.'

Joe Joe never even bother ask her if she want a drive, him just draw a gear and move off down the road, then him go inside him house and slam the door.

Before him drop asleep, it come to him that maybe what him should do was to find an American woman who wanted to live a simple life in Jamaica. Him know a rasta man who have a nice yankee woman like that . . .

CLYDE HOSEIN

◁ ■■■■■■■■■■■■ ◇ ■■■■■■■■■■■■ ▷

The Man at the Gate of the House of Refuge

The short policeman said, 'Out! Quick march!' He laughed when Zakir, clambering up, lost his foothold and clung to the tyre buffers.

The boatman teased: 'Bet you the first thing he do in town is find a sweet *jamette* woman.' He pushed Zakir up to the jetty and flung the flour sack of his possessions behind him.

The old man's legs wobbled upon the weathered planks; he scanned the wharf. Out of a customs shed rumbled a truck, its freight under a tarpaulin; stevedores hollered as they loaded the steamer docked beyond the signal station.

'How meself get-um Paradise?' he asked no one in particular.

The short policeman snatched the sack. 'How much money they give you?'

From the pocket of his new khaki shorts Zakir took the handkerchief, untied it. 'Twelve shilling.'

'Is only a dollar taxi fare to Paradise,' the taller policeman said.

The boatman argued, 'Man, fifty cents by train.'

The short policeman took all the coins but three. 'We don't use shillings any more. Nobody tell you?'

'It's we own dollars and cents now,' the boatman explained. 'We in power now, you know.'

Zakir received the seventy-five cents.

The taller policeman led him past the Harbour Master's office. They came to the fence along a street on which cars whizzed. Zakir had seen a car before but it had looked nothing like these metallic fishes. The man gave him back the three coins of the nine his colleague had divided. 'See the building with the pillars? That's the railway station.'

Zakir held to the world he had just left. Behind him, across the olive deep, lay the high walls and wheeling gulls whose cries persisted as did the pounding of the waves below his cell. Ahead rose tall buildings of a kind that had awed his child's imagination on the trip from the village to Calcutta before the ship had brought him and his family here.

He stood suspended between confusing times until an old man pushing a long box-laden handcart yelled, 'Move!' Zakir stepped without the gate.

At the roundabout circulating vehicles trapped and fascinated him and then a stream of workers caught him in their numbers and he crossed the road.

The station smelled of the swamp and dumping ground that lay to the left. A porter observed him wander through the waiting rooms and hall. The man seemed friendly. 'Paradise? You got to wait till one-thirty for the train going south.'

Zakir sat on a bench and watched the traffic go by.

The glass walls of the offices across the road threw glare and heat upon him. He rested his head in hands still hurting from his grasp upon the handrail as the launch had raced upon the sea, open but for fishermen's pirogues and a cluster of emerald islets, towards the sun-tipped peaks and white-veiled valleys of this the main island.

Eventually, he asked the porter, 'Where meself get-um cab call-um taxi?'

The speed terrified him. In the back seat of the Holden, between snoring men who tossed with every turn, Zakir shut his eyes against the blast.

Occasionally he opened them to the glistening road ahead on which oncoming vehicles seemed aimed at him, but always their drivers zipped and tucked into the stream of cars, trucks and donkey carts.

Cane fields came and then villages of high-stilted houses; he could tell the Hindu homes by the red and white prayer flags in their yards.

More miles of cane fields ended in yet another town. Something about the district made him sit up. Was this not Jacob's Junction? That wizened building? Indeed, it was Carvalho's Bar.

'Paradise-wa?' Zakir hardly heard his voice.

The driver laughed. 'Yes, old man, Paradise.'

'Give-um railway.'

The engine still sang in Zakir's head. He held to the wall of the station.

Was this really Paradise? Did Phulbassiya too have a big concrete house? Was she, her cat's eyes screwed against the dazzle, on her balcony watching the midday traffic?

The footpath beyond the station was now a two-lane road. He took it.

He came to a school, a church, then green and brown brick houses with galleries hidden behind potted palms and baskets of fern; no blanched wooden huts besieged the standpipe.

Rounding the bend, he saw that the barrack-house was gone. So were the palmiste, the caimat and the mango. A steelband was at practice where the front yard should have been between hedges of chigger-toe.

The unfamiliar music pierced him. He sat on the kerb. A throbbing vein in his eyelid made the sky pulse red. Suddenly, the music stopped on a high note and someone said, 'Jesu Joy of Man's Desirin' in their arse. Next week we learnin' Toccata and Fugue in D Minor by that genius, Batch!'

When Zakir came to, he was lying on the culvert, his sack folded under his head. An enormous black man leaned over him.

'Take it easy, old man. You just faint away.'

A short grey Indian pressed forward through the crowd that had formed about Zakir.

Zakir put up his shaking hand to shield his eyes. The Indian switched to Hindi, then to Bengali and Zakir replied in the latter, in a voice stumbling with the hopelessness of his position, about Phulbassiya, his jail term, and that he had no one to whom he could turn.

'Kaiser Kant is my name. I live in that house over there.' The little man spoke in English to the steelbandsman still kneeling at Zakir's side. 'Help me take him to the hammock, Valentine.'

Zakir's weightless body rocked past vines with each long stride the giant took in the trellised garden.

From the kitchen window a young woman called down, 'I hope you ent bringing another stray for me to mind.'

'Have some respect,' Kant said. 'This man is not feeling well.'

Valentine eased Zakir into the hammock and was gone.

Kant went up the stairs, came down and held a bowl of fish broth to Zakir. 'Have some lunch and then you will tell me all about it.'

He found her. He rounded the bushy bend and there she was, bent to the scrubbing board in the tub, a lard barrel sawn in two, washing clothes under the same mango tree outside the same partitioned barrack-house they shared with cane cutters like themselves. He handed her his day's pay; she tied the shilling and penny at the end of her veil with the ninepence she had earned the day before.

The soot of burnt cane was on his lips and he carried upon his blackened rags the stale-bread smell of parched earth. His cutlass mirrored beams of roasting sun that darted along the wooden gable and green wheels of leaves above. The anger leapt in him again that would send him looking for Ian Fraser, the estate overseer. Her grey eyes told him she had read his thoughts; she took the cutlass from him.

He awoke.

The steelband had struck up. Zakir threw his feet to the ground and struggled from the hammock to see through the gap in the hibiscus hedge his host, Kant, on the road talking to a man.

Zakir grabbed his sack, crossed the pebbled yard, followed the ochre track in Kant's kitchen garden and arrived at a plum tree beside a drain which he jumped to gain the street down which he had come from the railway station. He watched the steelbandsmen in penitential postures shake and nod in time with the shifting motions of their arms as they plunked their sticks upon their pans.

He saw that patch of earth before him in another time, as on another planet, when he would wake at four to find Phulbassiya already up with a sandwich of fried beans or chopped green mango, or any edible leaf or vine or fruit, or perhaps, the luxury of a tin of sardines from Canada. Carrying his cutlass and some food wrapped in a cloth, he would set off in advance of her for the field, walking barefoot on dew under the stars before the birds began to rage.

His own frenzy was no less voluble. He cursed and swore as he walked in the pristine dusk that cloaked tree and bush and rickety rusting roof clenched over the bitter smell of hurt that encircled men resigned to their fate and proud of it. He was tired of huddling, bleating and castrated, before the greedy gods who cowed him with the power of their sin.

The sun came up, ignited the leaves, pummelled him until his mind chafed as his hands did upon the handle of his swinging cutlass. Flash after flash, visions of water came, but it was four and one-half hours, no less, from the commencement of his task that the driver of his gang signalled the break for lunch.

Men imprisoned by their calm paid dearly for a break from grace. That is what had happened to him. But who had paid more dearly, he, for self-destructive sabotage of estate authority, or his father before him, who, in his sickness, took so many beatings that despair became a necessity?

Zakir cringed at the new sparseness of trees in the district, but his eyes connected with a vaguely familiar skyline. Keeping the samaans in sight, he walked a maze of streets interconnected by neat concrete drains and overhead electrical wires. Afar, the smoking factory stack came into view, in front him the house that had bloomed while others around it wilted with contagion and fatigue, the same overseer's quarters stood green-ringed behind white walls.

But the inhabitants had changed. Behind iron gates black children in pink jumpers ran about the now much bigger lawn.

It was some way up from here that he had surprised Ian Fraser, a lifetime ago.

He shook his head; he had seen enough. He retraced his steps. The steelband grew loud.

Kant came cycling around a corner. He let out in irate Bengali, 'I've been looking for you, where have you been?'

'Brother, the world is not the same,' Zakir replied. 'I'm lost. I don't know where to start looking.'

Kant dismounted and wheeled the cycle at Zakir's pace.

Zakir studied the gentle red eyes in the dark creased face. The man's friendliness seemed a thoughtless intrusion. Zakir wanted to break away to sit alone and think but, wiping the beads of perspiration from his brow, he allowed Kant to guide him. There was nothing else he could do.

With a sigh Zakir sat in the hammock. Kant shouted up the stairs, 'Ai girl, bring the Cockspur and glasses come!'

He drew up the stool. 'I came to live here in 1939. The war was just starting when I bought from Carvalho, the rumshop man. Barracks, cane, everything was gone when I moved here.'

His scowling daughter-in-law darkened them, put the bottle of rum and the glasses on a stair and left.

In Zakir's abstract gaze, the poured liquid rose to fill the jigger with gold. 'Will I ever know where my wife is?' Zakir threw back his head and choked on grog and exasperation.

Kant refilled the glass. He leaned conspiratorially. 'Sometimes a man must learn to live with himself, with his memories.'

Zakir saw with horror the stain of weals on the face in front him, its disfigurement clarified by the slanting light. A knowing look came to it and Kant said, 'My friend, since they sent you away buildings and ambitions have grown high. A flick of a switch will give you light, you can fly above the clouds; but sons still beat their fathers. No matter. Fire another with me.'

Kant drank as though he were imbibing some rare nourishment. 'You never heard anything about your brother? Maybe we could put an ad in the newspaper. We could ask the radio station to broadcast a message. And what about the police?'

The word struck such terror into Zakir that he lapsed into English. 'Meself no see why talk police. Them no help long time me ask. Sabbet all-you coolie give-um plenty trouble!'

Kant put his hand on Zakir's shoulder. 'Is your father-in-law's name Subnaik?'

Zakir's eyes radiated hope. 'Yes, yes.'

'My friend, I found out where your wife went. Listen to me. When you were sleeping I talked to a man, an old-old man who knows. He was already here when I came to this district. He told me Subnaik took his wife, his sons and their wives and Phulbassiya and went back to India.'

'*Aryavarta?*'

'Yes, *Bharat Varsha . . . Himavat-Setu-Paryantam.* I should have gone back myself.'

Zakir said, 'Who is this man? What does he know?'

'His name is Kishore. He says he used to live in your barrack-house.'

Zakir tried to put a face to the name.

Kant said, 'When the English were offering land in exchange for the passage to India, Kishore took property. He planted it and became one of the thousands of private cane farmers.

'He was lucky; not everybody got land or passage. *My* parents had to save. From their thirty cents a day, they saved in the government savings bank. They bought their land.' He swallowed his rum. 'Drink up, man. It's up to us now. We mustn't let the old people down.'

Zakir went into the yard. Red beams sent playing in the shivering grass long shadows of grafted oranges in a row. His jaw tightened till it pricked with a thousand needles.

While Zakir bent in agony Kant put his arm around his broken body. 'You can stay here. In this room downstairs. I'm minding a stray bitch but we'll put her and her litter on a bag outside the door.' He drummed consolations on Zakir's back. 'Stay here tonight, man. Tomorrow we will see.'

Zakir said, 'Show me how to get to Kishore's house.'

Kishore turned out to be a shrivelled, sour old man, living with a younger woman in a bushy lane, and, despite his deviousness, Zakir learned that Kishore had gone to live in the barrack-building after Zakir was sent up to prison.

'Good thing Subnaik daughter gone from the likes of you.'

Zakir was shocked that the man still thought him a dangerous criminal.

He returned to hear Kant's son upstairs. 'You have time to waste with every Tom, Dick and Harry crying some sad story. I hope that man not staying too long.'

The father's soft voice came, 'He only staying a few days.'

All night Zakir inhaled the pungency of rust.

In the dawn, he talked as to a child to the slavering bitch with the distended udders. He heard voices and an engine.

Kant came down the stairs. 'How did you sleep?'

'Very well. Look here, my friend, I'm leaving today. I'm going to search for my brother.' He threw his clothes into the sack. 'I have a feeling Munir is in Town.'

'Town is a big place and you're talking about forty–fifty years ago.' Kant grabbed the ornate iron bedhead, eased himself to the rumpled sheet. 'How much money do you have Zakir?'

Zakir showed him the two coins. 'You're crazy,' Kant said.

'I have to find Munir. I'm leaving now.'

When Kant saw there was no use arguing, he said, 'All right, wait,' and came back down from the kitchen with a brown paper bag which he gave to Zakir.

Zakir sniffed the warm bread.

Kant's hand opened over Zakir's, releasing a green note. 'Five dollars, a loan. Borrow it from me.'

A freight train went south, amazing Zakir with its shiny chemical containers and oil-field equipment that soared from its boxcars. At ten he was in the almost empty north-bound coach rushing through cane and rice that time after time would break to reveal a line of roofs under a line of trees. When the hills reared at his side, their excavations pained him. High towers loomed; the stink of swamp and garbage dump told him he had arrived.

Following the Calle Marina, he reached a car park flanked by a double row of palmistes; there the stench of fish and grime suffused the baking air. After the wholesale merchants' came rumshops and restaurants, then French colonial houses, their *portes cochères* leaning, their stables inhabited by staring women and barefoot children.

Zakir crossed to a street aimed at a tree-clad hill. He went by a tumbril packed with green coconuts among which an Indian stood wielding a cutlass as he hacked open a nut for a customer, a white woman with steel-blue hair.

Zakir kept to the walls dimmed by eaves and canopies. Cursing his deliberate steps, young men overtook him. Music blasted from a festooned grotto filled with dresses, pots and glassware. He came to bigger stores, their silk-fringed windows displaying things he had never imagined to exist.

The city seemed about to suck him into its maw. He turned and hurried back the way he had come.

At the end of the car park, he found a little square between two Canadian banks. He sat on a bench under a palmiste and studied a wizened woman who squatted at a pot on three sooty stones. Further away, an old man slept on a sheet of cardboard at the gnarled roots of a dying almond.

How would he find Munir?

Outside the Canadian Imperial, a Madrassi vended doubles from a bicycle. Zakir had eaten Kant's bread on the train and now the aroma of the spiced chickpeas and mango caused him to swallow.

He tendered the green note and ate the savoury with such relish that he smacked his hands clean of the thick sauce that had oozed between his fingers. He had left the change, red notes and silver and copper coins, on the lid of the food container; now he pretended to count. The man eyed him with amusement.

Ordering another doubles, Zakir said, '*Bhai*, me lose-um l'il brother long time. How me find-um?'

The man's expression hardened. 'Your brother?'

'Munir go-um small-small.' Zakir levelled a hand to indicate Munir's height then. 'One morning no find-um. Sabbet overseer take he, big khaki-wallah. Them beat Bap, him sick, can't cut cane. Munir gone, Ma cry, grieve. She dead, malaria.'

A queue began to form. The vendor said, 'Man, I don't know what to tell you.' He turned to serve his next customer. 'The papers does print up picture and thing about people missing. Try them, nah.'

The customer put in, 'Yes, go down by the *Times*.' He led Zakir to the corner and pointed out a white brick building.

Zakir shouldered his sack. Behind him the customers laughed. He shrugged off his fatigue.

He stepped off the green-guttered street into the foyer where he stood among brightly painted bins containing entries for competitions run by the subscription department. A screech assailed him. 'Get out of here!' The slant-eyed woman waved to a little guard who fingered a truncheon. The woman said, 'Look at him, he not so nasty like the rest, but bet you he drunk.'

The guard bore down upon Zakir. 'What you doing here?'

'Me come to find me brother, lost and found,' pleaded Zakir.

A man swept in from the street, was about to mount the stairs, but turned. 'You lost something, old man?'

'Me brother long time lose. Him go 'way. No see he no more . . .'

The man led Zakir up the stairs to a long office where rows of people sat behind typewriters under whirring overhead blades. He offered Zakir a chair at the side of his desk and as Zakir stumbled over the story of his search, the man alternately wrote and doodled.

Eventually he said, 'This is a sad story. I will put it in the papers tomorrow. Who knows? Your brother might see your picture and come here or phone in or something.' He signalled to someone in a cubicle.

Zakir balanced his sack on his knees, ran his fingers through his hair and assumed a deathly stare at the lens.

He shut his eyes against the headlights that searched the square. The night air nipped his ears, chilled his feet through his canvas shoes. The slats of the bench bored into his nape and spine, then into his ribs and temple. With a sigh at the winking stars, he got up.

The gas lamps of the food trucks and the corn vendors' flambeaux drew him. He walked a street of olfactory enticements: curries, fried chicken, boiling corn which gave off bouquets of onion and pepper. Where makeshift stalls sprinkled the sidewalk, the tang of oranges collided with odours of freshly shucked oysters.

In those commingled aromas under the rustling palmistes, night workers awaited route taxis to the suburban valleys and loiterers drank, munched and cracked jokes at the expense of uniformed chauffeurs and their broods of tourists going to and from the bars and clubs higher up the road.

Zakir stood at the edge of the lights. From the shadows came coughs and groans of derelicts whom, earlier, he had watched bedding down on the sidewalks under the shops' canopies. Consciousness of his bodily smirch grew until it assumed the proportions of a scar.

A clock struck twelve. Following the chimes between the French colonial houses, he came to the church. The sound of running water lured him to the back. In the asphalted yard he found the tap.

A thumping snapped him from fitful sleep. Wisps in the grey dawn, scavengers piled coconut husks and soft-drink bottles in the tray of their ramshackle truck. Their hurled patois rang with an elemental bliss that magnified Zakir's desolation. His limbs trembled, his lips quivered.

But the blaze of morning sanctified him. At eight he manipulated his washed body through the raucous streets.

At the *Times*, not finding the man who had helped him, Zakir bought a newspaper. He walked back to his bench and searched for his photograph. His staring expression seemed to blend conceit and guilt and give him a mad air.

In the car park, under a palmiste, a one-armed man was polishing a car. Zakir summoned his courage.

The man replied, 'Look, mister, you can't see I busy? Just now the owner of this car coming for it.'

Zakir sat on the low concrete wall. The man looked up and sucked his teeth. 'All right, all right.' He took the newspaper from Zakir and read haltingly.

As far as Zakir could gather, the facts were well reported.

The streets howled. Sun flagellated the overflowing sidewalks upon which Zakir fought his way. A man sidestepped him, stopped and asked, 'You find your brother yet?'

In the *Times* office the newsman said, 'If you can't find me the next time you come, talk to that lady, Mrs Jeaneau. I'm sorry we have nothing to tell you.'

At the bottom of the stairs, the buzzing grew in Zakir's ears; he held to the banister. His stomach hurt. A sour taste rushed to his lips. In the café around the corner he bought a bun and an orange crush.

In his wanderings that afternoon, he drove himself to find some mental pole around which he might revolve, yet he could not cease to alternate between hysteria and resignation.

When the wharves gave way to dilapidated sheds in weedy yards, strewn with junk, he turned back. Mrs Jeaneau had nothing to report.

The congestion and noise of the city inflamed him, drove him to the Calle Marina.

When he awoke amber rays touched the palmistes.

His meal, his nocturnal walk, his washing at the church tap. His aloneness demeaned him.

First thing in the morning, he went to the *Times* only to hear the same story. He petitioned merchants for some casual job. They hardly heard him out.

A morning without ruction came. It was Sunday.

Down to his last dollar, he forsook breakfast. Summoning new vigour, he walked north, his mind savouring the surety of other times that brought the ache for a face from the world he had known before he had gone to prison.

His feet went of their own volition till he had covered the three miles around the Savannah of whose beauty even he had heard. An impetuous indifference came to him that caused him to strut under the prodigious trees in the cool botanical gardens. He followed a guide leading a party of tourists. He hovered on the radius of their speech until they brought him, through light and shade, in a circle back to the cricket ground where taxi cabs waited.

◇

The crash of waves upon the rocks outside the prison walls pounded his temples. Viridian fields of waving cane beguiled him. A sluggish stream washed mustard leaf fleets and mud snakes between blue pataki banks. In an aged pipal glade, the koels called. At lamplight a thoombri mourned above tabla and harmonium.

◇

In the square all night he thought of going to see Kaiser Kant. But, in the morning, Paradise did not seem such a good idea.

'You didn't pick up?' The one-armed man came over to Zakir's bench. 'I mean a job.'

Zakir shook his head. 'Before meself ask they say go, go. All place me beg, say meself do-um anything. But, no . . .'

'Too Tall, that's my name. Yours?'

'Me? Zakir.' He spread over the backrest of the bench the shirt he had wrung dry.

'Okay, Zakir, how about getting me two buckets of water? I'll pay you twenty-five cents a bucket.'

After the second trip, Zakir sat and watched Too Tall, his strength concentrated in his one arm, rub the gleaming metal.

Too Tall said, 'A man like you shouldn't be out on the streets like this. You ent like them.' He pointed to a cardboard roll where a derelict lay. 'The government should look after people in their old age. You should ask at the office on Cabildo Street.'

Zakir spent one of the coins on doubles. Later, after Mrs Jeaneau had kept him waiting for over an hour, she roared at him, 'We can't make this Munir *appear*, you know.'

'Plenty thank-um you and the mister,' Zakir said. 'Tell him me not come back bother you no more. Brother dead or him gone away or can't read-um.'

Suddenly no structure, no line, no face was strange to him. The voices inside him grew louder than all the sounds of the city. He trudged towards Cabildo Street.

In the office, clerks, as if in slow motion, wrote and stapled papers together. A young man leaning on a counter talked to a woman who flipped the pages of a ledger.

'All you tell-um . . .'

She raised her eyebrows at Zakir. 'Come back later, we closing for lunch.'

Zakir sat on the steps below and put his head between his knees.

As soon as the door swung open, he followed the crowd in. His head seemed filled with the poachy earth of a cattlepen. He said, 'All-you tell-um me talk gov'ment about place for meself to stay?'

The woman behind the counter regarded him with horror. 'You don't see other people waiting? You think you can just walk in here and play boss? ' The whole office stared at him.

Zakir cowered under the sudden sting of their eyes and her vituperation.

Year after year, more houses went up across the road until only one vacant lot afforded a chunk of corrugated sea, whereas before the bay had been so exposed that he could have seen between the five islets the central hill of the prison island.

In his striped blue and grey cotton pyjamas, Zakir stood at his spot at the gatepost under the flamboyant and peered through the pikes at the road upon which evening traffic flowed. He heard the boys coming along the sidewalk and he stepped back for fear of what they might do.

They stopped at the locked gate. One said, 'Hey, Santa Claus, we want to give you a present.' The other boy picked up a fallen flamboyant pod and tried to poke Zakir.

The man on the veranda of one of the older houses, the high one with the shop on the ground floor, shouted across the street, 'You little scamps! That's what they teaching you in school!'

They sped away trailing a wake of laughter. Zakir saw what was perhaps a toothbrush moustache on the blur of the face across the road.

Following the wall of rusting zinc sheets, nailed to unpainted laths on wooden posts, some capped with monstrous ant nests, he came to the men's wing and mounted the steps of the once-grand estate house.

A dingy hall gave way to a long high-ceilinged room, the irregularity of plaster and paint between sash windows indicating the position of the original walls. He threw himself into his bed across which fell a glare from the fanlight above the door.

The chaos of hard little blue beds suffocated him. He fought off the after-images of iron pikes and gateposts.

His mouth watered for the biscuits and cocoa that should have been his since slanting rays had hit the press, the top shelf of which he shared with his neighbour, who lay staring. Zakir listened to the shuffle of feet along the veranda and then he too joined the congregation at the main door to the commons. A raw meat smell seeped through the crevices of the shuttered room. The cook screamed, 'Move back!'

She unlocked the door; the inmates streamed in to form a queue. From the kitchen came the clang and clatter of pots and pans. The aproned housemaids appeared, two toting the steaming cauldron, two carrying bowls and aluminium spoons which they set down in heaps upon the serving table. The bell summoned the indifferent from court-yard and sleeping quarters.

Dismissing the server's crusty manner, Zakir said, 'Give-um biscuit and cocoa, nah please, Missy, meself can't eat-um *ghose* meat.'

Still the server ladled into Zakir's bowl. 'You want biscuits and cocoa for tea, breakfast and dinner? Soup have good nourishment.' She took the next inmate's bowl.

Zakir grimaced. The salted pork and dumplings swam in a beige goo. He chewed on the dumplings. When they were gone he scooped a dice of meat, put it to his lips.

At once the act brought remorse. He scraped the bowl into the bin and rushed back to the men's wing.

But he could not lie still. The drone of traffic called him. Down he went into the parched courtyard and between droopy hibiscus to his post under the flamboyant.

Dark hung over the street and chunk of sea. Dim shadows played on curtains. Cars ran about under the impetuous and compelling urges of their invisible drivers. Streetlights went on.

Zakir sank into the whirlpool of his anger. The lit scene before him, its salt tang and all, dissolved to that blighted day and he was again tracking Ian Fraser in the roseau and wild banana.

Along the green trail Fraser rode slumped in the saddle. The pith helmet blackened his face, his jodhpured legs rested against the glistening flanks of the chestnut mare. In Zakir's wet palm, the wired haft of the cutlass slipped.

He said, 'I give-um up meself,' but the foam-headed inmate only continued to watch Zakir place shoots of grass into bead-sized holes in the dry flower beds and draw up worms. He spoke to the worms before, gently, he put them back.

Brushing dust from hands and knees, he took from his sack the now dehydrated slice of bread, threw bits of it into the shade of the flamboyant and laughed when the ground doves floated to the crumbs.

'I give-um up meself police,' he told the men on the sidewalk; they skirted the gateway. Behind them came an overdressed woman. Her white stockings reminded him of that first day, promoted from the children's grass gang, he herded the water buffaloes at the pond with Jattan and Jerrybandan. To show off his coming manhood, husbandry now, cane cutting shortly after, Zakir had left the green mud to dry white on his spindly legs. Deliriously happy, he had paraded about Paradise until night denied him further show of pride.

Paradise. There the natural world mitigated coarseness, uncertainty, self-hate. Despite the move from continent to island, sky, bush, sea were all the same. In these a man could trust. Was this Bap's vision?

Paradise. How much of himself had Zakir left there?

A young man's hopes. A bridegroom's naïvety. Phulbassiya's father had wanted for his only daughter a Hindu ceremony and Zakir did not mind. At the wedding he had worn silk jibba and lace dhoti. The holy men had put a string of marigolds, zinnias and oleanders around his neck and a dot of sandal paste in the middle of his brow.

'*O gul mohur!*' He touched the flamboyant. 'Tree, my sister!' He recalled laughter drilled to silence, the vast dusty plain waiting for rain and the roar of swollen rivers.

He saw now from a larger context, his view high above the earth. He searched for himself, even the dot he might be, and his nothingness overwhelmed him.

He said, 'Stone, here I am. Bird, here I am. Sky, here I am.' Under the flaming tree, he gripped the pikes.

How long ago they had brought him here he could not say. Life was a transit of days of overcrowded loneliness and long nights of sleepless chaos. A doppelganger mocked him. His mind collapsed from those draining rituals of nostalgia to which he clung for direction.

Triangular eyes, steel cold. Whose puffy-with-satisfaction face now mocked him? Whose smirk altered to a sneer?

Zakir lay on his bed, listened to the distant hum; then came the rattle and fingers of light lengthened across the ceiling.

Even before, even before . . .

Disembarking from the ship, he clutching his mother's skirt, she following his father, shunted from queue to queue, the immigration agents herding them with curses . . .

Zakir rose and felt for his sack.

In the tattered shroud of the sky multi-sized holes let in the blazing light beyond. The disembodied voice of a night walker crossed the deserted streets. With an angry whine another vehicle sped by. Released from its high beam the edges of darkness beyond the circles of weak streetlight reappeared to make his view yellow and black again as in the suffocating barrack-room with the oil lamp burning, only now the shadows did not dance.

Was this his gate? Was he born to stand here?

Another sun rose, burning the bushes on the shack-scarred slopes behind the House. By afternoon, the flamboyant had wilted. A passing cloud shot pellets of rain that stung his skin, sizzled on the asphalt. The steam assailed his nostrils. It brought back the hookah at which Bap, after work, changed into jacket, dhoti and turban, hunched puffing in the dark corner. It was his only consolation after Munir had disappeared and Mai had gone.

And when Bap's turn came, Zakir inherited the old man's debts, and the contents of the room that he was never to see since that fateful day.

It was in Muhurram and he had hurried from a distant field to the parade of the tombs in the traces between the canes. The throbbing drums, the rum, the rebellious march behind red, green and silver paper minarets and domes combined to lift him to a high that refused to wear off when he got home to find Phulbassiya still not returned from her cane cutting task.

He placed a pinch of *ganja* in the bowl, lit the hookah and let the cloying smoke invade him. He added pinch after pinch until his deadened tongue and singed moustache told him to stop.

But courage had come; his heart grew bold, the new man in him pointed a finger at Zakir's dereliction. 'A fine man you are!' Over and over he said it.

Contentious crows shot up and wheeled from Zakir's path. He stopped, listened. He heard only the sighing of the wind, the clacking of the smoke-blue leaves sharp to his skin as he moved through the bush.

He wiped his hand against his khaki shorts. On a green-bearded bough, a nun sang out her little heart. The roseau stalks shone gold.

Poor Phulbassiya, Zakir thought, wanting to take this to the *Panchayat*. What could a council of five elders do against a man like Fraser?

A jingle touched his ear. He stopped. Hoofbeats came. The man was talking to his mare. The faceless man slumped in the saddle. Sequins of light danced on the stirrups in which the glistening black wellingtons were splayed.

Hidden by the long grass, Zakir followed man and mount along a track so soft that he hardly heard himself. But a crack appeared in his resolve.

Let him ride away. Another time, he thought. But, to his surprise, Fraser reined the mare. He seemed to topple out of the saddle. Zakir ducked behind wild banana leaves.

He heard the sound of water falling. Through the broad leafage, he saw the mare grazing. From the coruscating equipment on her back, the holster declared the chance that Zakir took.

Cutlass raised high, he tore through the bush. 'Hai! Hai! Hai!'

The mare let out a frantic neigh and cantered off. Fraser turned. His hand flew up from his state of unzip. There, Zakir aimed.

Into a vortex Zakir spun.

He saw the helmet fall, the eyes' swollen lids, the quizzical look change, the naked pink sheath below, glistening wet, scandalously innocent.

Zakir's arm fell again. Again, the blade sank.

A grotesque assortment of objects reared. The cutlass thudded. Zakir saw *his* blood too.

His life rose to his mouth and he could have screamed himself out of existence. In the ditch the crumpled man lay still.

Depersonalised, incongruous to himself, Zakir too went down, reliving that other hand-to-hand encounter: Bap grovelling in the dust while the other overseer cracked the whip; Bap holding his head and shouting in Bengali, 'O God, don't beat me in front of my sons!'

Zakir tore his bloody shirt and tied the gash as he ran.

He came to the water buffalo pen. Some mud-splashed boys beat just-as-muddied beasts into submission. Jattan and Jerrybandan came to mind.

He circled the field and called from the waist-high cockroach plants to Jattan's barrack-room window. He saw the estate constable on his horse in the lane.

In blinding flight, Zakir regained the field. He let the tears fall. Obstinate, angry, debauched even in pain, the face in the ditch staggered him. He sank, leafslashed, into the welcoming canes.

An inconsequential little thrill sent needles through him: if Fraser were not dead, if they found him in time, O Phulbassiya, it would be

102

some time before he would say, 'Get Phulbassiya washed and send her up!'

◇

Even long after my discharge from the orphanage I did not know what my mother meant by 'Oho!' It took a Canadian, Reverend Knox, to put me in the know.

'Alas! Alas!' she was always saying, and if I cast my mind back to that dark corner, I can make out shadows of events that brought her regret after regret.

I remember the room, the thin walls went half-way to the roof, a big room with a curtain of flour sacks separating our beds from our parents', jute bags that I rolled up after my family had got up, cooked, had coffee with roti and beans and gone off into the dawn.

An old woman looked after me but she left me on my own for hours on end, exposed to the fears that undermined every second that I lived, nervous and silent.

There was constant quarrelling; not a day went by without some flare-up and always women crying and threats of cutlass chop-ups.

But worst of all was my father's asthma. It got so bad that at nights he would gasp and moan as he writhed on his bag. I feared the mornings he was so sick he could not move but sat in the sun, his chest caving in, and my mother with the Book, reciting prayer after prayer. But her petitions did not keep away the overseer. I can't remember his name either, but he was a gaunt, brooding man and you'd never think such fury lay beneath his milk-white skin.

Not until I had become a pupil teacher and read the commission of enquiry reports that Reverend Knox showed me did I begin to understand why my mother's face was always drawn and why my brother and I lived on fruit from trees we raided as we ranged far and wide in the cool evenings after he had finished work.

According to Reverend Knox, Father must have been charged with everything in the book: habitual idleness, refusing to begin or finish work, absent from work without leave, malingering, damaging employer's property, breach of hospital regulations, use of threatening words to those in authority. If our hunger was any indication of the state of affairs, then I'm sure that Father was fined for all of those charges.

As clear as my death is to me now is that day I ran. I heard the driver shouting outside. Father groaned on his bag. My brother and I got up and peered through the crack in the boards. I saw the overseer and

103

another white man on their horses, one snorting as if he too bore his master's rage.

The driver knocked over the coalpot that was on the steps, burst in, dragged Father by the heels into the yard and whipped him. All the while the white men reined their circling horses, and, through his laboured breathing, Father implored them to believe that his illness was real.

Then he stood up and after he had taken his cutlass, he touched my head. Just after he had gone, walking between their horses, I felt my burning brow and saw the blood that must have transferred from his hand.

The old woman had no time for me. The excitement had brought out into the yard the tenants who took up work later and children of my age not quite old enough to wield a sickle or husband a water buffalo. I slipped away down the rutted trace.

I wanted to put distance for a while between myself and all that pain. The bush was high and damp and the clearing to which I came was a railway track. Running from slipper to slipper, I arrived at a river. Over it was a bridge. When I crossed I saw the train. I slinked around it and, hearing voices, climbed into a car.

The engine whistled. I felt the judder; heard the clank of chains. I fought back my tears. My face and limbs burned with cuts from the razor grass.

When they found me I could not make myself understood. I knew only that I lived with my mother, my father and my brother in a long house with the smells of food and acrid pipes and the quarrels of each apartment invading the other.

Everybody at the orphanage was kind to me. There were other boys like myself; we all became Christians. I would say that it was the best thing that ever happened to me. Warren Grant: I liked the name they gave me. I said it to myself all the time when I was alone.

Look at me now. Despite my ups and downs, I've had a good life as a teacher and I've raised five children, all gone from Amina and me now. The last boy is teaching at Dalhousie.

Soon I'll retire; I'll be home all day with Amina. The pension is small but I have saved, bought insurance, my children are all doing well. And don't talk about the grandchildren! Amina and I go crazy when they visit.

Amina will still carry on the shop below. Who knows, one good day we might rent it out and just relax, take it easy.

Yes, I could have had a worse life than this. I could have ended up like that fellow across the road. What's going on in his head? Why does he stare? What does he think?

Sun or rain, day after day, sometimes even at night, he stands there at the gate of the House of Refuge.

AMRYL JOHNSON

◁ ■■■■■■■■■■■■■■■■ ◇ ■■■■■■■■■■■■■■■■ ▷

Yardstick

Is like the man don't sleep at all, at all. Don't matter how early I open the door, he there on he veranda, looking out.

'Morning, Mr Braffitt. How you?'

A toothless grin exposed the pink wealth of his gums.

'I dare, yes, Zelda girl. And yourself?'

His reply, the response was not always said. Sometimes, it was merely implied.

Today just like any other blasted Thursday. I have to wash the clothes, cook the food, get the first two ready for school in time, get myself ready for work then take the baby to the nursery. Her head was hot, she had to remember and—

Zelda went back to forcing clothes against the scrubbing board. She caught a glimpse of the old man in her line of vision just before she slapped the wet cloth against the board. He was still smiling.

Remember and—Then she had to—

'Yes Mr Braffitt. Is true. Is true.'

And when she finish doing that, she go have to—

'Is true. Is true what you saying, Mr Braffitt. I agree. I agree.'

Zelda was only half listening. Her answers came almost mechanically. This was habit. Part of an early-morning ritual which had started from the very first morning, the very first morning she had moved into the yard.

'The old man always want get you in some 'tory. Is like he always, always have something to say.'

Old talk. Five in the morning, every morning. The old man would be there on his veranda, waiting to tell her something. I hear he have false teeth. I only hear. I ain't yet see he with he teeth in. All I ever see he doing, is skinning up he gum. Zelda could not always understand what he was saying. At times, she found herself blatantly guessing.

'Pa Braffitt does want talk politics. He ain't happy at all, at all with the way they running things in the country.'

Mother Gloria who also lived in the yard, had laughed when she said it.

'He say he does remember when—. And the man travel all about, oui. He did work Panama Canal. The man go America, he go Canada, he go England. He—.'

'And he come back here?!!'

Zelda's interruption had been high-pitched with incredulity. Mother Gloria had looked at her as if she was being disrespectful.

'Trinidad is he home, child. When he done he travelling, where else he go go?'

Zelda thought Mr Braffitt a fool.

Here? Me? Even if I did have a house here waiting. Empty.

Every now and then, her thoughts would drift back to that particular conversation with Mother Gloria. If she was at home, she would look around her and schueps. She would look at her poverty and deprivation and suck air through her teeth. She would do so loud with contempt. Sometimes, she would say it aloud.

'When I get out, you think I ever coming back here? Here? Christ, I tell you when I gone, I gone.'

It was as if all her life had been spent in those two rooms he had taken her to when she was carrying their first child. Only for a while. Just a short while, he had said. Short while. Things were going to get better. Much better. And she had waited. More to the point, she had believed him. She had believed him. Ten years had gone by. Ten years of her sweet sweet life. Gone.

And Lord. And Lord, what? What, what, what? What did happen? What did go wrong, Lord? He in the same job he did have when I first meet he. And when last they give he a raise? I did think he have ambition. What ambition?

After a while, you done hoping. You done waiting for the rainbow. Every morning when you open your eye, you should feel good about life. Every day when I look up into the sky, was like every ray of sun less bright than the day before. And when you do hear the shout, you start to feel a tightening in your stomach even before you begin to open your eye.

Was how it was for a while. And sudden sudden one day, I leave that behind. My inside start to get hollow hollow. Was like I empty. Was like I real real empty. Everything I feel getting less and less. Then like nothing inside me. Nothing. Nothing. Then like was I can't feel nothing at all, at all, something else start welling up inside me 'til the thing get full full. And it hurting. The thing hurting. I start to wonder if the pain ever going to go. I ever going be free of this hurt? But it do. It leave me numb. I never going to feel nothing again. Everything I do from then on, I do it from duty. After that, every child I bring into this world, I shit out of me like vomit.

Zelda had not needed to go looking. She had found any, all yardsticks right there on her doorstep. Of late, she had taken to spending more and more time talking to herself.

'You see me, I not like Rosalie, eh. I still alive. I ain't dead.'

Rosalie make ten. She, the man, and the children that ain't leave yet still in the board house where she make the first. Now she breast so dry up and shrivel, they hanging to she waist. She ain't never have no pleasure. She ain't never tasted no joy. She spend she whole life making baby. Making baby have she chain to the house. I never see she dress up. I never see she going no place. I just have to look in Rosalie eye to remind myself how I don't want to be. Of late, is like the two of we always catching one another glance. She don't talk much. Rosalie don't say much but she don't have to. Is there. Is right there in she face. Everything. Rosalie not old. Rosalie not an old woman but every line on she face does tell she story. Rosalie don't wear no expression. She don't look happy. She don't look sad. She don't look nothing. If wasn't for all the lines, I would think is mask the girl wearing. Is not a real face at all, at all. I feel every line on Rosalie face is she state of mind. She hiding behind mask to try and shield sheself. I feel so. But is when I look in Rosalie eye that I want to bawl. I want bawl for she. I want bawl for all of we. Anger does take me down below. I look in Rosalie eye and she telling me she life done. She trap. She in prison. I look in she eye and I want to scream for she. One time, I look at Rosalie and I make my decision. After that, my crying done. All my regret over. Long time now I make a vow and I have Rosalie to thank for that. I done make my decision. I getting out. By hook or crook, I getting out.

'Is true, Mr Braffitt. Is true. What you say is true.'

The emphasis had now long since shifted. So much of what Zelda was doing was now done out of a sense of habit. No longer even duty.

'No, Mr Braffitt, I ain't think so. I sure the rainy season done.'

Every morning the same chupid conversation. And sometimes when I come to think on it, I sure the reply I giving he ain't a fart anything to do with what he telling me. But what I go do? What? What?

It had slowly dawned on her. The truth and this decision had become more certain. More fixed. She had acquired a new found resilience. Zelda now had the stamina, the strength to go through the daily rigmarole, step by step. It was this determination which had recently found her sneaking days off work to spend hours in crowded waiting rooms, waiting. Just waiting. Waiting. Waiting her turn.

'You think it easy?!! It ain't easy, you hear! It ain't easy. You only *think* it easy.'

It was his stock reply. Joseph had not shouted. He had only raised his voice. He had never been violent. He had never lifted a hand to Zelda or the children. While most women would have been grateful, it was this peaceful, to her mind docile, nature which had been the bone of contention in their marriage.

Too damn quiet for he own good. Too quiet and softy softy. People don't appreciate you for it. They does want take advantage. I ain't know how it is he ain't learn by now. They does take he for a fool again and again but the man never wise up. I did like he at first because he was gentle. He was gentle and nice. I did think sooner or later he go see you don't get nothing for nothing in this world. Yes, is true, when I first meet he, I did like he 'cause he quiet and gentle. But, Lord, when you see opportunity after opportunity slip through he finger 'cause he too softy softy to go out and fight and claw and devour, something does stick in your throat. And what the arse he know 'bout it? The man always giving me the same blasted reply. It ain't easy. It ain't easy. No, of course, it ain't easy. It have anything in life that easy? Tell me. Nothing in Trinidad going to come to we black people. We at the bottom of the ladder. Is not like the Indian and them. They helping one another. I tired telling he the stupidey little job he in since I know he, ain't worth nothing. When last he pay go up? Eh? Eh? When last? He working night watchman. Since I know he, he working night watchman for little little money. If wasn't for the job I holding down, I don't know how we would have manage. And the children does grow out of they clothes so fast. What sort of family we is, anyway? He working nights. I working in the day. On he days off, all he want do is sleep or he out with he boys and them. When the children and me does get to see he? Family? What family? We make three children together and is like he feel he work done. From the start, is like I alone doing the bringing up. I alone. I bathing them, I caring for them. I is the one does have to do the beating.

Is me alone having to do everything. Everything. Father? What father? He is any father? I more father to them than he.

I twenty-six years of age and is still a fire in me, I still hungry and I want get out of this place before it dead. Look at me, juk, juk jukking. Jukking clothes against the blasted scrubbing board but why I have to—?

Zelda's thoughts suddenly accelerated in time. She stood looking down at the clothes, her eyes almost glazed and her mouth now hung open with inspiration.

Girl, you stupid. You real real stupid, yes. You done. You fix-up, fix-up already. Don't wait 'til the end of the week. Why wait until the end of the week?

Zelda made an instant decision. The excitement she began feeling was reflected in her voice.

'Today a real special day, Mr Braffitt. You know that?'

He looked at her blankly for a few seconds as if trying to make sense of what she was saying.

'Is true, Zelda girl?'

Zelda always found it consoling when she and the old man were on the same wavelength.

'Yes, Mr Braffitt, today a real special day and tomorrow morning you go see why.'

Zelda offered a broad smile. It tempted his own. At the best of times, his smile was never far from the surface.

Yes, Mr Braffitt, let we smile. Let we smile, you blasted old fool. What you think it is at all? You travel quite England. You travel quite America. You travel quite Canada. And when you done, you come back here? To this? Man, you real mad, oui. Old man, you real real chupid. You a vrai chupidy, yes. And I not too far short. Wait? No, man, my waiting done. I done run out of time. My time done. I pay my due. I serve my sentence. Yes, Mr Braffitt, let we smile together 'cause if wasn't for you, Mother Gloria and Rosalie, I would never've taken this thing so far. Every time I see the three of all you is like the devil and he fork chuking me, chuking me. He chuk, chuk, chuking me. He telling me, he reminding me that if I ain't take stock I going to end up like all of all you.

'Yes, Mr Braffitt, today is a real special day.'

Zelda and the old man continued to smile at each other for a while longer. He seemed oblivious to the contempt which twisted her smile into a grimace.

◇

Zelda cocked her head, listening to the seconds of a clock as it made its loud progress towards the bewitching hour. Midnight. Zelda sat waiting. A packed suitcase by her side. The room was in darkness. The moon's light through the open curtains seemed to highlight just one feature. A vase of plastic flowers on the small table by the window showed almost daylight colours. The glow also fell on the slip of white paper on the table next to the vase. The note read, simply.

> BOY, I GONE
> I NOT COMING BACK
> THEY IS YOUR CHILDREN TOO

Zelda went over recent events as she waited.

I have my papers. I done fix-up, fix-up. I get my passport. I get my visa from the American Embassy. I ready. I didn't plan to go 'til Saturday night. Straight from here to the airport. But something in me did snap when I pick up that piece of clothes. I know I didn't want spend no three more mornings slapping no one set of clothes against no jukking board and having to scrub it. I going now, tonight self. I go spend the rest of my time 'til the flight by Kevin and them. That is the last place he go think to look for me. And who say he go look?

Zelda heard the car as it screeched to a halt. Picking up the suitcase, she walked out of the door and, without a backward glance, closed it firmly behind her.

JAMAICA KINCAID

◇

My Mother

Mother as nurturer / Destroyer

Immediately on wishing my mother dead and seeing the pain it caused her, I was sorry and cried so many tears that all the earth around me was drenched. Standing before my mother, I begged her forgiveness, and I begged so earnestly that she took pity on me, kissing my face and placing my head on her bosom to rest. Placing her arms around me, she drew my head closer and closer to her bosom, until finally I suffocated. I lay on her bosom, breathless, for a time uncountable, until one day, for a reason she has kept to herself, she shook me out and stood me under a tree and I started to breathe again. I cast a sharp glance at her and said to myself, 'So.' Instantly I grew my own bosoms, small mounds at first, leaving a small, soft place between them, where, if ever necessary, I could rest my own head. Between my mother and me now were the tears I had cried, and I gathered up some stones and banked them in so that they formed a small pond. The water in the pond was thick and black and poisonous, so that only unnameable invertebrates could live in it. My mother and I now watched each other carefully, always making sure to shower the other with words and deeds of love and affection.

◇

I was sitting on my mother's bed trying to get a good look at myself. It was a large bed and it stood in the middle of a large, completely dark room. The room was completely dark because all the windows had been boarded up and all the crevices stuffed with black cloth. My mother lit some candles and the room burst into a pink-like, yellow-like glow. Looming over us, much larger than ourselves, were our shadows. We sat mesmerised because our shadows had made a place between themselves, as if they were making room for someone else. Nothing filled up the space between them, and the shadow of my mother sighed. The shadow of my mother danced around the room to a tune that my own shadow sang, and then they stopped. All along, our shadows had grown thick and thin, long and short, had fallen at every angle, as if they were controlled by the light of day. Suddenly my mother got up and blew out the candles and our shadows vanished. I continued to sit on the bed, trying to get a good look at myself.

111

My mother removed her clothes and covered thoroughly her skin with a thick gold-coloured oil, which had recently been rendered in a hot pan from the livers of reptiles with pouched throats. She grew plates of metal-coloured scales on her back, and light, when it collided with this surface, would shatter and collapse into tiny points. Her teeth now arranged themselves into rows that reached all the way back to her long white throat. She uncoiled her hair from her head and then removed her hair altogether. Taking her head into her large palms, she flattened it so that her eyes, which were by now ablaze, sat on top of her head and spun like two revolving balls. Then, making two lines on the soles of each foot, she divided her feet into crossroads. Silently, she had instructed me to follow her example, and now I too travelled along on my white underbelly, my tongue darting and flickering in the hot air. 'Look,' said my mother.

◇

My mother and I were standing on the seabed side by side, my arms laced loosely around her waist, my head resting securely on her shoulder, as if I needed the support. To make sure she believed in my frailness, I sighed occasionally – long soft sighs, the kind of sigh she had long ago taught me could evoke sympathy. In fact, how I really felt was invincible. I was no longer a child but I was not yet a woman. My skin had just blackened and cracked and fallen away and my new impregnable carapace had taken full hold. My nose had flattened; my hair curled in and stood out straight from my head simultaneously; my many rows of teeth in their retractable trays were in place. My mother and I wordlessly made an arrangement – I sent out my beautiful sighs, she received them; I leaned ever more heavily on her for support, she offered her shoulder, which shortly grew to the size of a thick plank. A long time passed, at the end of which I had hoped to see my mother permanently cemented to the seabed. My mother reached out to pass a hand over my head, a pacifying gesture, but I laughed and, with great agility, stepped aside. I let out a horrible roar, then a self-pitying whine. I had grown big, but my mother was bigger, and that would always be so. We walked to the Garden of Fruits and there ate to our hearts' satisfaction. We departed through the southwesterly gate, leaving as always, in our trail, small colonies of worms.

◇

With my mother, I crossed, unwillingly, the valley. We saw a lamb grazing and when it heard our footsteps it paused and looked up at us. The lamb looked cross and miserable. I said to my mother, 'The lamb is cross and miserable. So would I be, too, if I had to live in a climate not suited to my nature.' My mother and I now entered the cave. It was the dark and cold cave. I felt something growing under my feet and I bent down to eat it. I stayed that way for years, bent over eating whatever I found growing under my feet. Eventually, I grew a special lens that would allow me to see in the darkest of darkness; eventually, I grew a special coat that kept me warm in the coldest of coldness. One day I saw my mother sitting on a rock. She said, 'What a strange expression you have on your face. So cross, so miserable, as if you were living in a climate not suited to your nature.' Laughing, she vanished. I dug a deep, deep hole. I built a beautiful house, a floorless house, over the deep, deep hole. I put in lattice windows, most favoured of windows by my mother, so perfect for looking out at people passing by without her being observed; I painted the house itself yellow, the windows green, colours I knew would please her. Standing just outside the door, I asked her to inspect the house. I said, 'Take a look. Tell me if it's to your satisfaction.' Laughing out of the corner of a mouth I could not see, she stepped inside. I stood just outside the door, listening carefully, hoping to hear her land with a thud at the bottom of the deep, deep hole. Instead, she walked up and down in every direction, even pounding her heel on the air. Coming outside to greet me, she said, 'It is an excellent house. I would be honoured to live in it,' and then vanished. I filled up the hole and burnt the house to the ground.

My mother has grown to an enormous height. I have grown to an enormous height also, but my mother's height is three times mine. Sometimes I cannot see from her breasts on up, so lost is she in the atmosphere. One day, seeing her sitting on the seashore, her hand reaching out in the deep to caress the belly of a striped fish as he swam through a place where two seas met, I glowed red with anger. For a while then I lived alone on the island where there were eight full moons and I adorned the face of each moon with expressions I had seen on my mother's face. All the expressions favoured me. I soon grew tired of living in this way and returned to my mother's side. I remained, though glowing red with anger, and my mother and I built houses on opposite banks of the dead pond. The dead pond lay between us; in it, only small invertebrates with poisonous lances lived. My mother behaved towards

113

them as if she had suddenly found herself in the same room with relatives we had long since risen above. I cherished their presence and gave them names. Still I missed my mother's close company and cried constantly for her, but at the end of each day when I saw her return to her house, incredible and great deeds in her wake, each of them singing loudly her praises, I glowed and glowed again, red with anger. Eventually, I wore myself out and sank into a deep, deep sleep, the only dreamless sleep I have ever had.

One day my mother packed my things in a grip and, taking me by the hand, walked me to the jetty, placed me on board a boat, in care of the captain. My mother, while caressing my chin and cheeks, said some words of comfort to me because we had never been apart before. She kissed me on the forehead and turned and walked away. I cried so much my chest heaved up and down, my whole body shook at the sight of her back turned towards me, as if I had never seen her back turned towards me before. I started to make plans to get off the boat, but when I saw that the boat was encased in a large green bottle, as if it were about to decorate a mantelpiece, I fell asleep, until I reached my destination, the new island. When the boat stopped, I got off and I saw a woman with feet exactly like mine, especially around the arch of the instep. Even though the face was completely different from what I was used to, I recognised this woman as my mother. We greeted each other at first with great caution and politeness, but as we walked along, our steps became one, and as we talked, our voices became one voice, and we were in complete union in every other way. What peace came over me then, for I could not see where she left off and I began, or where I left off and she began.

My mother and I walk through the rooms of her house. Every crack in the floor holds a significant event: here, an apparently healthy young man suddenly dropped dead; here a young woman defied her father and, while riding her bicycle to the forbidden lovers' meeting place, fell down a precipice, remaining a cripple for the rest of a very long life. My mother and I find this a beautiful house. The rooms are large and empty, opening on to each other, waiting for people and things to fill them up. Our white muslin skirts billow up around our ankles, our hair hangs straight down our backs as our arms hang straight at our sides. I fit perfectly in the crook of my mother's arm, on the curve of her back, in the hollow of her stomach. We eat from the same bowl, drink from the same cup; when we sleep, our heads rest on the same pillow. As we walk through the rooms, we merge and separate, merge and separate; soon we shall enter the final stage of our evolution.

The fishermen are coming in from sea; their catch is bountiful, my mother has seen to that. As the waves plop, plop against each other, the fishermen are happy that the sea is calm. My mother points out the fishermen to me, their contentment is a source of my contentment. I am sitting in my mother's enormous lap. Sometimes I sit on a mat she has made for me from her hair. The lime trees are weighed down with limes – I have already perfumed myself with their blossoms. A hummingbird has nested on my stomach, a sign of my fertileness. My mother and I live in a bower made from flowers whose petals are imperishable. There is the silvery blue of the sea, crisscrossed with sharp darts of light, there is the warm rain falling on the clumps of castor bush, there is the small lamb bounding across the pasture, there is the soft ground welcoming the soles of my pink feet. It is in this way my mother and I have lived for a long time now.

Mother earth?
– "Mother" is more than just a person here

JOHN ROBERT LEE

◁ ■■■■■■■ ◇ ■■■■■■■ ▷

The Coming of Org

For Roderick Walcott

After midnight mass Papa's yard would be bright with lanterns and flambeaux and warmed by the blazing fire over which a huge pot of meat was stewing. The women with their many-coloured madras worn proudly like crowns would be busy loading the table in the middle of the front room of the house with bottles of sorrel and ginger beer and rum and whisky. At this time of the year, no self-respecting family was without plenty for neighbours and visitors. As for the children, they would be out of bed and in the way of everyone. The musicians would be

115

settling themselves in a corner of the house; then, in their own good time, the chantwelle and the musicians would begin to call out 'Vive la Rose!' because they belonged to the society of la Rose and they had always been loyal to the Roses. They would respond to the chantwelle's sung challenges to the rival society of la Marguerite with fervour and with joyous shouts of triumph. Vive la Rose! And they would dance the old dances until they were hungry. And later they would all gather around the wooden steps that led down into the yard and everyone would grow quieter as the violon wailed sweetly and sadly. And as they gazed into the leaping flames of the wood fire, deep within them the music would make their hearts soft and yearning for what they couldn't say. Then Mama would call to Papa who sat among the musicians with the shac-shac on his lap: 'Eh bien Papa, when you was youth, you had hear your grandpapa talk about when Ti Jean had leave the home of his mother and go and look for his brothers and had to swim the big sea?' And everyone would call to Papa, 'Oui, oui Papa, quittez l'histoire dit,' let the story tell, and they would sit even nearer together. Papa would say, with a wide grin and a tremendous flourish of the long shac-shac: 'Eh bien messieurs, mesdames, e dit kreek' and they would shout happily into the night, 'Krak!' and for the next few hours before daybreak the old contes and songs, the stories and histories of these ancient scattered people would fill the small dirt yard. Ti Jean and his adversaries, Compere Lapin and his tricks, the real history of the village and its long-dead characters, familiar spirits of good and evil, they would all move among the shadows that lurked outside the edges of the protecting firelight. The children, now afraid to go to sleep, would move closer to the skirts of their mothers as boloms and soucouyants and cloven-footed old men of dark forests shrieked and screeched and howled outside the hibiscus and croton hedges that encircled the yard.

At another festival once, they had heard a stranger, a wandering drum-maker, tell of one he called Org. He had spoken suddenly from his dark corner and when the people expressed ignorance, no one had heard speak of Org, he had gone on to speak intensely and in a low sharp-edged voice of this mysterious person: it was certain that everyone had to meet him some day.

'Ah, Org, c'est Basil,' someone said confidently.

'Non, is not Basil, is not la mort. But a man can die when he meet Org. Man, woman or child can see Org. Mais no one else see him but you. When a man meet Org, that man can die or he can disappear. Org does make a man change. Some get better. Some get worse. Non! Org not

God or the Saviour or the Devil! But Org can appear a beast. Org can be creature, or Org can be human being.'

'M'sieu, ou ka parler bêtise! Is stupidness you talking!'

'Listen!' The stranger ignored the interruption. 'Org can live around a man all his life. Org can be part of your living. You, all your life, see this other person. A person as far as you knowing, with a life, a family, a job, toute bagai, everything. But one day, you will discover that is only you ever know this person. One day you will know, you will not guess, you will know this is Org. Appearing in front of you. And you will never be the same!'

The people were silent. The night was full of snapping fire, the cracking wood, the smell of stewed meat, the insistent cacophany of all the insect sounds and the far-off barking, barking, ceaseless barking of someone's dog. The people wanted to be nearer to each other, but Org stood between them.

Finally a voice said, a little too loudly: 'M'sieu Tambou, Mister drum-maker, peut-être c'est ou qui c'est Org-là. Maybe it is you who is Org.'

The people laughed. Several comments were heard. Papa called the stranger to come and get some rum and some more meat. The short, fat red-skin man came forward into the light, fixing his hat on to his head and looking slyly at everyone, with his large protruding eyes. Then everyone wanted something to eat or drink and soon they were beginning to leave for their nearby homes as the dark night slowly began to turn purple and dawn lit the tops of the humped hills.

They never saw that stranger again, but the new spirit of Org had arisen out of their hearts to take his place among the other heroes of this dispersion. Who he was, no one could exactly say, but the mystery of him made young and old a little more thoughtful in their lives.

Each man who heard the story of Org knew it was truth. A great private question was answered that had brooded unasked in his spirit. He began to look for the coming of Org. He understood better now the strangeness that had come upon many of them for many generations. God, the Saviour, the Devil and Death were known and respected. But Org? Who really was he? An answer out of a dark abyss at the bottom of which growled and snarled the unknown statement of their deepest troublings. So familiar and yet mysterious. Mysterious as he was, or perhaps because his mystery was his power, he established a firm rule over the festival fires and the moonlit yards and the wakes for their dead.

◇

Tison closed the door of the apartment quietly. He stood on the third-storey veranda looking up at the stars. Over the roofs opposite he could see the lights of ships and small yachts in the harbour. He watched the lighthouse beam flash regularly into the distant clouds. It was about one o'clock. Except for the occasional car or distant barking dog, it was quiet. Below, the street was deserted.

Tison felt good. Marcia was snoring softly when he slipped out. A short note to say he loved her, a kiss on the closed eyes. Yes, that was the way to treat a woman. Treat them good. Love them good. With little gifts, little notes, little surprises, a man kept a woman under control. Yes. It was an art. He felt proud that he had taught himself well.

He wasn't yet ready to go to the small comfortable house he rented just outside the town. It was still early. He would go up to the ghetto yard a couple of streets away where there would be people and reggae music and good herb. And maybe that Rasta daughter he had been keeping an eye on would be there. He felt in the mood for that kind of company. Tonight he felt sharp and in control. Yes, Tison was feeling good.

He moved quickly now, happily, eagerly, down the several flights of stairs and into the street. In the cool night, he tucked himself warmly into his tight dark-blue denim jeans and jacket, pulled his closed-neck sweater up around his throat, drew his red beret close over his hair, trying for the Che Guevara effect. His high heels loud against the pavement gave him a feeling of power. His long slim legs made large strides past the small doll-like houses and late-night bars. He tucked his hands deep into his pockets and glanced often at his smooth dark baby-faced handsomeness in the glass windows of the uptown stores.

The yard was off a narrow alleyway and as he turned into the alley from the main road, he was hailed by the youths who lounged along its length. He was popular here. He played the music they liked on his afternoon programmes. The smell of herb was everywhere and several youths approached him with their long flat tins, offering the best of Columbian or Jamaican or local weed. He walked jauntily on towards the yard, humming the music of Bob Marley's latest album that played very loudly from a nearby house. He moved with the certain ease of a popular man, smiling at everyone and greeting many by name.

He turned to the right off the alleyway now, went through a high wooden gate between two houses and passed into the large enclosed yard. Several groups and individuals were scattered around. From a huge stereo speaker reggae dub music throbbed. Tison bought some joints from his favourite pusher, then settled near one of the groups to smoke and listen to their conversation. It was a mixed group of Rastamen and others and talk ranged from police brutality to the quality of the herb to the latest reggae tunes. Tison felt warm with sympathy for their causes. He enjoyed being here with them. He enjoyed their admiration.

He pulled deeply on his second joint and began to look around for the young Rasta girl. His feeling of well-being and self-satisfaction was increasing and he began to think that he would seek out the girl, buy enough herb and invite her up to his house.

He saw her sitting by herself on a small bench, her back against the high concrete wall that encircled the yard. Her eyes were closed, hands folded in her lap.

'Hail, daughter,' he said, settling near her, smiling.

She opened her eyes and turned slowly to look at him.

'Hail, man, Meester Dee Jay. Iree?' She smiled slowly and he thought how truly black and beautiful she was. Dimples were deep in her cheeks.

'Yes-I', he drawled, offering one of the joints, lighting it with his small lighter.

'Thanks-I.' She did everything slowly and deliberately. A wave of tender emotion swept over him. She was nice.

She sucked on the joint appreciatively. 'Some good local in the yard tonight,' looking at the joint, holding in the smoke, and then, long and wreathed in smoke, 'Praise Jah.'

Praise Jah, daughter, leaning back against the wall, climbing with the herb to move in glowing, warm fantasies and visions, with her beautiful at the centre. He glanced through the sweet smoke at her face, strong, dark and beautiful under her red, gold and green tam, and began to think of how he could speak the invitation to his house. From where he sat, he could see her strong thighs and firm good legs thrust out from the bench and he wanted very much to stroke their strong black beauty.

She passed her joint to him and he could see her young firm breasts move freely under her bodice.

Tison began to talk about how he didn't like this Babylon city and in fact did she know that he was from the country he only came here to get the white man schooling and because he didn't like the shitstem that was why he lived outside the shitty, where it was like the country. Yes, he was roots. He described his fruit trees and told her about the ital vegetables growing in the kitchen garden of his landlady and how quiet and cool it was up there and how he enjoyed living by himself where he could smoke and meditate and read his Bible in private without anybody to disturb him. She must come and visit his yard sometime.

'Yes-I', she agreed, she must do that sometime. 'Yes-I, some herb, some ital, some music, that was all the I needed to praise Jah and live in inity and peace and love. Yes-I. Praise Jah.'

She rolled some herb of her own and as they smoked again, him feeling most irey now, and speaking with great enthusiasm and joy, he said, as if suddenly inspired, Look, it was still early, why didn't they take a walk and go up to his house now, it wasn't far, he had his stereo, some tapes with his best patois programmes, plus Bob's latest LP, also he had ital food, they could cook a jot, and they could get some more herb, he had the dunza, so if she wanted, they could go up now.

She turned to him. Slow. She looked directly into his eyes, red now and heavy-lidded from the herb. He suddenly felt uncomfortable and terribly exposed. At the same time, he became very aware of a group of bare-headed Rastamen standing silently near them. And when she laughed, her teeth white in her dark face, he was certain she was mocking him.

'Another night, Meester Dee Jay man. Not dis time.' Too quickly he stammered something about it being all right, it was cool, cool, don't dig nutten. And when one of the young Rastamen, hair long and thick around his head and shoulders came up to speak to her, ignoring him completely, he began to feel threatened. When she moved off with the Rastaman, not saying anything to him again, Tison felt as if the whole yard knew what had happened between him and the girl.

He sat by himself for a while, everything now falling rapidly into confusion, the heavy bass of the nearby music now unbearably loud and him whirling in his head feeling hurt, rejected, vexed with himself. He didn't want to smoke again, but he tried to keep a cool front and dragged on the joint in his slow, superior manner.

Tison left the yard when he felt enough time had passed. As he went by a group outside the gate, they laughed, and he was sure they were laughing at him. The alleyway was deserted now, except for the pushers watching everyone carefully who entered or left the yard. No one hailed him. He put his head down and walked quickly towards the main road.

All his well-being was gone now. The happy high had left him and he began to feel more and more afraid. It was the nameless fear of a bad trip. He recognised it. It seemed as if everything he heard and saw was against him. Snippets of conversation seemed to be aimed at him.

Signs all seemed to carry a message especially for him. Words leaped up from scraps of newspaper at his feet. Judgement was all around.

A cold sweat broke out over his body. His heart began to miss beats. The scene with the girl gnawed at his mind and was at the centre of his confused emotions. He tried achingly to find his way back to the earlier calm. Should he go back to Marcia's? He stopped on the sidewalk, feeling a great indecision. No, he wanted only to get home now. His home was safe and he could sleep off his bad high.

Tison took the road on the outskirts of the town that would lead him directly home. It was a dark road, with street lamps at long intervals, not much used at this time of night. He was the only person on it now. But it was the shortest way home. He began to move quickly. He tried to focus his mind on something definite: he tried to go over his conversation with the girl, rationalising that it wasn't as much of a rejection as he had first imagined, that no one had really heard them and furthermore he was only inviting her to listen to some programmes. He saw her legs again, thrust out from the bench, smooth, firm and dark. He walked more briskly. Her laughter and her abrupt departure left him empty within, hurt and ashamed.

His mind felt like a deep hole into which everything was falling and he couldn't fix anything at all. He couldn't concentrate on anything. The irrational fear beat its way inside his stomach.

Tison was now about half-way up the road. At the approaching bend that turned on a small bridge it was the darkest part. After this it was well lit all the way to his house. He wanted to be inside, the door shut behind him. He hurried towards the bridge, anxious to be past it. He fought off the paranoia that filled his head with frightening thoughts and made him stumble. A couple of times he looked back to make sure no one was following him.

He let out a sharp involuntary squeal when he heard the sudden noise out of the darkness ahead. He felt his hair crawl across his scalp. His heart lurched painfully and he stopped.

Demonic creatures of all shapes raced through his mind. The long-shut doors of childhood memory were flung open and all the ghosts of dark nights beyond firelight yards rushed out, screaming and cackling.

The sound came again, more loudly, more different from anything he had ever heard. Tison began to whimper in his throat for God. He knew he was utterly terrified. Part of his mind realised he was near the bridge, over the edge of which was a deep ravine. He broke wind. He groaned and trembled in the chill of his sweat. The girl's face and mocking laughter flashed clear before his eyes. The dreadlocks who had gone off

121

before with her was now waiting with a cutlass near the bridge. That must be it. Why wasn't he more careful, he regretted with all his heart. And old women with the bodies of beasts and peeling skins chattered through his tortured consciousness.

Despairingly, he turned around to run fast. But suddenly a hand with claws that scratched his neck hard took hold of the back of his collar and dragged him down. He knew he was screaming. He could not hear himself. He felt his body pressed against the edge of the stone bridge and then he was lifted and slammed a number of times on it until he lay terror-shocked and still. His head was over the ravine far below and he could hear the water of the small stream flowing through it. His face was cold. His teeth chattered uncontrollably. His face was wet with tears.

The hand with the claws pulled at him again, and somewhere behind it the terrifying noise increased. He slumped over to lie on his back, his face to the stars and to the moonlight just now edging over the tall, dark, creaking bamboo trees.

Tison saw everything from a long way off now, far through the pain and fears and the herb that still whirled around in his head and his stomach, far through the voices and absurd scenes clear in his eyes and the jingles from his radio show.

In the whitening night he now saw over him (with a far, absolute incomprehension) one of the town's well-known derelicts, Fanto, naked as night, eyes wide and unseeing, spittle foaming at the mouth, straddling him: Fanto, slobbering and muttering incoherently, tearing at his throat with both hands, and from far away, but still too close, with a strange and absolute clarity, Tison observed: in Fanto's face a horrible fullness of mad lust, fixed, no more man: beast, crazed, depraved utterly: he heard the mocking laughter of the girl again and saw her smooth black legs and he felt Fanto's tongue obscenely slaking his mouth: and he saw Marcia's face, eager, mouth open, eyes shut, labouring: and his whole soul and mind and body revolted and drew themselves together inside of him for one almighty puke but he could not move: and he felt Fanto tighten his legs around him all the time chattering through his dribbling, toothless mouth: and he saw the dimpled backside of Joan the pilot's wife and heard the giggling of Margaret the high school student and his mouth and nose and eyes and ears were filled with the stench and stink and slobbering and wheezing of Fanto: and Tison remembered himself. And he screamed down through his soul for the horror of himself and when Fanto stretched frantically along his body and began to flail on him with his head and

122

arms and legs and belly, Tison left it all far away and tried to die but he couldn't and he realised, at last, that he had met his Org.

Papa sat looking through the window into the yard, while Mama busied herself with breakfast. Papa watched his son pause over the fork he was pressing down with his foot into the small kitchen garden, and look up to the great mountain La Sorcière whose top was covered with mist today. The young man's locks were almost down to his shoulders now and as Mama stopped for a moment by her husband to look at her son, she sighed again as she had so many times in the past months.

'But why the boy have to do that to himself, eh Papa, tell me. We sacrifice to give him a good schooling in town, he get a good job in town, everybody know him, and he leaving it to turn Rasta and come back here to say he diggin' garden.'

She sucked her teeth in annoyance.

'Eh, Papa. And you wouldn't speak to him. Make him stop that stupidness. Everybody saying he mad, is something they do him, a intelligent boy like that.'

Papa poured himself some water from the clay goblet. He drank deeply before he spoke.

'Mama, I tell you already. The boy not mad. Leave the boy.'

He looked out to where his son was turning the earth again.

'Is so it is when a man knowing himself. Not all reach man the same.'

He leaned on the window and looked up to the top of the mountain.

'Some never reach. Some never reach.'

Mama sucked her teeth again and returned to the kitchen muttering. One of the children ran into the house crying and Papa lifted her up.

'OK, doodoo, what happen, eh?'

'Papa, Papa, brother say that if I don't go away from him and the others, he will call Org for me. I just want to play with them. But I 'fraid Org, Papa.'

'Hush, doodoo, hush. Org won't take you. Hush.'

Papa looked out to where his son had just pushed the fork firmly into the ground and had flung his green shirt over his shoulder. He came to the window and told Papa that he was going up to the hills.

Papa watched him stride away on his long legs.

The child called out, 'Rasta, you not 'fraid Org take you when you go in the hills?' The young man did not turn around.

Papa said: 'Hush child, hush.' Papa thought: 'My son meet Org already. Maybe now he going to meet God.'

He held the child in his arms as Mama came out with a saucepan in her hand to stand by him and they watched their son walk slowly down the path, go through the gate in the hibiscus hedge, the flowers bright red in the early light, and move towards the hills.

EARL LOVELACE

Shoemaker Arnold

Shoemaker Arnold stood at the doorway of his little shoemaker shop, hands on hips, his body stiffened in that proprietorial and undefeated stubbornness, announcing, not without some satisfaction, that if in his life he had not been triumphant, neither had the world defeated him. It would be hard, though, to imagine how he could be defeated, since he exuded such a hard tough unrelenting cantankerousness, gave off such a sense of readiness for confrontation, that if Trouble had to pick someone to clash with, Shoemaker Arnold would not be the one. To him, the world was his shoemaker shop. There he was master and anyone entering would have to surrender not only to his opinion on shoes and leather and shoemaker apprentices, but to his views on politics, women, religion, flying objects, or any of the myriad subjects he decided to discourse upon, so that over the years he had arrived at a position where none of the villagers bothered to dispute him, and to any who dared maintain a view contrary to the one he was affirming, he was quick to point out, 'This place is mine. Here, I do as I please. I say what I want. Who don't like it, the door is open.'

His wife had herself taken that advice many years earlier, and had moved not only out of his house but out of the village, taking with her their three children, leaving him with his opinions, an increasing taste for alcohol, and the tedium of having to prepare his own meals. It is possible that he would have liked to take one of the village girls to live with him, but he was too proud to accept that he had even that need, and he would look at the girls go by outside his shop, hiding behind his dissatisfied scowl a fine, appraising, if not lecherous, eye; but if one of them happened to look in, he would snarl at her, 'What you want here?' So that between him and the village girls there existed this teasing challenging relationship of antagonism and desire, the girls themselves walking with greater flourish and style when they went past his shoemaker shop, swinging their backsides and cutting their eyes, and he, scowling, dissatisfied.

With the young men of the village his relationship was no better. As far as he was concerned none of them wanted to work and he had no intention of letting them use his shoemaker shop as a place to loiter. Over the years he had taken on numerous apprentices, keeping them for a month or two and sometimes for just a single day, then getting rid of them; and it was not until Norbert came to work with him that he had had what could be considered regular help.

Norbert, however, was no boy. He was a drifter, a rum drinker, and exactly that sort of person that one did not expect Arnold to tolerate for more than five minutes. Norbert teased the girls, was chummy with the loiterers, gambled, drank too much, and, anytime the spirit moved him, would up and take off and not return for as much as a month. Arnold always accepted him back. Of course he quarrelled, he complained, but the villagers who heard him were firm in their reply: 'Man you like it. You like Norbert going and coming when he please, doing what he want. You like it.'

More than his leavings, Norbert would steal Arnold's money, sell a pair of shoes, lose a side of shoes, charge people and pocket the money, not charge some people at all, and do every other form of wickedness to be imagined in the circumstances. It must have been that because Norbert was so indisputably in the wrong that it moved Arnold to exhibit one of his rare qualities, compassion. It was as if Arnold needed Norbert as the means through which to declare not only to the world, but to declare to himself, that he had such a quality; to prove to himself that he was not the cantankerous person people made him out to be. So, on those occasions when he welcomed back the everlasting prodigal, Arnold, forgiving and compassionate, would be imbued with the idea of his own goodness, and he would feel that in the world, truly, there was not a more generous soul than he.

Today was one such day. Two weeks before Christmas, Norbert had left to go for a piece of ice over by the rumshop a few yards away. He had returned the day before. 'Yes,' thought Arnold, 'look at me, I not vex.' Arnold was glad for the help, for he had work that people had already paid advances on and would be coming in to collect before New Year's

Day. That was one thing he appreciated about Norbert. Norbert was faithful, but Norbert had to get serious about the right things. He was faithful to too many frivolous things. He was faithful to the girl who dropped in and wanted a dress, to a friend who wanted a nip. A friend would pass in a truck and say, 'Norbert, we going San Fernando.' Norbert would put down the shoes he was repairing, jump on the truck without a change of underwear even, and go. It wasn't rum. It was some craziness, something inside him that just took hold of him. Sometimes a week later he would return, grimy, stale, thin, as if he had just hitchhiked around the world in a coal bin, slip into the shop, sit down and go back to work as if nothing out of the way had happened. And he could work when he was working. Norbert could work. Any shop in Port of Spain would be glad to have him. Faithful worker. Look at that! This week when most tradesmen had already closed up for Christmas there was Norbert working like a machine to get people's shoes ready. Appreciation. It shows appreciation. People don't have appreciation again, but Norbert had appreciation. Is how you treat people, he thought. You have to understand them. Look how cool he here working in my shoemaker shop this big Old Year's Day when all over the island people fêteing.

At the door he was watching two girls going down the street, nice, young, with the spirit of rain and breezes about them. Then his eyes picked up a donkey cart approaching slowly from the direction of the Main Road which led to Sangre Grande, and he stood there in front his shoemaker shop, his lips pulled back and looked at the cart come up and go past. Old Man Moses, the charcoal burner, sat dozing in the front, his chin on his chest, and the reins in his lap. To the back sat a small boy with a cap on and a ragged shirt, his eyes alert, his feet hanging over the sides of the cart, one hand resting on a small brown and white dog sitting next to him.

Place dead, he thought, seeing the girls returning; and, looking up at the sky he saw the dark clouds and that it was going to rain and he looked at the cart. 'Moses going up in the bush. Rain going to soak his tail,' he said. And as if suddenly irritated by that thought, he said, 'You mean Moses ain't have no family he could spend New Year's by,' his tone drumming up his outrage. 'Why his family can't take him in and let him eat and drink and be merry for the New Year instead of going up in the bush for rain to soak his tail? That is how we living in this world,' he said, seating himself on the workbench and reaching for the shoe to be repaired. 'That is how we living. Like beast.'

'Maybe he want to go up in the bush,' Norbert said. 'Maybe he going to attend his coal pit, to watch it that the coals don't burn up and turn powder.'

'Like blasted beast,' Arnold said. 'Beast,' as if he had not heard Norbert.

But afterwards, after he had begun to work, had gotten into the rhythm of sewing and cutting and pounding leather, and had begun the soft firm waxing of the twine, the sense of the approaching New Year hit him and he thought of the girls and the rain, and he thought of his own life and his loneliness and his drinking and of the world and of people, people without families, on pavements and in orphanages and those on park benches below trees. 'The world have to check up on itself,' he said. 'The world have to check up . . . And you, Norbert, you have to check up on yourself,' he said broaching for the first time the matter of Norbert's leaving two weeks before Christmas and returning only yesterday. 'I not against you. You know I not against you. I talk because I know what life is. I talk because I know about time. Time is all we have, boy. Time . . . A time to live and a time to die. You hear what I say, Norbert?'

'What you say?'

'I say, it have a time to live and a time to die . . . You think we living?'

Norbert leaned his head back a little, and for a few moments he seemed to be gazing into space, thinking, concentrating.

'We dying,' he said, 'we dying no arse.'

'You damn right. Rum killing us. Rum. Not bombs or cancer or something sensible. Rum. You feel rum should kill you?'

Norbert drew the twine out of the stitch and smiled.

'But in this place, rum must kill you. What else here could kill a man? What else to do but drink and waste and die? That is why I talk. People don't understand me when I talk; but that is why I talk.'

Norbert threaded the twine through the stitch with his smile and in one hand he held the shoe and with the other he drew out the twine: 'We dying no arse!' as if he had hit on some truth to be treasured now. 'We dying . . . no arse.'

'That is why I talk. I want us . . . you to check up, to put a little oil in your lamp, to put a little water in your wine.'

Norbert laughed. He was thinking with glee, even as he said it, 'We dying no arse, all o' we, everybody. Ha ha ha ha,' and he took up his hammer and started to pound in the leather over the stitch. 'Ha ha ha ha ha!'

Arnold had finished the shoe he was repairing and he saw now the pile of shoes in the shoemaker shop. 'One day I going to sell out all the shoes that people leave here. They hurry hurry for you to repair them. You use leather, twine, nails, time. You use time, and a year later, the shoes still here watching you. Going to sell out every blasted one of them this New Year.'

'All o' we, every one of us,' Norbert chimed.

'That is why this shoemaker shop always like a junk heap.'

'Let us send for a nip of rum, nuh,' Norbert said, and as Arnold looked at him, 'I will buy. This is Old Year's, man.'

'Rum?' Arnold paused. 'How old you is, boy?'

'Twenty-nine.'

'Twenty-nine! You making a joke. You mean I twenty-one years older than you? We dying in truth. Norbert, we dying. Boy, life really mash you up.' And he threw down the shoe he was going to repair.

'We have three more shoes that people coming for this evening,' Norbert said, cautioning. 'Corbie shoes, Synto shoes and Willie Paul sandals.'

Arnold leaned and picked up the shoe again. 'Life ain't treat you good at all. I is twenty-one years older than you? Norbert, you have to check up,' he said. 'Listen, man, you getting me frighten. When I see young fellars like you in this condition I does get frighten . . . Listen. Norbert, tell me something! I looking mash up like you? Eh? Tell me the truth. I looking mash up like you?'

Norbert said, 'We dying no arse, all o' we everybody.'

'No. Serious. Tell me, I looking mash up like you?'

'Look, somebody by the door,' Norbert said.

'What you want?' Arnold snapped. It was one of the village girls, a plump one with a bit of her hair plastered down over her forehead making her look like a fat pony.

'You don't have to shout at me, you know. I come for Synto shoes.'

'Well, I don't want no loitering by the door. Come inside and siddown and wait. I now finishing it.' He saw her turn to look outside and she said something to somebody. 'Somebody there with you?'

'She don't want to come in.'

'Let her come in too. I don't want no loitering by the door. This is a business place.' He called out, 'Come in. What you hanging back for?'

The girl who came in was the one that reminded him of rain and moss and leaves. He tried to look away from her, but he couldn't. And she too was looking at him.

'You 'fraid me?' And he didn't know how his voice sounded, though at that moment he thought he wanted it to sound tough.

'A little,' she said.

'Siddown,' he said, and Norbert's eyes nearly popped open. What was he seeing? Arnold was getting up and taking the chair from the corner, dusting it too. 'Sit down. The shoes will finish just now.'

She watched him work on the shoe and the whole shoemaker shop was big like all space and filled with breathlessness and rain and moss and green leaves.

'You is Synto daughter?'

'Niece,' she said.

And when he was finished repairing the shoes, he looked around for a paper bag in which to put them, because he saw that she had not come with any bag herself. 'When you coming for shoes you must bring something to wrap it in. You can't go about with shoes in your hand just so.'

'Yes,' she said. 'Yes.' Quickly as if wanting to please him.

He found some old newspaper he was saving to read when he had time and he folded the shoes in it and wrapped it with twine and he gave it to her and she took it and she said 'thank you' with that funny little face and that voice that made something inside him ache and she left, leaving the breathlessness in the shoemaker shop and the scent of moss and aloes and leaves and it was like if all his work was finished. And when he caught his breath he pushed his hand in his pocket and brought out money and said to Norbert, 'Go and buy a nip.' And they drank the nip, the two of them, and he asked Norbert, 'Where you went when you went for the ice?' And he wasn't really listening for no answer, for he had just then understood how Norbert could, how a man could, leave and go off. He had just understood how he could leave everything and go just so.

'You had a good time?' Though those weren't the right words. A good time! People didn't leave for a good time. It was for something more. It was out of something deeper, a call, something that was awakened in the blood, the mind. 'You know what I mean?'

'Yes,' Norbert said, kinda sadly, soft, and frightened for Arnold but not wanting to show it.

Arnold said, 'I dying too.' And then he stood up and said sort of sudden, 'This place need some pictures. And we must keep paper bags like in a real "establishment",' and with that same smile he said, 'Look at that, eh. That girl say she 'fraid me a little. Yes, I suppose that is correct. A little. Not that she 'fraid me. She 'fraid me a little.'

When they closed the shop that evening they both went up Tapana Trace by Britto. Britto was waiting for them.

'Ah,' he said, 'Man reach. Since before Christmas I drinking and I can't get drunk. It ain't have man to drink rum with again. But I see man now.'

They went inside and Britto cleared the table and put three bottles of rum on it, one before each one of them, a mug of water and a glass each, and they began to drink.

Half an hour later the *parang* band came in and they sang an *aguanaldo* and a *joropo* and they drank and Norbert started to sing with them the nice festive Spanish music that made Arnold wish he could cry. And then it was night and the *parang* band was still there and Britto wife family came in and a couple of Britto friends and the women started dancing with the little children and then Josephine, Britto neighbour, held on to Arnold and pulled him on to the floor to dance, and he tried to dance a little and then he sat down and they took down the gas lamp and pumped it and Britto's wife brought out the portion of *lappe* that she had been cooking on a wood fire in the yard and they ate and drank and with the music and the children and the women, everything, the whole thing was real sweet. It was real sweet. And Norbert, more drunk than sober, sitting in a corner chatting down Clemencia sister picked up another bottle of rum, broke the seal and about to put it to his lips, caught Arnold's eye and hesitated, then he put it to his lips again. He said, 'Let me dead.' And Arnold sat and thought about this girl, the one that filled the world with breathlessness and the scent of aloes and leaves and moss and he felt if she was sitting there beside him he would be glad to dead too.

IAN McDONALD

◁ ◆ ▷

The Duel in Mercy Ward

Benjie and Beepat arrived in the ward at Mercy about the same time. This ward was for chronic, not exactly terminal, cases. One or two used to make a kind of recovery and totter out into the land of the living. But generally when you went in there you only came out on the long journey. Benjie was wheeled in one morning. Beepat the same afternoon, and ever afterwards Benjie made his seniority a point to emphasise and exaggerate.

'I was here long, long before you come in making trouble,' Benjie would say.

'You old fool,' Beepat would respond. 'We come in the exact same time.'

And that would be good for an hour or two of satisfying, acrimonious debate.

But that was just a very small bone in the huge pot of contention that Benjie and Beepat soon began to cook up. They argued about everything. They drove the nurses to distraction. They were in next-door beds at first but they soon had to be separated. They still found ample ways to meet and quarrel and suck teeth at each other's views.

They made as many as possible in the ward take sides, which added to the confusion. The halt and the lame and the nearly blind, not to mention the dying and the nearly dead, were summoned to make a choice. It was World Cup Final every day, Benjie's team against Beepat's team, and you better have helmets because bouncers bound to fly.

Everything was a case of competition between Benjie and Beepat. They had some big rows about politics – how the other one's party was full of vagabonds and fools. They had some big rows about religion – how Hindus have so many thousands and thousands of Gods they even have a God for water-snake and carrion-crow and how Christians like cannibals, wanting to drink the blood of Jesus Christ. And they had some big rows about race – how Indians mean and sly and can't take their liquor and how black people only like to fête and play with women. But somehow in these rows you had the feeling they were rowing for

131

rowing's sake. It was Beepat so Benjie had to say one thing and it was Benjie so Beepat had to say the other thing. But they didn't seem to want to put their heart in it. Politics, religion and race really were not worth getting worked up about. Life was too short.

Cricket was the cause of more important rowing. Right at the beginning they made a mistake and in one argument both said, while the other was also saying, how Kanhai was the greatest batsman in the world. So from then on they had to forget Kanhai in the rowing and row instead about who the second best was. And if Benjie selected a team not one man could be the same as in the team Beepat selected. And if a man had a good cover-drive for Benjie, no, he only had a good hook-shot for Beepat. And when they were listening to Test Match cricket there were always three commentaries – Benjie's commentary which was giving one view, Beepat's commentary which was giving a view as if it was a different game, and the real commentator's commentary which, to tell the truth, wasn't half so interesting or quarter so scandalous as Benjie's and Beepat's commentaries.

But even cricket wasn't all that much. What Benjie and Beepat really put their hearts into were rivalries that could be decided definitely and specifically right there in the ward on a daily basis.

Like the rivalry to see who was the most popular patient in the ward. This amounted to seeing who could get the most visitors to come at visiting hour. The story started when one of Beepat's cousins and five nieces and nephews happened to come and visit at the same time when his old brother and sister-in-law were there. That made eight people around Beepat's bed. And Benjie only had two people visiting him. So Beepat made a big thing about how some people so bad-natured they don't have any family or friends left to visit them while some other people at least could say a lot of friends and family still think highly of them and show their devotion.

Well, you can imagine Benjie's response. It only took about three days before ten people turned up around Benjie's bed at visiting hour and only four by Beepat's bed that same day. Benjie didn't forget to rub the salt in the wound, and what could Beepat say? He stayed quiet and planned his own counter-attack. He sent word out by his cousins and by his cousin's cousins. I am sure I don't have to describe all what happened then: more and more people coming in to visit Benjie and Beepat. Benjie drew from all over town and up the East Bank; Beepat drew from the East Coast mostly but as far away as Crabwood Creek too. Benjie even sent out and hired a bus to bring visitors in one day after competition was going about a month. By this time only a few of the visitors were actually getting in to Benjie and Beepat, but that didn't prevent both of them getting a count of how many had turned up to visit and then each announcing, like an election official, the total number that had tried to pay a visit to their beloved Benjie/Beepat. It was a hard battle and visiting hour was an exciting time for the whole ward until a stop had to be put to all the nonsense, the authorities cracked down, and Benjie and Beepat had to find another contest in which to test wits and belligerence.

That ward is more often than not a place of anguish and despair where people at best lose their grip on life and quietly fade away and at worst die in a hopeless, lonely agony which shakes the soul to think about too long. But in the era of Benjie and Beepat a little more of something like a last vital spark was preserved a little longer in all those hopeless, discarded cases. It wasn't much and it wasn't for long but it was something and it was for a while and in life can you be sure that in the end there is much more than that? I don't know.

And that leads directly to by far the intensest rivalry between these two obscure but determined representatives of the life-force, Benjie and Beepat. Neither of them was going to be the one to die first. That was the ultimate competition. Benjie, you could say, would rather have died than pass away before Beepat. And Beepat felt exactly the same way. They put their last surge of will-power into this battle to the last breath not to be first to go.

They kept an eager eye on each other to see what signs of wear and tear might be appearing – further wear and tear, I should say, because you can imagine that Benjie and Beepat were both worn and torn a good bit already by the time they were brought into the ward at Mercy. If one of them coughed an extra amount in the night the other started up at once and the next morning was sure to make a comment. They kept an eye on each other's bowel movements. Nothing they would have liked better than to get a sight of each other's urine samples to see if they were clear or cloudy. They each had ancient village remedies to supplement the despised hospital medicine and they both made sure the other knew a new and extra-potent cure was being smuggled in which would give the recipient an edge in the struggle to survive.

Twice they had to take Beepat down to the operating theatre.

'He gone now,' Benjie said. 'Old Beepat gone. I don't know how he last so long, he was so sickly-looking. But now he gone.'

But Beepat returned both times and continued the fight to the death. Once Benjie in his turn had to be given blood and saline, right there in his bed. A doctor and some nurses bustled about setting up the apparatus and plastic bottles and Benjie in truth looked gone, lying with his eyes closed and a deadly waxen look in his face. It was Beepat's turn to intone the last rites.

'Benjie could never make it now. When you see those bottles hook up like that in a man, that is the end. The end. He can't make it any more. It was only mouth when he said he was feeling so good yesterday. Now look at that face, it could be in a coffin already.'

But Benjie pulled through.

One morning at crack of dawn Beepat was amazed to see Benjie trying to do what appeared to be push-ups on the floor by the side of the bed. The word went round that Benjie was feeling so good that he had decided to begin a regime of light exercises every morning and evening. It was good psychology, and had the effect of shaking up Beepat and putting him on the defensive for a while. But it turned out to be counter-productive. After a couple of mornings Benjie couldn't make the grade and had to put the get-fit regime in cold storage. In fact he had a bad relapse and couldn't even get out of bed for a few days, which gave Beepat the chance to make a special effort to walk around the whole place and show how strong he was.

It would be good to tell how the story ended with Benjie and Beepat walking out one fine day, good for a few more years' rowing. But, in truth, life isn't like that, not for you, not for me, and not for Benjie and Beepat. The day came when Benjie began to go down. It was Diwali and Beepat had got some clay diyas and put them glimmering around his bed. It looked beautiful. Beepat was very proud. Normally Benjie would have had some comment to make, but he was silent and still. Beepat was surprised. From that time Benjie couldn't get out of bed any more. He tried hard one or two more times but he couldn't raise himself to take the bait. Beepat began to get silent.

Benjie had a bad case of sugar and it had got to the time when the doctors couldn't even slow down the ravages of the disease. The legs were going bad. They had to operate and cut and try to keep the rest of Benjie whole. But the sickness was too far gone and Benjie was too old. You can't live only on strong will. In the last month they cut him down four times, but he still hung on. The first time Beepat made a joke at Benjie's expense, but after that he didn't make any more jokes. Every time they cut Benjie, Beepat grew more quiet. The whole ward grew silent: no more Benjie and Beepat rowing. The time for that was over.

When they cut Benjie for the fourth time they brought him back up to the ward with his legs cut off just above the knees. He was hardly living any more but he was still alive. Beepat lit a diya in front of the greatest of his Gods before he lay down for the night. During the night you could hear Benjie's breathing across the ward. The diya by Beepat's bed flickered out and he fed it with oil a few times. Beepat lay awake late and then he composed himself to sleep. It was strange. When the nurses made their second morning round, when the birds had just begun to sing, they found that Beepat's sleep had eased into dying. It was recorded that his heart gave out, after respiratory troubles, and he died at 9.02 am. Benjie lasted until noon that day.

EARL McKENZIE

◁ ◆ ▷

Fear of the Sea

Before that outing Ossie had never seen the sea. He had heard grown-ups talk about it, and they had described it as a big deep thing made of water, which was sometimes very rough, and in which people caught fish. Those descriptions, however, did not tell him very much. Perhaps the best description he got was from an old man who said it was like the biggest field of cabbage one could imagine.

One year, a few weeks before Easter, a man named Mass Aston went around the district selling tickets for an outing to the beach. Ossie's father bought tickets for the three members of his family. Ossie had never been on an outing and began to itch all over with excitement. During the days that followed, his parents had only to threaten not to take him along and he would rush to do anything they requested.

The day before the outing he got up early and completed all his chores. Then he bathed in the river which ran near their house. He regarded this river as an enormous quantity of water, and he found it hard to believe when people told him that compared with the sea it was almost nothing. They said it was just one of the hundreds of little rivers which flowed into the big rivers which in turn flowed into the sea. Ossie wondered about this strange thing which they said was like the sky but made of water, which had the colour of the mountains but was flat and rolling, and which was so irresistible people paid to visit it time and time again.

Near sunset he went to the square to see what was happening there. The truck in which they would be travelling had already returned from its daily trip to Kingston, and it was now parked at its usual spot beside the wooden two-storey building at the northern end of the square. One of the sidemen was washing the cab, and two others were bent over the spare tyre and pumping air into it. Some of the people in the square stood around the sidemen and watched; others were moving in and out of the shops in haste, going home to prepare food for the trip.

Ossie left the square at dusk and began running home. His feet were light with anticipation as he ran. He swung around a kerb and crashed into Adassa.

'Boy, why you don't look where you going?' she shouted angrily as she shoved him away.

In the half-light he noticed that her normally pretty face was contorted with anger, an anger too deep to be entirely the result of his bumping into her.

'Sorry, ma'am,' said Ossie.

'Cho!' she said as she brushed past him.

'I didn't see you,' he called after her.

She didn't answer and the grey form of her dress and headtie quickly disappeared around the bend.

A little further down the road he saw Caswell, her boyfriend, sitting on a bank with his head and hands bent over his knees. Ossie said 'Good evening' as he passed, but Caswell did not answer.

At home his mother and one of his aunts were in the kitchen preparing food for the outing. Ossie went into the house and sat by the window where he could smell the fried chicken and rice and peas, and where he could listen to the women's voices while he watched the flickering of the fire behind the rows of bamboo wattling.

He slept lightly that night; he woke up at the slightest sound, and he interpreted every crowing of a cock as a sign of daylight. When it was finally daybreak he was sleeping soundly and had to be awakened. It was still dark outside, but his parents had surer ears and noses for the sounds and smells of morning than he had.

They got up, dressed, and had breakfast. Then they set off for the square. They had the food in a bamboo basket with a lid, and they took turns carrying it up the hill.

The square was full of colourfully dressed people who were greeting each other, chatting and laughing. The truck was now out on the main road between two of the shops; the back-board was lowered and people were climbing in. People were also climbing in through the side-door to the left. Ossie's mother and father climbed in through the side-door, and he left them to join in the scramble for a seat on the back row. These seats were in great demand since you got a better view from them. Ossie managed to squeeze in between two of his friends. There was a space in the middle to let people through, and one of the sidemen asked that it be saved for him. Ossie settled down comfortably and waited for the trip to begin.

Neville, the driver of the truck, lived in a rented room on the top storey of the wooden building. A few minutes later, he and Adassa appeared at the top of the outside stairway. Adassa was wearing a tight-fitting red dress, and her thick hair was combed back with only a few plaits and pins to keep it in place. Her face was fixed in a defiant smile, and she kept close to Neville as they walked down the stairway.

The image of Caswell sitting alone on the bank came back to Ossie, and he tried to remember if he had seen him since arriving at the square. Ossie stood up and looked around the square, then inside the truck. Caswell was sitting in the right corner four rows away, and he was watching the square through the space between the wooden bars at his eye level. He seemed to be staring vacantly, without focusing on anything or anyone in particular. Ossie turned and noticed that Neville and Adassa were about to walk along the right side of the truck. He remained standing to see if Caswell would react to them. They came into his view and his body shook. Then he turned away from them and pretended to be watching the sidemen who were collecting baskets over the wings of the truck. He turned away from the sidemen, and, with bowed head and drooping shoulders, he stared at the floor of the truck. Most of the passengers were chatting and laughing. But Caswell was the loneliest person Ossie had ever seen.

Then everyone could hear Neville and Mass Aston having an argument outside.

'I want mi wife and myself to drive in the cab,' said Mass Aston. 'Is me in charge of this trip.'

'Is only Adassa I want inside there with me,' said Neville. 'If I don't drive unu can't go.'

When they saw Mass Aston and his wife coming through the side-door they knew that Neville had had his way.

Mass Aston stood in front and counted the passengers. He ordered the sidemen to pull up the back-board. Then he reached over the wings and pulled the cord attached to the bicycle bell close to the driver's seat.

The truck started and people began waving to those who were staying behind. Some were watching with obvious envy. Others showered them with so many blessings and good wishes it was as if they were leaving for a foreign country.

The truck stopped a few times to pick up additional passengers. Soon they were out on the open road. Conversation slackened and they began singing. They sang 'Roll Jordan Roll' and 'Chi-Chi Bud O'. When they began driving on asphalted road they broke into the gear-box song:

Mass Aston	Mr Driver!
Passengers	Drop in a gear for me.
Mass Aston	Mr Driver!
Passengers	Drop in a gear for me.
	For when you are driving
	Remember your gear-box
	Drop in a gear for me.

Neville was famous for being a 'sweet-foot' driver, and at the end of each round of the song he changed gears with so much music and rhythm the people shouted with pleasure. He also tapped out the rhythm of the song on his horn.

Later they drove past enormous cane fields, and large pastures in which herds of cattle grazed. They drove beside a large river which began to open Ossie's eyes to what the grownups had said about rivers and the sea. Then they began climbing into hilly territory. Ossie noticed the many small and thickly forested hills which were so different from the large mountains he was accustomed to seeing.

Ossie will never forget his first sight of the sea. Suddenly an enormous stretch of deep indigo hit his eyes; it seemed as if it had risen up suddenly out of the earth, then it fell again. People rushed to the wings. 'The sea, the sea!' they shouted. 'Look at the sea!' The truck turned away and the wide expanse of blue quickly shrank to a long strip before it was swallowed up into the vegetation. Ossie found that his heart was pounding, that he was breathing heavily, and that his palms were moist.

For several minutes the sea seemed to be playing hide-and-seek with them. Sometimes they were so close to it they could see the white spots people in the truck said were waves. The next time they saw it, it was a mere strip in the distance. It took some time for Ossie to realise that they were seeing the same sea from different directions as they followed the winding road along the coast.

Suddenly they were right up beside the sea, separated from it only by a concrete wall. Ossie looked out at the vast expanse of blue-green water, and he felt nostalgia for the friendly intimacy of his little village stream. Now he could see the waves crashing against the wall, and he could hear the sea breathing and panting as if it were alive. They drove in silence as if it were somehow irreverent to laugh and sing in the presence of the awesome being beside them.

After a few minutes they turned into a side entrance, and they drove through a colonnade of coconut trees until they came to an open area where a number of vehicles, including a bus and a truck, were parked. At the far end of the open area Ossie could see a strip of white sand; beside it the sea lay quietly as if it had suddenly fallen asleep.

There were three buildings beside the beach: two thatched huts which were used as dressing rooms, and a large club-house, also thatched, which contained a restaurant, a bar and a place for dancing. The beach was already crowded with people from the other vehicles. There were also a few tourists with cameras. Some of the tourists had a motor boat and they were taking turns going out into the sea and coming back.

Most of the members of Mass Aston's party assembled in families and began eating. Later, a few changed into swimsuits and went into the sea. Very few of them could swim, so they splashed around at the edge of the water, or sat on the sand. As soon as they were through eating, most of the men headed for the bar.

Ossie did not go into the water; he had no swimsuit and he could not swim. He also felt a growing fear of the sea. So he walked along the shore with his friends and collected shells and driftwood.

Later in the afternoon a wind started blowing, and Ossie noticed the increased intensity of the waves. He heard a man telling his listeners that the waves had the power to pull you in, and if they did, they would bring you back to the shore twice, but after the third pull you would be gone for ever.

When they were tired of the beach, Ossie and his friends went into the club-house. There was a jukebox and people were dancing. Neville and Adassa were by themselves in a corner and they were close-dancing. Neville had a bottle of beer in his left hand and he hugged Adassa with his right. Their cheeks were pressed together as they danced.

After watching the dancers for a few minutes, Ossie and his friends turned their attention to the jukebox. They were admiring the way the jukebox changed records when they heard the sound of someone screaming outside. The screams got closer and a woman rushed into the club-house.

'Caswell drownin'!' she cried. 'Caswell drownin'!'

People stopped dancing and rushed out of the club-house. Ossie and his friends followed. The beach was lined with people who were all looking out into the sea.

When Ossie and his friends got to the front they saw a tall black man coming towards the shore with Caswell's body slung sideways across his shoulders. The man lay Caswell's body face down on the sand. Caswell was wearing only his striped underpants.

One of the tourists, a middle-aged woman with red hair, went forward and knelt beside the body. She rested her palms on his back and began moving forward and backward as she tried to squeeze the water from his body. Each time she pressed forward the water spouted from his nose and mouth.

The woman who had taken the news to the club-house began describing what she had seen:

'I noticed that he wasn't lookin' too happy since mornin'. But is not my business what goin' on. Everybody can see what goin' on between Adassa and Neville. That is their business. But when I saw Caswell goin' into the sea I thought he was just going in to bathe. It didn't occur to me at the time that he might have something else on his mind. Then a little later I looked out and didn't see him any more. Then I spread the alarm.'

A few minutes later the tourist got to her feet with a dejected look on her face. 'I'm sorry,' she said. 'I've done everything I can. I'm very sorry. But he's dead.'

The woman began wailing. 'Look at the news we goin' 'ave to carry back! Look at the news we goin' 'ave to carry back to his parents!'

The tourists hitched their boat to their car and prepared to leave. The man who had taken Caswell's body from the sea asked them to report the death at the nearest police station. Most of the people began heading towards their vehicles. A number of vehicles left the beach. The people who came in the bus had to wait; the man who had taken Caswell from the sea was a member of their party and he would be required to give a statement to the police.

As Ossie walked back to the truck he noticed that Neville and Adassa were sitting in the cab. Neville's eyes were red and he was pulling hard at a cigarette and inhaling deeply. Adassa was leaning back in her seat and her face was cold and expressionless.

It was almost dusk when the police finally arrived. Ossie did not want to see what they were doing so he remained in his seat at the back of the truck. It was getting uncomfortably cold. Finally he heard the bus and the police van leaving the beach. The members of their party who had watched the examination and removal of the body began climbing into the truck. Soon afterwards the truck began retracing its path through the colonnade of coconut trees.

As they drove along the coast Ossie had his final glimpses of the sea, the sea that had taken Caswell. He glimpsed sections of its sad and immense loneliness. Each time he saw it he shivered at the thought of its unimaginable depths. He heard its panting as it intimidated the shore. Again, they kept moving closer and away from it; gradually it merged into the encapsulating darkness.

They drove in silence for many miles. Then they began to sing. The truck became a wake on wheels. For Ossie the songs were as sad as his memory of the sea. And every time he thought of the sea, he felt a cold fear approaching his heart.

ROOPLALL MONAR

◁ ■■■■■■■■ ◇ ■■■■■■■■ ▷

Bahadur

This Bahadur couldn't read and write at all people say, but he gat more commonsense than most estate people who uses to wuk in the backdam from soon-soon morning until six o'clock in the evening, when cricket and night beetle does croak inside the cane field, by the beezie-beezie and the blacksage bush-corner.

And too besides, them ole people say that this Bahadur was damn independent. You couldn't dare eye-pass he or want fo push yuh finger in he face, else was real trouble. And he don't stand fo nonsense from them driver and overseer and backraman, never mind they been control the estate at that time. And beside, Bahadur was lil fussy chap. True-true, if he ain't feel to wuk one day he staying home, and the next day he get excuse in he sleeve long time to tell driver and overseer. So it come that them estate people does say Bahadur is a real sense man.

Well, it so happen that soon after Bahadur get married he start to think serious about building he future. He know that if he continue wukking in the Creole gang, then move to spray gang, then shovel gang, by the time he reach forty he body turn like packsawal mango. True, he might lose he manhood like one-two sugar worker and he still gon live in logie. And pardna, if you couldn't wuk Sunday to Sunday in the sugar estate, you on the brim of starvation. Tings always hard guava season. And though sugar had good price in Europe because of the war, in backdam money been still too small.

So one Wednesday night while he on he bed, Bahadur tell he wife Sumintra that he gon leff cane wuk and start fo hustle fish, because he ain't like the damn slavery going-on in the estate. And too beside he can't stem the blasted advantage them driver and overseer does take on them good-looking coolie and black woman who does wuk in the weeding gang.

'But is not all time fish does run, Bahadur,' Sumintra say, and though she eye brighten up, she face serious.

'And is not fo all time people does keep they strength fo wuk in backdam. People is no engine,' Bahadur say while he stroking Sumintra round face and she long hair, which run down till by she hip.

'But you can think up something better?' Sumintra ask. She want make sure they future build up step by step.

'Arite woman, gimme some time,' Bahadur say. You see he didn't want fo displease Sumintra, he like she too bad. Is the first woman he had you know. So after they make a lil sweetness, he assure she that he gon think up some smart way fo earn he bread and live in better logie, or he name not Bahadur.

And he been thinking that whosoever get ranger wuk in the estate come damn independent. Ranger wuk get authority, and you does get lil bit privilege with Big Manager, and the work easy too. But only brave and trustful men like Sugrim and Mutton, who been serve estate faithfully like them backdam mule ever since them was small boys, could get that sort of job, so Bahadur couldn't dream fo get ranger wuk until he prove heself faithfully. And too beside, Bahadur daddy or uncle is not a driver so they na able fo sweet-talk Big Manager to get Bahadur ranger wuk. But if one smart man wuk he brain good, he must get ranger wuk, Bahadur tell heself.

And day-in, day-out, while Bahadur still wukking in creole gang, he thinking-thinking. Some day when sun real hot and them creole boys and Bahadur sweating like donkey working in the thick-thick sugarcane, Bahadur does feel to curse the driver and walk off the job. But when he mind flash-back pon Sumintra he does clam up he mouth. True, he don't want Sumintra to feel he lazy and good-fo-nothing.

And one-two day when rainy season heavy, and sandfly, cap-cap and scorpion reigning like king in them cane field, and try fo suck out yuh blood while yuh throwing manure on them young caneroot, Bahadur does leggo some stinking mumma cuss and attempt fo smash them cap-cap forthwith which does sting he. Then he does say kiss-me-rass, to hell with backdam wuk. But when he mind flash at Sumintra, he passion does cool down, and then he does strain he brain-nerve fo think up quick-quick how he could get one ranger wuk.

Then one morning when Bahadur wake up, he get one bright idea, but he ain't tell Sumintra, who been cooking on the chulaside in the rickety front-shading which been join the logie. And throughout the day while Bahadur wukking in the backdam, he shuffling the idea in he mind just like he shuffling card at wakenight. After dinner he decide fo work forthwith on the idea.

Round nine o'clock night time when he notice that moonlight come out, he tuck in one white flour-bag bed-sheet inside he shirt, which he dig out from the trunk in the bedroom unknown to Sumintra. Then he walk by Sumintra while she darning he shirt by one hand-lamp and say, 'Gal, I now remember Das ole man want see me important tonight-tonight, so I gat fo go out.'

Sumintra agree, but she advice he that he must be careful by Cabbage-Dam side, cause she hear that it does have one jumbie there that does frighten people.

'None jumbie ain't dead yet fo frighten me, gal,' Bahadur say as he walk out.

When Bahadur pass Cabbage-Dam, and turn in the next dry mud-dam which running behind the sugar factory compound, he notice the dam clear. Is only the estate cowpen, surround partly by some fruit tree and beezie-beezie bush he seeing. This time the two ranger-watchman, Sugrim and Mutton, patrolling cowpen like security guard; one-two time they gaffing, then they smoking and laughing.

Good, Bahadur shake he head and say. Then Bahadur hide heself behind one cork tree which been growing aside the mud-dam donkey years now, while he studying the surrounding like one tief-man before he go fo tief. Twenty minutes later Bahadur tek out the sheet and throw it over he self. Now he does look like one judge-night people you does see on the road preaching. Only thing is that he face cover, though Bahadur make sure he seeing through the sheet. When he certain the mud-dam clear, and is only Sugrim and Mutton he seeing around the cowpen, he step on the mud-dam from out the cork tree and start fo walk slow-slow toward the cowpen. This time he tip-toeing and stretching one-two time so he could look tall, while the breeze flapping the sheet flap flap flap . . .

Meanwhile Sugrim and Mutton bussing-down one gaff. True, they saying that since Head Ranger place them to watch cowpen one year now, they never see jumbie, although backdam people say too much jumbie does reign round this side. But that is chupidness they say. And if you hear how they boasting and bragging, eh-eh, you gon think they could strangle one lion if it materialise in front of them.

And Mutton start talk how some watchman is cockroach . . . they just frighten they own shadow, especially Ramdat. Sametime Sugrim raise he eye and it happen to drop on this thing in white, walking slowly toward the cowpen. Eh-eh, Sugrim puke. And he still watching this thing as though he hypnotised. When Mutton notice that Sugrim ain't listening to he, he follow Sugrim eye and he too spot the white thing.

This time Bahadur done notice Sugrim and Mutton reaction, and he know that they frighten-frighten. So he start walk more slow, tip-toeing and stretching heself like Moongaza.

'Shit, dat is what?' Mutton ask while he getting cold sweat and he teeth knocking.

'That is no people. That is something strange,' Sugrim talk while he mind reflect that some jumbie does look just like this, but he ain't tell Mutton.

Meanwhile Bahadur still walking slow, and when he about to reach the cowpen he leggo one screech like night owl. Then he chuckle and laugh in one big tone ha ha ha, and then he turn back.

'O Gawd, Mutton, is a Dutchman,' Sugrim say. 'And me hear Dutchman is bad-bad.'

Soon as Mutton hear that he scramble he dinner bag and bolt to factory side, saying, 'To hell wid cowpen. Me ain't want Dutchman kill me tonight.'

And don't matter how much Sugrim saying, 'Hold on, hold on, Mutton,' Mutton ain't stopping. Eh-eh, he speeding more. Then sametime as Sugrim shout that Dutchman jumbie disappear, he hear the screech and see the white thing coming toward the cowpen again.

'O Gawd, this gat to be one Dutchman. Me ain't want dead tonight,' Sugrim shout, and start fo gallop like jackass toward the factory, hollering, 'Mutton, Mutton, wait, boy Mutton . . .'

When Bahadur see the rigmarole he want buss-down one laugh. He plan working exactly how he'd seen it. One hour later while he on the bed, and Sumintra sleeping and snoring as though she work whole day in the backdam, Bahadur start plan how he gon operate the next night.

Come morning, whole estate know one Dutchman jumbie been frightening Sugrim and Mutton, and they had was to run fo they life. And don't matter how much time Big Manager and Head Ranger telling Sugrim an Mutton that it ain't gat nothing name jumbie, that is only vision, still Sugrim and Mutton insist that they want keep watch somewhere else that night, and begging Head Ranger that he must place two other watchman by cowpen. At last Head Ranger agree, and decide to place Ram and Pooran by the cowpen.

All time when people talking bout this Dutchman jumbie, Bahadur cool like cucumber, though he laughing in he mind. And people been too occupy with this jumbie, so they ain't have time to notice Bahadur.

When night come, round nine o'clock Bahadur tell Sumintra he belly griping bad-bad, and he going to the latrine which been situate about twenty-five rod away from the logie.

'But careful of this Dutchman jumbie, you hear, man,' Sumintra warn Bahadur as he left the logie.

'Me na frighten na jumbie, gal,' Bahadur say.

This time moonlight bright like day and the place look silvery. When Bahadur certain the mud-dam clear he go behind the tree and throw the sheet over he self. Coupla minute after he walk slow-slow toward the cowpen, and he howling like dog does howl when they see jumbie.

And like Ram and Pooran been on the look out. True, when they spot the white thing they done know is the very Dutchman jumbie, and like it really mean to kill them the way it howling. So pardna, they ain't tek chance at all, they grab they dinner bag and scoot toward the sugar factory like athlete, screaming all the way. They ain't want this Dutchman jumbie ketch them at all. They always hearing them ole people say is yuh neck them jumbie does break first and yuh does die like fowlcock. And they ain't want to die this way because them ole people say that if is so yuh soul don't get prappa resting.

Meantime Bahadur head to he logie and walk in easy like cat, and when he certain Sumintra sleeping he take out the sheet and put it inside the drawer next the bed.

Next morning, news spread like wildfire. Big Manager and Big Ranger come worry. True, if they ain't place watchman by estate cowpen, certain-sure it have people like Black, Sumeer and Nizam bound to tief one-two young calf and bull, slaughter them and sell it quick-quick to them butcher in Good Hope befo' morning come. And Big Manager know that if calf or bull short in estate, them overseer and manager gon be disgruntled because they like to eat they beef every Gawd day.

And don't matter how much trap Big Manager and Head Ranger been set, they never catch Black, Sumeer and Nizam red-handed. Estate people does say them boys does smell the rat. And you can't accuse them on suspicion. Eh-eh, you have to catch them. And them boys know the law. And too beside they slippery like ochro.

By afternoon time every watchman refuse point blank to keep watch by the cowpen. They say they ain't mind going back to wuk in backdam, which they argue is better than if you does dead by one Dutchman jumbie. And don't matter how tempting is the sweet-talk and pay increase coming from Big Manager mouth, still them ranger an watchman hold they end. At last Big Manager turn to Head Ranger Sambo.

'Take your deputy and pass the night there until we work out something,' Big Manager say.

'Yes, Boss,' Sambo reply. But in he mind he frighten, specially of this Dutch jumbie. But he gat to obey Big Manager else he might be sent back to backdam wuk, and he ain't want that. Head ranger wuk give Sambo authority, and too beside Sambo greasing palm with driver and overseer, plus he getting sweet-talk with women.

By afternoon time news spread that Big Ranger Sambo and second Ranger Burt self going to watch cowpen, and they mean to put one end to this jumbie. All time Sambo and Burt beetie yapping like suction pump, but they acting brave-brave. By eight o'clock night time, whole estate done bolt up inside they logie, because they ain't want tengle with this jumbie. By nine o'clock Bahadur tell Sumintra he gat one message fo Khan and he must deliver it tonight-tonight. This time he done tuck in the white sheet inside he shirt long time since.

When Bahadur bank Cabbage Dam Turn and enter the dry mud-dam, he notice them two ranger in front the cowpen smoking, so he duck down by the parapet and throw the sheet over he self. Then he raise-up and start walk slow-slow toward the cowpen.

Soon as Sambo and Burt spot the white thing, big-big sweat start drop down they forehead blop blop, and by the time word come out from Sambo mouth, 'You is who?', Bahadur screech like one night owl, then he laugh with one strange big sound . . . Eh-eh, Sambo and Burt skin come heavy and they inside come cold like ice while they heart beating bap bap bap like water pump. They done know this is a bad jumbie and they can't tek chance. So by the time the white thing turn back and laugh, Sambo and Burt crawl through the bush which grow round the cowpen, reach one dry mud-dam, then head straight to they logie more quick than one cat with dog on he tail.

Next day news spread like wildfire. This time Sambo and Burt sick in bed, and every hour they screaming out as though they seeing this Dutchman in front they eye. Soontime fear done strike the estate so bad that even during the day the backdam people stop walking by the cowpen, while three other strong man had to accompany Khan and Paul fo clean cowpen. And soon as cowpen done clean them men vanish.

Big Manager try whole day to get two watchman fo watch the cowpen, but everybody refusing. Now Big Manager in one prickle, especially when he think bout Black, Sumeer and Nizam. By one o'clock he detail one message to all field worker saying that which male worker willing to watch cowpen that night gon get extra money. But everybody refusing, don't matter how much them driver sweet-talk them.

Then Bahadur notify the gang driver that he, Bahadur, taking up the challenge.

'Bahadur? Ah-eh, one pinnie-winnie thing like he gon watch cowpen?' some people talk when the news break out.

'Bahadur gat fo be mad,' other people say.

And in order to certain that Bahadur ain't get away from cowpen, some men set up sentry by Cabbage Dam unknowing to Bahadur. And as the night hour going from ten to eleven to twelve in the bright moonlight, them men by Cabbage Dam only seeing cowpen, but they ain't seeing the jumbie. Two hour later them get baffle and left. Next day was rigmarole in estate. People saying Sambo, Burt, Mutton and Sugrim ain't see any damn jumbie. And don't matter how much Mutton and Sugrim saying that they did, estate people believe they lying.

But when Big Manager ask some men at order-line to help keep watch at the cowpen they tremble lil-bit and say no no . . . So was Bahadur had to watch the cowpen again. Three night later when Big Manager and Second Manager check by cowpen at twelve o'clock midnight, Bahadur in position in front the cowpen brave like one tiger, and all the cattle safe.

'The only brave person we have in this damn superstitious estate is Bahadur,' Big Manager tell Second Manager next morning by order-line. And from that day one, Bahadur was confirm as Head Ranger.

And one morning two-three week later when Bahadur and Sumintra lying on they bed, and Bahadur stroking she smooth round face and she long hair which run down till she hip, he tell she how he get the Head Ranger job. She look at he real proud, while in she mind she saying that her man ain't going to lose he manhood like them other backdam worker what get shrivel up by hard-wuk and the sun. And she smile at he and they do they lil sweetness.

VELMA POLLARD

My Mother

For Marjorie

The Lexington Avenue train raced into Fourteenth Street station like a runaway horse and miraculously came to a stop; belching forth such an army of fast-moving bodies that I flattened myself against the stair-rails in sheer terror. But I survived, and after the first flight of stairs, stood near a tiny candy shop in the station, to let them all pass.

I stared, but only at the blacks – the strangers whom this heartless machine had rushed out of Harlem, out of the safety of the familiar 125th Street and into this alien city; to dingy stores and tiny disorganised offices or to other vague connections: Canarsie, Long Island, Jamaica, etc. They were all running, in some way or other – in careless abandon or in crisp, short, overbred paces; the women's girdles and eventually their coats, controlling the obviousness of the movement; the men's coat tails flapping at the inevitable slit below the rump.

The men, whether they were briefcase types or lunchpan types, all wore little hats with short brims. It was a cold morning. In New York twenty-three degrees is considered cold. The women didn't need hats. Cheap, curly wigs hugged their temples protecting their black youthfulness and hiding their kinky strands. Fifty acknowledging thirty, needs a wig. For some reason the real hairline tells a story even when it is dyed black. And here the merciful cold allowed for the constant sweater or the little scarf that covers the tell-tale neck.

Everybody was running and everybody looked frightened. But you could see that all this had become natural. This speed was now normal and because they couldn't see their own frightened faces, they couldn't recognise their fright. When you answer long enough to a name that for one reason or another is wrong, and when you live long enough with a face that is always wrong, a frightened look grows on you and becomes an inseparable part of you. I looked at them and became numb with a kind of nameless grief. For I had seen my mother for the first time in all those tense women's faces, in all those heads hiding their age and gentleness beneath the black, curly wigs.

◇

The little journey was a ritual. Very early, the first or second Saturday morning of the month, my grandmother and I would walk to Anne's Ridge and get in the line at the bank. I would sign my name on the money order made out to me and we would soon move from the Foreign Exchange line to the Savings line. I never knew how much money came, for the exchange from dollars to pounds was too much for me to handle; and I never knew how much was saved. But I always felt, one Saturday every month, that we were rich.

Sometimes we stopped in the big Anne's Ridge stores in town and bought a new plate or two, sometimes dress material and v-e-r-y occasionally, shoes. Then we stopped in the market for the few things Gran didn't plant and Mass Nathan's shop didn't stock.

The journey home was less pleasant. I never ever noticed the hills on the way back; not because they were so much less green but because it took all my energy to think up little stories to help me block out Gran's monthly lecture. It always had to do with ingratitude. I'm not sure now how she knew the extent of my ingratitude long before I even understood the concept of gratitude. It had to do with the faithfulness of her daughter working hard in America to support me so I could 'come to something' and my not trying to show thanks. I was no great writer; but Gran saw to it that I scratched something on an airletter form to my mother every month and that something always included thanks for the money.

Gran never made it clear in what non-verbal ways I should express thanks. I had to do well at school; but the teachers had a sort of foolproof mechanism for assuring that – those were the days of the rod and I meant to be a poor customer for that. So school was okay. But the guidelines at home were less clear. An action that one day was a sign of ingratitude was, next day, a normal action. It seemed that the assessment of my behaviour was a very arbitrary and subjective exercise and depended partly on Gran's moods.

Now I understand what Gran's dilemma was like. She herself did not know what she had to produce from the raw material she was given if her daughter's sacrifice was not to be meaningless. She had been set a great task and she was going to acquit herself manfully at all costs; but she was swimming in very strange waters. And her daughter could only work and send money; she couldn't offer guidelines either – only vague hints like the necessity for me to speak properly, however that should be.

◇

Every year we expected my mother home on vacation and every year she wrote that she was sorry she couldn't make it. But she always sent, as if to represent her, a large round box that people insisted on calling a barrel. It was full of used clothes of all sorts, obviously chosen with little regard for my size or my grandmother's size. I never went to the collecting ceremony. This involved a trip to Kingston and endless red tape. I merely waited at the gate till the bus turned the curve, gave its two honks and slid along the loose stones to a halt to let my grandmother out. Then the sideman would roll the barrel along the top of the bus and shove it to his comrade. Immediately the bus would honk again and move one.

Nothing smells exactly like my mother's boxes. It was a smell compounded from sweat and mustiness and black poverty inheriting white cast-offs. I still remember one of those dresses from the box. With today's eyes I can see that it was a woman's frock; a woman's short voile frock for cocktail parties or an important lunch. And I was nine or ten then. But I wore it with pride, first to the Sunday School Christmas concert and then to numerous 'social' events thereafter. And even now, that low-slung waist or anything resting lightly on the hips has particular charm for me whether or not the beholder's eye shares my judgement . . . There were blouses and shoes and hats; something to fit almost everyone in my grandmother's endless chronicle of cousins. We accepted our ill-fitting fits and wore them with surprising confidence.

Every year we expected my mother home on vacation. But she never came. The year I was in third form they flew her body home. I hadn't heard that she was ill. I felt for months afterwards that my very last letter should have said something different, something more; should have shown more gratitude than the others. But I could not possibly have known that that would be the last.

When the coffin arrived it was clear that nobody from Jamaica had touched that coffin. Sam Isaacs may have kept it a few days but that was all. The whole thing was foreign – large, heavy, silvery, straight from the USA. And when they opened the lid, in the church, so she could lie in state and everybody could look and cry, it was clear that my mother too had been untouched by local hands. She had come straight from the USA.

When my mother left Jamaica I couldn't have been more than five or six, so any memory I had of her was either very vague or very clear and original – carved out of my own imagination with patterns all mixed up, of other people's mothers and of those impersonal clothes in the annual barrel. The woman in the coffin was not my mother. The woman in the purple dress and black shoes (I didn't even know they buried people in shoes), the highly powdered face, framed by jet black curls and covered lightly with a mantilla, was not like any of the several images I had traced.

The funeral couldn't be our funeral. It was a spectacle. I don't suppose more than half the people there had actually known my mother. But it was a Sunday, and the whole week that had elapsed between the news of her death and the actual funeral made it possible for people from far and near to make the trip to our village. Those who were from surrounding districts but had jobs in the city used one stone to kill two birds – visit the old folks at home, and come up to 'Miss Angie daughter funeral'.

It wasn't our funeral. It was a spectacle.

The afternoon was hot; inside the church was hotter. Outside, I stood as far as I could from the grave and watched several of them pointing at me, their eyes full of tears: 'Dats de little wan she lef wid Miss Angie.' Near to me was a woman in a fur hat, close fitting, with a ribbon at the side. She wore a dress of the same yellow gold as the hat, and long earrings, costume jewellery, of the same yellow gold.

I could hear the trembling voices from the grave –

> 'I know not oh I know not
> What joys await me there . . .'

– and fur hat, beside me, trying to outdo them so her friend could hear her:

'A didn't know ar but a sih dih face; is fat kill ar noh?' (My mother was rather busty but that was as far as the fat went.)

She didn't wait for an answer but continued: 'A nevva sih wan of dese deds that come back from England yet.' (No one had taken the trouble to tell her it was America not England.)

'But de reason why a come to see ar is becaaz I was dere meself an a always seh ef a ded, dey mus sen mih back. Is now a sih ow a woulda look! But tengad a lucky a come back pon me own steam . . . An you sih dis big finneral shi have? she wouldn't have get it in Englan' you know. Since one o'clock she woulda gaan an' if they cremate ar, while we drinking a cuppa tea, she bunnin'.'

'Wat?' asked her audience at last. 'Deh gives tea? an peeple siddung?'

'Man, deh put dem in someting like ovin, an by dih time we jus' drink dih tea, you get dih ashes an' you gaan . . .'

They had stopped singing about my mother's joys; the slow heavy dirge was now 'Abide with me', sung with the Baptist rhythm sad and slow, though I hardly think it is possible for that particular song to be anything but sad and slow, Baptist or no Baptist. I looked towards the crowd. They were supporting my grandmother. I knew she wasn't screaming. She was never given to screaming. She was just shaking as great sobs shook her body and her hands seemed to hold up her stomach. It was pointless my trying to comfort her; they wouldn't let me. Two old women were holding her, Miss Emma, her good friend, and Cousin Jean who was more like a sister than a cousin.

Next day I went alone to my mother's grave to push my own little bottle with maiden-hair fern into the soft, red earth. When all their great wreaths with purple American ribbons had long faded, my maiden-hair fern started to grow.

I had never known my mother. I had known her money and her barrels and my grandmother's respect for her. I had not wept at her funeral. But that morning, in the subway station at Fourteenth Street, in the middle of nowhere, in the midst of a certain timelessness, I wept for her, unashamedly, and for the peace at Anne's Ridge that she never came back to know, after the constant madness, after the constant terror of all the Fourteenth Street subway stations in that horrifying work-house.

I saw my tears water the maiden-hair fern on her grave to a lush green luxuriance. I was glad I was a guest in the great USA and a guest didn't need a wig. I would take no barrels home with me. I saw my mother's ancient grave covered again with its large and gaudy wreaths. Like the mad old man in Brooklyn, I lifted from a hundred imaginary heads a hundred black and curly wigs and laid them all on the ancient grave. And I laid with them all the last shapeless, ill-fitting clothes from the last barrel. The last of the women had hurried away. I wept for my mother. But I rejoiced that the maiden-hair fern was lush and that we had no longer need for gaudy wreaths.

LAWRENCE SCOTT

◁ ■■■■■■■■ ◇ ■■■■■■■■ ▷

King Sailor One J'Ouvert Morning

'It's a feeling which comes from deep within,
A tale of joy or one of suffering,
It's editorial in song of the life we undergo,
That and only that I know is true calypso.'

MIGHTY DUKE

'Come down J'Ouvert morning, find yourself in a band', the first line of the long-time calypso was an insistently repeated refrain: at first hummed; humming breaking into simulated pan; 'ping pong, ping pong', hummed again; 'ping a ling, ping a ling ping pong, ping a ling, ping a ling ping pang, pang pang', hummed by Philip Monagas with pressed lips as he felt the spirit rising inside of himself this carnival Sunday morning as he stepped out on to the cool terrazo floor on the veranda of the modern concrete apartment up in the Cascade Hills overlooking Port-of-Spain.

'Come down J'Ouvert morning, find yourself in a band', Philip whistled. He could whistle the tune too but he could not remember the rest of the words and no one else seemed to sing them either, this long-time calypso. Just the one line and then the humming which accompanied the way he found himself walking and moving these days, easy and fluid, and then almost on tiptoe wanting to spring into the air. 'Come down J'Ouvert morning, ping a ling ping p'ding.' It was a kind of invocation, a prayer repeated many times like a mantra which induced and welcomed the madness of the masquerade, Carnival.

Since returning to the island Philip Monagas had been looking forward to the carnival.

He wasn't a tourist and he didn't want anyone taking him for a tourist. He was from here and he wanted to be seen and known for that. It would have to emanate from him, himself inhabit a costume which would come alive when he moved. He saw wings, the wings of the red devil and the butterfly Papillon, Moco Jumbie reaching for the sky on his long stilt legs. He would have to come out and be, be from here. He didn't want anyone to say that he was moving like a tourist, and yet, he didn't want anyone to suspect that he was forcing it, trying to be a local and being anyone but himself.

Like this morning self outside Mr Elcock's parlour when he went to buy the *Express*: 'Honky'. He didn't acknowledge it. His eyes slit and he kept looking straight ahead into the parlour at the pile of *Express* newspapers on the counter. He felt the blood rising into his cheeks. When he turned around he would have to face the fellas. He would have to walk the gauntlet of the fellas on the bridge. 'Honky.'

'Reds.' Did that feel better? A red skin for a white skin? You couldn't belong if you were white. He didn't believe that, and was that the point anyway? Colour. 'Reds.' He felt a tinge of, well at least they think I belong.

He wasn't a red nigger. How did he know that? Did he know that for sure? He was made to understand that through the elaborate mythology of story; those teatime stories told with guava jam, cheese and Crix biscuits. Uncle Andresito had spent months down in vaults of the Cathedral of the Immaculate Conception sorting through the dusty archives until he found the marriage certificate of the first Monagas with the official stamp PERSONAS BLANCAS. Why was Uncle Andresito so concerned? But, what about the other story that his great-grandfather had confessed to the parish priest that they were negro after all? When a particular member of the family turned out dark: 'That is a throwback, child,' they would laugh and say, 'He turn out bad, eh boy.' They would laugh, their laughter ringing the veranda with peals of laughter. They said, too, that it was the Corsican blood. If there was a little crinkly hair they said it was the Spanish blood. Anything but. The insistence. The obsession. And now, here, this morning, on the bridge in Cascade, big carnival Sunday two hundred years later, clutching his *Express* newspaper, Philip Monagas, great-grandnephew of Phillipe Monagas who could only write sad stories, burnt with an anger raging in himself with himself in the burning sun. Two hundred years since they come and no racial mix. He didn't believe that. The whole Diego Martin valley populated with black Monagas. Oh, but that is slave masters giving their names to slaves, and yes, Uncle Bertrand had a little thing on the side up on the cocoa estate, but still we pure. Pure white.

'Reds, you ain't look at me yet man.'

Philip turned. 'Yes, yes man, how you doing? I go see you.' He wanted to say, 'Man I isn't an American, you know,' but with a wave of the hand Philip plucked out of his head his carnival mantra, 'Come down J'Ouvert morning, find yourself in a band,' and bounced up the hill wondering what he looked like to the fellas on the bridge, but feeling better in himself for the picong.

◇

This year he would play J'Ouvert. He would play a J'Ouvert mas.

◇

Early morning still. The pan in the valley had started up: ping pong, ping pong. Coming up the valley with the shacks. The sound was iron, iron on iron. Now was not the time for the fine tenor pan like clear crystal drops in Cascade's waterfall Cazabon had painted up the valley. It was a deeper sound, a sound from the belly and the groin calling the people to a meeting with iron beating on iron:

> *Mooma, mooma your son in the grave already*
> *Your son in the grave already*
> *Take a towel and band your belly*

another song, another tune, reaching up from the soul of a village, Calinda's festival, the stick fight in the gayelle, the circle under the rum-shop. 'Mooma, mooma, your son in the grave already, your son in the grave already, take a towel and band your belly.' Philip hummed the tune.

Philip didn't know where these feelings came from, making his heart want to burst. He wasn't brought up to have these kinds of feelings. He was brought up to distrust those drums, any drums, the steel band when he was a child, but the excitement and wonder got into his blood in spite of it all, 'That noise'. But then, later, 'Oh, our people are really clever. We have real talent in this island, you know,' when they started to play classical music, and they themselves didn't even play classical music or read books in their house either. Then too, Tassa: 'Josephine, shut those windows the heat will be unbearable, but that noise. Those people will drive me mad with their drumming.' Tassa, coolie drums, coolie music. All Sunday after mass Indian wedding in the afternoon. All night drumming down in the barracks. Tassa, coolie drums, waking terrified. All night, Tassa. 'Can't those people stop that dreadful noise?'

The noise of enslavement and indentureship.

Yes, this year he would play J'Ouvert. He would play King Sailor. Weeks now it was in his mind to play this mas. 'Come on Philip man, come down J'Ouvert morning and find us man.' These were his pardners from up Petit Valley and Maraval, not real friends but fellas

155

and young girls who would greet him as if they knew him from long ago before he went away, school pardners, who wanted him to belong, yes, to belong because they too strove to belong, and by having him in their group would extend them and their sense of belonging.

He wouldn't play pretty mas in one of the big bands Monday and Tuesday during the day. He would play J'Ouvert and then he would lime. Why King Sailor? He had, is truth, a deep urge to play a real dirty mas, to daub himself, his white skin in the blackest coal and shoe polish (you can't get molasses these days) with streaks of blue rinse powder for his face to become a mask and his whole body to transform itself with a fork in his hand, a tail in his arse and an iron chain dragging behind. 'Jab jab. Pay de devil jab jab.' This spectre from his childhood loomed up in his mind to terrify and to excite. Jab Molassi.

'You don't think I should play Jab jab, boy?' Philip asked his friends.

'No man, Jab jab too dirty, play a King Sailor. It go suit you.' But then they too played in mud bands with brown clay and leaves to cover their naked white bodies. 'Yes man, that is the thing, King Sailor will be the thing exactly for you.'

This same Sunday morning as he stood barefoot on the cool terrazzo floor of the veranda, rocking to the persistent iron on iron of the pan in the valley, he remembered what it was like to be small again and waiting with excitement and fear for the first Jab jabs to come up from the barracks and villages on the sugar cane estate where he grew up. He was swinging from the veranda ledge with his bare feet hardly touching the cool concrete, squeezing his pennies to throw for the Jab jab. He shook his legs with excitement as they came up the gap, beating their iron chains and brandishing their forks. 'Pay de devil jab jab,' beating the rusty bread tin. He threw the pennies into the yard at their feet and they scrambled them up while still continuing their threats, 'Pay de devil jab jab, pay de devil jab jab.' And Josephine, his nurse, hugged him up and together they laughed and cried for them to come back.

There had been envy then too to belong with those little boys; to be one of those who could throw terror into the neighbourhood, but also bring laughter and madness to the day. In the weeks leading up to carnival he had been taken along to the children's carnival shows, dressed up by his mother to try and win the prize at the company club. They would do the circuit: Red Cross, Guaracara Park, Queens Park Savannah and maybe even the Country Club. One year he had been dressed up as a Usine St Madeleine milk bottle with Bristol board, cellophane and a little silver cap, another time as one of the Pope's Swiss Guards and then once on a float as Peter Pan in Kensington Gardens. But what he wanted to be was a Jab jab and to be with those boys from the barracks down the gap out into the estate with bare bodies in the baking sun terrorising the world or at least the estate.

He would play King Sailor. He had improvised some tufts of coloured ribbon as pom poms for his shoes and streamers for his sailor cap and more streamers for the white stick he would use for the special dance, the King Sailor dance. He could see himself chipping down, shuffling and spinning round the white stick, making his entrance into town for J'Ouvert. 'Come down J'Ouvert morning, find yourself in a band.' Yes, he was feeling good.

He pressed out the white cotton sailor shirt and hung it on a wire hanger behind the bedroom door. Then he pressed the old pair of white sailor pants with the bell bottoms. He sewed the pom poms on to the front of his washy congs. He put them at the foot of the bed and laid out the bell-bottom sailor pants on the bed with the legs flapping over the side and just touching the edge of the washy congs with the pom poms made from ribbons. He was ready, almost. Then he pinned the ribbons into his white stick, trying out the dance, shuffling around and then leant it up in the corner behind the door. He could do the dance. He was ready. Only thing was the sailor cap which sat on the bed all piquéd up with a pink pom pom on top looking like a birthday cake. He was ready for town. 'I coming down, I coming down.' These were the songs of bravery when he was alone. He was nervous like hell.

Four o'clock Monday morning. That was the magic hour. It felt like going to bed and getting up for midnight mass. It had that feeling like going to church. And instead of the litany: Tower of Ivory, House of Gold, Ark of the Covenant pray for us, it was his carnival mantra, 'Come down J'Ouvert morning, find yourself in a band.' Jam Jam Jam.

He shut the door behind him easy and went out into the four o'clock darkness resplendently white with ribbons and pom poms: King Sailor, with only the amber street light for a moon. He was walking down into town from up in the Cascade Hills. Dogs barking. Cock was crowing since midnight so that was nothing special. Shuffling feet. He could hear the slap of washy cong on the pitch. People coming down. Massing. More people by the savannah. This was more people than midnight mass Christmas time even with the parang mass they have now. This was more people than Easter vigil, even if they giving new fire and water.

Already he thought that everyone was watching him. And then it was easy because he was watching everybody. People coming out, showing themselves. There was no distinction now. Some people might think that he was a tourist, but they have plenty black tourists too from Brooklyn and Queens, he thought.

People were looking good. Even those who were not playing mas and just had on jeans and T-shirt looked special. This was it. He had been told about it and he had read about it: Carne Vale, Canboulay, Emancipation. J'Ouvert was all these and he was here in the long line and belonging to it. The little steel bands were coming down from the hills behind Port-of-Spain and there was the sound ahead; a sound which was the massing of people and the scraping of pans on the ground, the hooking up of pans on to their sheds and then the final tuning and the fringes on the pan sheds fluttered in the dawn breeze and glittered. A strange quiet. He saw a bat and a skeleton float by. And then it was sudden, in absolute unison, pan pan pan, jam jam jam, as Invaders began to move down Tragarete Road.

Philip couldn't see anybody he knew. Yes, he knew that fella and he waved and said, 'How you going?' to this one and that one there who he now noticed. But they were not the people he had arranged to meet. This was not the band he was supposed to play in. He wanted to step out to look for the people he was supposed to be with, but he couldn't. A stronger force pulled him back, carried him along. When he looked up he could see the tops of the pan sheds like giant hosays rocking and the crowd pressing round. This was J'Ouvert. He didn't have place to do his sailor dance. He expected to have space and then he would be able to do the special dance. He could do the dance. Give him the space he could do the dance.

Then all of a sudden he was pressed right up against the big bass pan and the fella in charge of the section shouted, 'Come man, push. We need you to push.' Philip didn't think that he could have been referring to him so he hesitated and the fella came alongside him and began to push where he was standing and said, putting his arm round Philip's shoulder, 'So pardner, so, push.' Philip began to push. He dropped his King Sailor stick right there in the gutter. He felt a little sorry for that but it did not last long as he continued to push. Then he saw the excitement on the faces of the children who were hanging from bars inside the sheds above the pan players, taking a ride. He was inside and the music was inside him. He was pushing the pan down into town.

'Monagas.' He saw a fella from the band he was supposed to be in. It flashed through his mind where he was supposed to be. Then he was gone.

$\diamond$

By Green Corner he got squeezed up on to the pavement. He grabbed a Carib beer from a fella just managing to prize the money out of his sailor pants pocket, and then he was gone, taken along pressed up against people and the sweat of this whole town, chipping down, ping p'ding, jumping up all the way down into Port-of-Spain.

Philip saw the sun rise over Laventille as he stood up in Nelson Street. He stayed with the pan for the whole J'Ouvert on a journey during which he saw the mamaguy and pappyshow of a people playing a mas of defiance and mockery, irony and disguise, in which they enacted their own terrible enslavement and indentureship, transforming it and offering it now as a gift of celebration for all.

He was heady with the excitement, the ritual and the fact of his belonging. The vision he had had of himself resplendently white in pom poms and ribbons with his stick and his fine stick dance was not what he saw at all. He had to laugh for truth as he looked at his King Sailor shirt tied round his neck and his bell bottom pants rolled up to his knees. He laughed and said to himself as he pushed the pan right back into the pan yard, 'Like I play Jab jab after all.'

OLIVE SENIOR

The Two Grandmothers

I

Mummy, you know what? Grandma Del has baby chickens. Yellow and white ones. She makes me hold them. And I help her gather eggs but I don't like to go out the back alone because the turkey gobbler goes gobble! gobble! gobble! after my legs, he scares me and Mr SonSon next door has baby pigs I don't like the mother pig though. Grandma lives in this pretty little house with white lace curtains at all the windows, Mummy you must come with me and Daddy next time and you can peek through the louvres Grandma calls them jalousies isn't that funny and you can see the people passing by. But they can't see you. Mummy why can't we have lace curtains like Grandma Del so we can peek though nobody ever goes by our house except the gardeners and the maids and people begging and Rastas selling brooms. Many many people go by Grandma Del's house and they all call out to her and Grandma Del knows everyone. My special friend is Miss Princess the postmistress who plays the organ in church she wears tight shiny dresses and her hair piled *so* on her head and she walks *very slow* and everybody says she is sweet on Mr Blake who is the new teacher and he takes the service in church when Parson doesn't come and Miss Princess gets so nervous she mixes up all the hymns. Mr Mack came to fix Grandma's roof and Grandma said 'poorman poorman' all the time. Mr Mack's daughters Eulalie and Ermandine are big girls at high school in town though Eulalie fell and they don't know what is to be done. Mummy, why are they so worried that Eulalie fell? She didn't break her leg or anything like that for she is walking up and down past the house all day long and looks perfectly fine to me.

Mummy, I really like Grandma Del's house it's nice and cosy and dark and cool inside with these big lovely oval picture frames of her family and Daddy as a baby and Daddy as a little boy and Daddy on the high school football team, they won Manning Cup that year Grandma says did you know that Mummy? And Daddy at University and a wedding picture of Daddy and you and me as a baby and all the pictures you send Grandma every year but those are the small pictures on the side table with the lovely white lace tablecloth in the picture frame on the wall is Great-grandpapa Del with a long beard and whiskers he makes me giggle and he is sitting down in a chair and Great-grandmama is standing behind him and then there is a picture of Grandma herself as a young lady with her hair piled high like Miss Princess and her legs crossed at the ankles she looks so lovely. But you know what, Mummy, I didn't see a picture of Daddy's father and when I asked Grandma she got mad and shooed me away. She gets even madder when I asked her to show me her wedding picture. I only want to see it.

Mummy do you know that Grandma sends me to Sunday School? And then we stay over for big church and then I walk home with her and all the people it's so nice and only Parson comes to church in a car. Mummy did you go to Sunday School? I go with Joycie a big girl next door and Grandma made me three dresses to wear. She says she cannot imagine how a girl-child (that's me) can leave her home with nothing but blue-jeans and T-shirts and shorts and not a single church dress. She has this funny sewing machine, not like Aunt Thelma's, she has to use her feet to make it go just like the organ in church Miss Princess pumps away with her feet to make it give out this lovely sound she works so hard you should see her and the first time I went to Grandma's church I was so scared of the bats! The church is full of bats but usually they stay high up in the roof but as soon as the organ starts playing on Sunday the bats start swooping lower and lower and one swooped so low I nearly died of fright and clutched Grandma Del so tight my hat flew off.

Did I tell you Grandma made me a hat to go to church with her own two hands? She pulled apart one of her old straw hats, leghorn she said, and made me a little hat that fits just so on my head with a bunch of tiny pink flowers. Grandma didn't send it with me though or my Sunday dresses she says she will keep them till I return for she knows that I am growing heathenish in town. When Grandma dresses me up for church I feel so beautiful in my dresses she made with lace and bows and little tucks so beautiful and my hat, I feel so special that my own Grandma made these for me with her own two hands and didn't buy them in a store. Grandma loves to comb my hair she says it's so long and thick and she rubs it with castor oil every night. I hate the smell of castor oil but she says it's the best thing for hair to make it thick and soft and after a time I even like the smell. Grandma Del says my skin is beautiful like honey and all in all I am a fine brown lady and must make sure to grow as beautiful inside as I am outside but Mummy how do I go about doing that?

Nights at Grandma's are very funny. Mummy can you imagine there's no TV? And it's very, very dark. No street lights or any lights and we go to bed so early and every night Grandma lights the oil lamps and then we blow them out when we are going to bed, you have to take a deep breath and every morning Grandma checks the oil in the lamps and cleans the shades. They have 'Home Sweet Home' written all around them. So beautiful. She cleans the shades with newspapers. She says when I come next year I'll be old enough to clean the shades all by myself. Grandma knows such lovely stories; she tells me stories every night not stories from a book you know, Mummy, the way you read to me, but stories straight from her head. Really! I am going to learn stories from Grandma so when I am a grown lady I will remember all these stories to tell my children. Mummy, do you think I will?

161

II

Mummy you know Grandma Elaine is so funny she says I'm not to call her Grandma any more, I'm to call her Towser like everybody else for I'm growing so fast nobody would believe that she could have such a big young lady for a granddaughter. I think it's funny I'm practising calling her Towser though she is still my grandmother. I say, 'Grandmother, I mean Towser, Grandma Del introduces me to everyone as her Grand-daughter she calls me her "little gran" and Grandma Elaine says, 'Darling, the way your Grandmother Del looks and conducts herself she couldn't be anything but a Grandmother and honey she and I are of entirely different generations.'

Grandma Elaine says such funny things sometimes. Like she was dressing to go out last night and she was putting on make-up and I said 'Grandma' – she was still Grandma then – I said, 'Grandma, you shouldn't paint your face like that you know, it is written in the Bible that it's a sin. Grandma Del says so and I will never paint my face.' And she said, 'Darling, with all due respect to your paternal Grandmother, she's a lovely lady or was when I met her the one and only time at the wedding, and she has done one absolutely fantastic thing in her life which is to produce one son, your esteemed father, one hunk of a guy, but honey, other than that your Grandmother Del is a country bumpkin of the deepest waters and don't quote her goddamn sayings to me.' Mummy, you know Grandma Elaine *swears* like that all the time? I said, 'Grandma you mustn't swear and take the name of the Lord in vain.' And she said, 'Honeychile with all due respect to the grey hairs of your old grandmother and the first-class brainwashing your daddy is allowing her to give you, I wish my granddaughter would get off my back and leave me to go to Hell in peace.' Can you imagine she said that?

She's really mad that you allow me to spend time with Grandma Del. She says, 'Honey, I really don't know what your mother thinks she is doing making you spend so much time down there in the deepest darkest country. I really must take you in hand. It's embarrassing to hear some of the things you come out with sometimes. Your mother would be better advised to send you to Charm School next summer you are never too young to start. Melody-Ann next door went last year and it's done wonders for her, turned her from a tomboy into a real little lady.' (Though Mummy, I really can't stand Melody-Ann any more, you know) 'And your mother had better start to do something about your hair from now it's almost as tough as your father's and I warned your mother about it from the very start I said "Honey, love's alright but what about the children's hair?" If you were my child I would cut it right off to get some of the kinks out.' Mummy, you won't cut off my hair, will you? Daddy and Grandma Del like it just the way it is and what does Grandma Elaine mean when she says my hair is tough, Mummy?

Anyway, Mummy, can I tell you a secret? Gran, I mean Towser, told me and says it's a secret but I guess since you are her daughter she won't mind if I tell you. Do you know that Towser has a new boyfriend? He came to pick her up on Saturday night, remember I told you Joyce was staying up with me and we watched TV together while Towser went out? That's the time she was painting her face and she put on her fabulous silver evening dress, you know the strapless one and her diamonds with it, the ones her husband after Grandpapa gave her, and I was so proud she was my grandmama she looked wonderful like a million dollars and when I told her so she let me spray some of her perfume on myself before Mr Kincaid came. He is a tall white man and he kissed Towser's hand and then he kissed my hand and he had a drink with Towser and was very nice and they drove off in this big white car like what Uncle Frank drives Mummy, a Benz, and Towser was looking so pleased the whole time and before Mr Kincaid came she whispered and said her new boyfriend was coming to take her to dinner and he was so nice and handsome and rich. Towser was looking as pleased as Eulalie did when the mail van driver was touching her when they thought nobody was looking but I was peeking through the louvres at Grandma Del's and I saw them.

But Mummy, I don't know why Towser wants me to spend more time with her for she is never there when I go; always rushing off to the gym and the pool and dinners and cocktails or else she is on the phone. I love Towser so much though, she hugs me a lot and she says things that make me laugh and she gives me wonderful presents. Do you know she made Joyce bake a chocolate cake for me? And my new bracelet is so lovely. It's my birthstone you know, Mummy. You know what, Grandma Elaine, I mean Towser says she is going to talk to you about taking me to see my cousins Jason and Maureen in Clearwater when she goes to do her Christmas shopping in Miami. Oh Mummy, can I go? You know all the girls in my class have been to Miami and you've never taken me. Mum, can we go to Disneyworld soon? I'm so ashamed everyone in school has been to Disneyworld and I haven't gone yet. When Towser goes out Joyce and I sit in the den and watch TV the whole time except I usually fall asleep during the late show but Joyce watches everything until TV signs off, and next morning when she is making me breakfast she tells me all the parts that I missed. Mummy, can't we get a video? Everyone in my class has a video at home except me. You know Towser is getting a video she says she is getting Mr Kincaid to give her one as a present. Towser is so much fun. Except Mummy, what does she have against my hair? And my skin? She always seems angry about it and Joyce says Grandma is sorry I came out dark because she is almost a white lady and I am really dark. But Mummy what is wrong with that? When I hold my hand next to Joyce my skin is not as dark as hers or Grandma Del's or Daddy's even. Is dark really bad, Mummy?

III

Mummy, did you know that a whistling woman and a crowing hen are an abomination to the Lord? That's what Grandma Del told me and Pearlie when Pearlie was teaching me to whistle. Don't tell Grandma but I *can* whistle. Want to hear me? -! -! -! Ha ha. Mummy, can you whistle? Pearlie is my best friend in the country she lives near to Grandma in this tiny house so many of them and all the children sleep together in one room on the floor and Mummy, you know what? Pearlie has only one pair of shoes and one good dress and her school uniform though she hardly goes to school and some old things she wears around the house that have holes in them. Can you imagine? And you should see her little brothers! Half the time they are wearing no clothes at all. Mummy can you send Pearlie some of my dresses and some of my toys but not my Barbie doll? She doesn't have any toys at all, not a single one.

And Pearlie is just a little older than me and she has to look after her little brothers when her Mummy goes out to work. She has to feed them and bathe them and change them and while she is changing the baby's nappies her little brothers get into so much trouble. And when they break things when her mother comes home she beats Pearlie. Poor Pearlie! She can balance a pan of water on her head no hands you know. I wish I could do that. She goes to the standpipe for water and carries the pan on her head without spilling a drop. Sometimes I go with her; I borrow a pan and though it's smaller than Pearlie's I always end up spilling the water all over me and the pan gets heavier and heavier till I can hardly bear it before we get to Pearlie's house. Pearlie can wash clothes too. I mean real clothes, not dolly clothes. Really. Her baby brother's nappies and things and she cooks dinner for them but the way they eat is really funny. They don't have a real kitchen or anything she has three big rocks in the fireplace and she catches up a fire when she

164

is ready and she has to fan it and fan it with an old basket top and there is a lot of smoke. It makes me sneeze. Then when the fire is going she puts on a big pot of water and when it is boiling she peels things and throws them in the water to cook – yams and cocos and green bananas and that's what they eat, no meat or rice or salad or anything. Pearlie uses a sharp knife just like a big person and she peels the bananas ever so fast, she makes three cuts and goes zip! zip! with her fingers and the banana is out of its skin and into the pot. She says you must never put bananas and yams to boil in cold water for they will get drunk and never cook. Did you know that?

Once I helped her to rub up the flour dumplings but my dumplings came out so soft Pearlie said they were like fla-fla and she won't let me help her make dumplings again. Pearlie has to do all these things and we only get to play in the evenings when her mother comes home and can you imagine, Mummy, Pearlie has never seen TV? And she has never been to the movies. Never. Mummy do you think Pearlie could come and live with us? I could take her to the movies though I don't know who would look after her baby brothers when her mother goes to work. You know Pearlie doesn't have a father? She doesn't know where he is. I'd die without my Daddy. Grandma Del says I'm to be careful and not spend so much time with Pearlie for Pearlie is beginning to back-chat and is getting very force-ripe. Mummy, what is force-ripe?

Sometimes I play with Eulalie's baby. His name is Oral and he is fat and happy and I help to change his nappy. He likes me a lot and claps his hands when he sees me and he has two teeth already. He likes to grab hold of my hair and we have a hard time getting him to let go. Mummy why can't I have a baby brother to play with all the time? Eulalie and Ermandine love to comb my hair and play with it they say I am lucky to have tall hair but Grandma Del doesn't like Eulalie and Ermandine any more. She says they are a disgraceful Jezebel-lot and dry-eye and bring down shame on their father and mother who try so hard with them. Sometimes my Grandma talks like that and I really don't understand and when I ask her to explain she says, 'Cockroach nuh bizniz inna fowl roos' and she acts real mad as if I did something wrong and I don't know why she is so vexed sometimes and quarrels with everyone even me. She scares me when she is vexed.

You know when Grandma Del is really happy? When she is baking cakes and making pimento liquor and orange marmalade and guava jelly. On, she sings and she gets Emmanuel to make up a big fire out in the yard and she gets out this big big pot and we peel and we peel guava – hundreds of them. When we make stewed guava she gives me a little spoon so I can help to scoop out the seeds and I have to be real careful to do it properly and not break the shells. Mummy, right here you have this little glass jar full of stewed guavas from Grandma Del that I helped to make. Grandma gets so happy to see her kitchen full of these lovely glass jars full of marmalade and guava jelly. But you know what? Grandma just makes it and then she gives it all away. Isn't that funny? And one time she baked a wedding cake and decorated it too – three cakes in different sizes she made and then she put them one on top of the other. Grandma is so clever. She allowed me to help her stir the cake mix in the bowl but it was so heavy I could barely move the spoon. When it was all finished she let me use my fingers to lick out all the mixing bowls. Yum Yum. Why don't you bake cakes so I can lick out the bowls, Mummy?

And this time I found that I had grown so much I couldn't get into the church dresses Grandma made for me last time and Grandma made me some new dresses and she says she will give the old dresses to Pearlie. Mummy can you believe that everyone in church remembered me? And they said: 'WAT-A-WAY-YU-GROW' and 'HOW-IS-YU-DAADIE?' and 'HOW-IS-YU-MAAMIE?' till I was tired. Mummy that is the way they talk, you know, just like Richie and the gardener next door. 'WAT-A-WAY-YU-GROW'. They don't speak properly the way we do, you know. Mummy, Eulalie and Ermandine don't go to church or school any more and Ermandine says when I come back next year she will have a little baby for me to play with too and Eulalie says *she* will have a new little baby.

IV

Mummy, you know what the girls in school say? They say I am the prettiest girl in school and I can be Miss Jamaica. When I'm big I'll go to the gym like you so I can keep my figure and I must take care of my skin for even though I have excellent skin, Towser says, I must always care for it. Towser spends hours before the mirror every morning caring for her skin and her new boyfriend Mr Samuels is always telling her how beautiful she looks. Towser really loves that. Mr Samuels is taking her to Mexico for the long Easter weekend and Towser is going to Miami to buy a whole new wardrobe for the trip. She says she is going to bring me all the new movies for the video. Mummy, when I am old like Grandma will men tell me I'm beautiful too? Can I have my hair relaxed as soon as I am twelve as you promised? Will you allow me to enter Miss Jamaica when I am old enough? You know Jason likes me a lot but he's my cousin so he doesn't count. Mom, am I going to Clearwater again this Christmas to spend time with Jason and Maureen? Maureen is always fighting with me you know but Jason says she's jealous because she isn't pretty like me, she's fat and has to wear braces on her teeth. Will I ever have to wear braces? Mom, when I go to Miami can I get a training bra. All the girls in my class are wearing them and a make-up starter kit? Mom, when are we going to get a Dish?

V

Mom, do I have to go to Grandma Del's again? It's so boring. There's nothing to do and nobody to talk to and I'm ashamed when my friends ask me where I'm going for the holidays and I have to tell them only to my old grandmother in the country. You know Gina is going to Europe and Melody-Ann is spending all of her holidays in California and Jean-Ann is going to her Aunt in Trinidad? Mom, even though Grandma Del has electricity now she has only a small black and white TV set and I end up missing *everything* for she doesn't want me to watch the late show even on weekends, and Grandma's house is so small and crowded and dark and she goes around turning off the lights and at nights Grandma smells because she is always rubbing herself with liniment for her arthritis she says and it's true Grandma is in terrible pain sometimes. Mummy what is going to happen to Grandma when she is real old? She's all alone there.

She got mad at me when I told her I didn't want her to rub castor oil in my hair any more because I was having it conditioned and the castor oil smells so awful. And on Sundays Grandma still wants me to go to church with her. It's so boring. We have to *walk* to church and back. It's *miles* in the hot sun. I can't walk on the gravel road in my heels. If a parent passed and saw me there among all the country bumpkins I would die and Grandma says I am far too young to be wearing heels even little ones and I tell Grandma I'm not young any more. I'll be entering high school next term and everybody is wearing heels. She criticises everything I do as if I am still a baby and she doesn't like me wearing lip gloss or blusher though I tell her you allow me to wear them. And Grandma still wants me to come and greet all her friends, it's so boring as soon as somebody comes to the house she calls me and I have to drop whatever I am doing, even watching TV, and I have to say hello to all these stupid people. It's so boring Mom you wouldn't believe it, there's nobody but black people where Grandma lives and they don't know anything, they ask such silly questions. And they are dirty. You know this girl Pearlie I used to play with when I was little she is so awful-looking, going on the road with her clothes all torn up and you should see her little brothers always dirty and in rags with their noses running. I can't stand to have them around me and Pearlie and everybody is always begging me clothes and things and I can't stand it so I don't even bother to go outside the house half the time. When anybody comes I can see them through the louvres and I just pretend I am not there or I am sleeping. And everybody is just having babies without being married like Pearlie's mother and they are not ashamed. The worst ones are those two sisters Eulalie and Ermandine, you can't imagine how many babies they have between them a new one every year and Grandma says not a man to mind them.

But Mummy, something terrible happened. That Eulalie and I got into an argument. She's so ignorant and I told her that it was a disgrace to have babies without being married and she said, 'Who says?' and I said, 'Everybody. My Mummy and Grandma Elaine and Grandma Del for a start.' And she said, 'Grandma Del? Yes? You ever hear that she that is without sin must cast the first stone?' And I said, 'What do you mean?' And she said, 'Ask your Grannie Del Miss High-And-Mighty since her son turn big-shot and all. Ask her who his father? And why she never turn teacher? And why her daddy almost turn her out of the house and never speak to her for five years? And why they take so long to let her into Mothers' Union?' And Eulalie wouldn't tell me any more and they were so awful to me they started singing 'Before A married an' go hug up mango tree, A wi' live so. Me one'. You know that song, Mummy? I went home to ask Grandma Del what Eulalie meant, but Mummy, when I got home it was just weird I got so scared that I got this terrible pain in my tummy, my tummy hurt so much I couldn't ask Grandma Del anything and then when I felt better, I couldn't bring myself to say anything for I'm scared Grandma Del will get mad. But Mummy, do you think Grandma Del had Daddy without getting married? Is that what Eulalie meant? Mummy, wouldn't that make Daddy a bastard?

VI

Mummy, please don't send me back to stay with Auntie Rita in

Clearwater again. Ever. Nothing, Mummy . . . It's that Maureen. She doesn't like me.

◇

Mummy, am I really a nigger? That's what Maureen said when we were playing one day and she got mad at me and she said, 'You're only a goddamn nigger you don't know any better. Auntie Evie married a big black man and you're his child and you're not fit to play with me.' Mummy, I gave her such a box that she fell and I didn't care. I cried and cried and cried and though Auntie Rita spanked Maureen afterwards and sent her to bed without any supper I couldn't eat my supper for I had this pain in my tummy such a terrible pain and Uncle Rob came into the bedroom and held my hand and said that Maureen was a naughty girl and he was ashamed of her and *he* thought I was a very beautiful, lovely girl . . .

But Mummy, how can I be beautiful? My skin is so dark, darker than yours and Maureen's and Jason's and Auntie Rita's. And my hair is so coarse not like yours or Maureen's but then Maureen's father is white. Is that why Maureen called me a nigger? I hate Maureen. She is fat and ugly and still wearing braces . . .

◇

Mummy, why can't I have straight hair like Maureen? I'm so ashamed of my hair. I simply can't go back to Clearwater.

VII

Mom, I don't care what Dad says I can't go to stay with Grandma Del this summer because the Charm Course is for three weeks and then remember Towser is taking me to Ochi for three weeks in her new cottage. Do you think Towser is going to marry Mr Blake? Then I am going with you to Atlanta. You promised. So I really don't have any time to spend with Grandma this summer. And next holidays remember, you said I can go to Venezuela on the school trip? I don't know what Dad is going on about because if he feels so strongly why doesn't he go and spend time with his mother? Only that's a laugh because Daddy doesn't have time for anybody any more, I mean, is there a time nowadays when he is ever at home? I know Grandma Del is getting old and she is all alone but she won't miss me, she quarrels with me all the time I am there. Mom, I just can't fit her in and that is that.

OK. You know what? I have an idea. Why don't we just take a quick run down to see Grandma this Sunday and then we wouldn't have to worry about her again till next year. Daddy can take us and we can leave here real early in the morning though I don't know how I am going to get up early after Melody-Ann's birthday party Saturday night, but we don't have to stay long with Grandma Del. We can leave there right after lunch so we will be back in time to watch *Dallas*. Eh, Mom?

JAN SHINEBOURNE

◁ ━━━━━━━━━━━━ ◇ ━━━━━━━━━━━━ ▷

The Maid in Bel Air

The Vincent child was still there – none of my business, thought Vera and put it out of her mind as she emptied the washing machine. But the sink was near the window and it was her habit to glance outside as she rinsed the washing.

Bel Air was as quiet as an empty country church at this time of the morning. Most servants came to work later but it meant that they left later too. She preferred to start early and leave in time to catch the three o'clock bus at Stabroek Market. By three-thirty when the bus reached Plaisance, the market would still be open. By quarter-to-four she could start the cooking. It left time for the gardening, the chickens, some sewing and the radio before the generator shut down.

Vera took the washing outside. The Vincent child was still there. Why was the child standing exposed in her nightgown in the broad daylight? Her thoughts turned to her own child, Susan. She always reminded Susan to get to the standpipe by six o'clock or else after six o'clock the whole village seemed to want water at the same time. At six o'clock the estate turned on the water supply. At eight they turned it off again. It came on again at noon the next day before it was turned off at two o'clock. She always reminded Susan too to clean the house and sweep the yard, and look after Winston and Marcus. She did her best to discipline the children but when she was not there it was in God's hands what became of them. Mrs Batson next door kept her eye on the house and children as best she could, once she was feeling well enough. Mrs Batson had no more grandchildren to mind. If work could be found in Plaisance she would have preferred to work near home but Plaisance had no work, Georgetown had all the work. The whole of last year she had to work with the merchants in Water Street. The job was picking out rotten onions, potatoes and garlic and selling the ones they let her keep. She used to walk up and down Water Street in the hot sun, selling onions and garlic the whole day. This job with Mrs Semple was better, it was God-sent. Bel Air was a clean place. The maid's uniform saved on clothes-spending and nobody to overseer you whole day and the whole quiet and peaceful house to yourself although Mrs Semple made sure she had enough work to keep her busy whole day. That hot sun, that walking up and down Water Street, the begging people to buy – was terrible.

Soon, Mrs Semple would be down to open the kitchen door. The Vincent child next door was still there; she must be ill but her mother wouldn't let her stand outside in her nightgown like that. Vera returned to the laundry room. She washed and dried the sink and washing machine. She swept and wiped the floor then she washed her face and changed into her uniform.

The Vincent child was standing at the other end of the veranda now. Vera had to stand on tiptoe and crane her neck to see the child. She opened the window a little wider. The child was nearly a young woman. Her hair was not even combed. She was wearing a scarf round her head. She probably hadn't bathed yet.

The Semples were up now. She could hear their footsteps on the floorboards above. The shower was running now. Now voices. Soon Mrs Semple would let her into the kitchen to start the breakfast.

'Morning Vera,' Mrs Semple called.

'Morning ma'am.'

After that, Vera had no time to think. She cooked the bacon, eggs and toast and made the coffee. Mr Semple and the children ate in a hurry as usual. By eight, they were in the car. Other families in Bel Air were on their way out too. Vera could hear the gates opening, voices calling out, cars driving away. It was rush hour now in Georgetown. Schools and offices were filling up.

Mrs Semple took her time. Sometimes she did not leave the house until eleven. Her father owned an insurance company. Mrs Semple

171

worked for him. Mrs Semple's shower lasted a long time. Once it stopped running, Vera knew that Mrs Semple would be down soon to give the day's orders. Mrs Semple took only coffee in the morning. She was on a diet.

She did not hear Mrs Semple come downstairs. Vera was washing up at the sink. Mrs Semple came to the sink, stood next to her, opened the window and asked Vera: 'You see the Vincent child on the veranda?' Vera did not reply. Mrs Semple would think she did not mind her own business if she said yes. Vera took the kitchen mat outside. She shook it out and returned to the kitchen.

Mrs Semple said, 'Vera, the electrician is coming to fix the fridge today. Make sure it is working before he goes away.'

'Yes ma'am.'

'And if the fish-lady comes round and has fresh prawns get a dollar's worth.'

'Yes ma'am.'

'Look, here's fifteen dollars on the kitchen table. Don't spend it all. We need fresh fruit in the house. If no prawns, get some fish at the market. Whatever, clean, salt and freeze it. I can't stand the supermarket fish. It taste like paper.'

'Yes ma'am.'

'Why is that child on the veranda? The car is not under the house either.'

Vera made her way outdoors. The vacuum cleaner was kept in the laundry room. She always took it upstairs about now, on her way to start the tidying and cleaning, beginning with airing and making the beds, then the dusting and vacuuming upstairs, then downstairs.

Vera was dragging the vacuum cleaner from the laundry room when Mr Vincent's car appeared. He was a reckless driver. He drove the car right up to the gate. It was unusual for him to be arriving home at this time. In the mornings, he always left with the children for school about the same time as Mr Semple and the children. Mr Vincent called up to his daughter: 'Margaret go inside!' He hopped from the car and opened the gates. He returned to the car, drove it under the house, got out again and ran up the front stairs. Vera heard the front door slam shut.

In the kitchen, Mrs Semple was craning her neck to peer up at the Vincents' house. She asked Vera, 'Vera, you see Mr Vincent come in? I haven't seen Mrs Vincent this morning. I wonder if she gone to the university yet?'

While Vera made the beds, Mrs Semple did her exercises. After that, she would put on her make-up. Vera would watch her out of the corners

172

of her eyes. Mrs Semple's ablutions fascinated Vera. The final touch was Mrs Semple's choice of dress for the day. Mrs Semple would spend a few minutes studying her wardrobe before she decided what to wear.

Vera switched on the vacuum cleaner and Mrs Semple called out, 'Vera, switch off that thing!' When it was switched off, Mrs Semple instructed her, 'Do the downstairs first. I can't stand that noise. Wait until I leave.'

'Yes ma'am.'

The telephone rang. 'I'll get it Vera,' Mrs Semple said. 'You dust the vanity. I'm finished there.'

'Yes ma'am.'

'Gordon?' That was Mr Vincent. The Semples and Vincents used first names with each other. 'Yes man. Mmh hmm. No, it's all right. What? Oh my God! No! Oh my God Gordon! What are you telling me? No! Oh my God have mercy on us what in heaven's name is this? I don't believe you. Oh my God Gordon I am so so sorry, so sorry my good heavens! But just so? I saw Margaret on the veranda and I felt in my bones unconsciously . . .' Mrs Semple sat on the bed and doubled up, one hand over her mouth now, the other hand holding the receiver to her ear. The shock in Mrs Semple's voice chilled Vera. 'Yes, all right. Yes. I will come over. Right away. I must phone and tell Harry. Right away. I'll be over.'

Mrs Semple put down the phone, picked it up again and dialled rapidly. 'Vera!'

'Yes ma'am?'

'Stop what you are doing. We have to go over to the Vincents. Mrs Vincent died this morning.'

Mrs Semple was telling Mr Semple over the phone: 'Harry you would never believe this. Hilda has died. Yes. Gordon just telephoned to tell me. Look, I am going over this instant. I don't know. I don't know the details. God man I hear just this second, this instant, this moment. I am going over. I knew something was up. Yes, all right. Call him. OK.'

Mrs Semple went to her wardrobe. She sucked her teeth. 'I better wear this one.' Quickly, Mrs Semple pulled on the dress. Vera felt her own legs heavy and wooden. She could not imagine Mrs Vincent dead.

'Vera, come along.' Mrs Semple slipped on her shoes and led the way from the bedroom.

Downstairs, Mrs Semple collected her things together: handbag, shopping bag, keys, letters, handkerchief, pen. 'Vera, don't just stand there man. Lock the back door. Shut the windows. We will have to forget about the electrician. He will just have to come back another time.

The fridge will have to wait. God have mercy on us. Out of the blue. Out of the blue. I saw the woman coming in from university only yesterday. I didn't know she was ill.'

Vera did as she was told. She couldn't take it in. She thought of Mrs Vincent alive, not dead. Such a young woman. Mrs Vincent was kindness itself. From the moment she met her last year, Mrs Vincent had taken an interest in her. Mrs Vincent came originally from the country, from Plaisance, from 'your part of the world' she had told Vera. Twice, Mrs Vincent had baked her a cake, and three times given her a cardboard box filled with clothes for herself and the children. Then there were other presents: schoolbooks, pens and soursop and mangoes from the trees that grew in Mrs Vincent's yard. Mrs Vincent was concerned about the children; she used their names when she asked Vera about them: 'How is Susan doing at school? And Winston? Marcus?'

Mrs Vincent's concern rubbed off on her. It alerted her to the children's welfare. Vera was not ungrateful for Mrs Vincent's attentions but it made her even more careful not to be familiar with her. The greater Mrs Vincent's warmth and friendly gestures, the more formal Vera became. She never refused a present. She answered all Mrs Vincent's enquiries after the children. But she made sure that in her mind she never expected anything from Mrs Vincent. Never mind Mrs Vincent came from the country too. There was the matter of age too. Mrs Vincent was thirty-seven, fifteen years younger. It made it even more important for Vera to know her place. She admired Mrs Vincent greatly. She was a beautiful black woman, well-dressed and well-spoken, with a handsome husband and two children who were a credit to her. It was difficult to believe that Mrs Vincent came from the country. Now her death was a bolt out of the blue.

'Mistress, Mrs Vincent dead?'

'Yes Vera. You heard me.'

Vera put her hands to her mouth. The chill she first felt when she heard the shock in Mrs Semple's voice had not left her. It was sitting on her still. Goose pimples were breaking out on her arm. The soles of her feet were cold.

'For God's sake Vera!' Mrs Semple snapped. 'Come along man!'

Vera followed Mrs Semple to the Vincent house. They entered by the back stairs, through the kitchen. Vera hesitated at the door.

'Come through Vera, come through,' Mrs Semple urged impatiently. 'What is the matter with you?'

Vera took off her sandals.

'Vera what are you doing?'

'Taking off my shoes ma'am?'

'What for? Vera! Put your shoes on. No one told you to take off your sandals. What is the matter with you?'

'I didn't want to dirty the floor ma'am.'

'Well wipe your feet on the mat. Come with me. Let us go and hear what Mr Vincent needs doing in the house. Come along.'

In the living room, Mr Vincent and his daughter sat together on the settee. The sliding door that led to the veranda was open. The sunlight fell in a large square on the floor. He rose to greet Mrs Semple. Vera hung back and waited while the couple talked. Mrs Semple held Mr Vincent's arm and whispered in a soft voice. Then she turned and spoke to Vera.

'Vera, make coffee.'

Vera returned to the kitchen. Mrs Vincent's handbag was lying on the dresser. It was a leather handbag, well-used. Mrs Vincent used to carry it on her shoulders. She was never without it. Coming in from work, going out to work – Vera could see Mrs Vincent, with the handbag. If Mrs Vincent saw her she always waved and said something.

Mrs Vincent's daughter, Margaret, came to the kitchen. Vera put the kettle on and searched the cupboards for cups.

'Look, here, in this cupboard,' the child said, pointing.

'Yes ma'am.'

The child stood in the doorway with her arms folded and one leg crossed over the other. She watched Vera as she washed and dried the cups. Now Mrs Semple came to the kitchen.

Mrs Semple put her arm round the child and said, 'Margaret go and change out of your nightie.'

The child replied, 'I'm all right.'

Mrs Semple coaxed her, 'Go. People will be coming soon.'

The child shrugged. 'Oh, all right.'

'You have everything in your room?' Mrs Semple asked her.

'Yes,' the child replied, and left the kitchen.

Mrs Semple instructed, 'Vera you had better make a large pot of coffee. The doctor is here.'

'Yes ma'am.'

There were footsteps on the front stairs. The doorbell rang and Vera could hear their voices. The telephone rang and a car's horn sounded at the gate. Mrs Semple left the kitchen and returned a minute later to give Vera more instructions: 'Vera, nine coffees.' Then she was gone again.

The tray was laid when Mrs Carew, Mrs Vincent's best friend, came to the kitchen. Her eyes were red. Mrs Carew said, 'Vera look what befall us.' Mrs Carew shook her head and bit her underlip. 'Vera we will need two more cups. Come, I will help you serve.'

They served the coffee. Vera felt sorry for Mrs Carew, Mr Vincent and the child. Mrs Carew always gave Mrs Vincent lifts in her car. Both women worked at the university. They were always chatting. Sometimes they sat together in the car and chatted for a long time before Mrs Vincent got out. Both would wave to each other as the car pulled away. If Mrs Carew passed her on the street, she always stopped and said, 'Come Vera, I will give you a lift.' Mrs Carew was like Mrs Vincent, friendly, chatty and bright.

Mr Vincent helped himself from Vera's tray. There was a cigarette between his lips. His eyes were red. His white short-sleeved shirt was crumpled. He looked tired. All the people here she knew by their coming and going to and from the Vincent house. They were not Mrs Semple's friends. Mrs Semple had her own circle. Mrs Semple liked to talk a lot about Mr and Mrs Vincent and their circle. Vera often overheard them. Mrs Semple had a deep curiosity and she liked to talk and speculate about people. She and her friends spent a lot of time drinking, playing cards and joking.

Vera spent the next hour listlessly in the kitchen. The waiting, boredom and atmosphere of death made her morose. To escape it, she went outside to sit on the landing. The sun was sharper but the landing was shaded by the tree that grew near it. There was a breeze and Vera lost herself in the pleasure of resting in it. But awareness of Mrs Vincent's death returned to her when she caught sight of Mrs Vincent's bedroom window. The bedroom was next to the kitchen, like Mrs Semple's house. The louvre panes were open. The curtains were open too. Vera reflected that all the light of day and breeze were pouring in through the open window over Mrs Vincent's corpse. Vera began to weep.

Mrs Carew came to the kitchen. She joined Vera on the landing. She stood near her and put her hand on her shoulder. Vera dried her eyes with her apron. Then Mrs Carew began to weep. Mrs Carew wept noiselessly, her white hankerchief balled in her fist, mopping her eyes. Eventually, Mrs Carew ceased weeping. But Vera's weeping turned to sobbing. Mrs Carew waited patiently for Vera's grief to abate. However, Vera's sobbing turned to a rocking that shook her entire body, and her rocking turned to swaying until no longer able to contain herself, Vera, still seated, began to wail softly and flail her arms helplessly as she swayed and rocked.

Mrs Carew's alarm grew by the second. Her slender frame could hardly support Vera's. 'Vera!' Mrs Carew cried out.

Vera wailed, 'Oh Lord ma'am, oh Lord! Mrs Vincent was so kind to me! She was such a young woman to die!'

'All right Vera, all right.'

Vera emitted a strangled cry. The noise froze Mrs Carew. Mrs Carew became resentful.

Vera groaned, 'Lord, Lord!'

'Vera for God's sake stop this at once!' Mrs Carew ordered.

Vera's mourning brought Mrs Semple, Mr Vincent and the child to the kitchen. They watched the scene with wonder. Vera continued to bawl out her grief. Mrs Carew threw up her hands in despair. Vera clutched Mrs Carew's skirt and wept into it.

Mrs Semple's voice rose loud above Vera's: 'Vera!' Vera did not hear. Mrs Semple repeated: 'Vera!', her voice a near shriek. 'Vera stop this at once. Do you hear me?'

Mrs Semple's commands penetrated Vera. Slowly, her sobbing, rocking, swaying and foot-stamping ceased. Shame replaced her grief. Mrs Carew sighed with relief. Vera took her weight off Mrs Carew. Mr Vincent and his child returned to the living room.

'Vera, honestly!' Mrs Semple scolded.

Mrs Carew said, 'I think we should put away Hilda's things now, before the undertaker arrives.'

'Yes,' Mrs Semple agreed. 'Gordon says he can't face it. There's her jewellery. We should make sure it's safely locked away. Vera, you come with us. Collect the laundry from the bathroom. Take it over to our place for washing.'

'Yes ma'am,' Vera murmured, and rose to follow the two women.

In the bedroom, the green curtains were now drawn. Mrs Vincent's corpse lay straight and immobile on the bed. The women paused at the sight, but quickened by resolve, Mrs Semple and Mrs Carew moved deeper into the room. Mrs Carew opened the wardrobe, and began to empty the contents. Mrs Semple searched the vanity table. It was left to Vera to make her way to the bathroom, but she stood rooted to the spot. An immense dread possessed her. It emanated from her and filled the room. In Mrs Vincent's corpse, Vera could see an image of her own future death. It aroused her memories of other deaths.

Mrs Carew and Mrs Semple watched, hypnotised by the drugged expression on Vera's face as she moved like a sleepwalker towards Mrs Vincent. Vera bent over the corpse and placed her face close to Mrs

Vincent's as if to place a kiss on her cheek and she said in awe and reverence: 'Mrs Vincent ma'am, I ask you to blow a good breeze on me and my family ma'am. I begging you to blow a very good breeze on us ma'am.'

NOTES ON CONTRIBUTORS

OPAL PALMER ADISA (Jamaica, born 1954) is a poet and playwright as well as an accomplished story writer. She has lived for some years in the USA where she has taught at San Francisco State University and University of California, Berkeley. She has published two books of poems, *traveling women*, 1989; *Market Woman*, 1979; a children's book, *Pina, The Many-Eyed Fruit*, 1985; and the collection that 'Duppy Get Her' is taken from, *Bake-Face and Other Guava Stories* (Kelsey Street Press, 1986).

F. B. ANDRÉ (Trinidad, born 1955) lives in Canada, where his work has appeared in such journals as *The New Quarterly* and *West Coast Review*.

JAMES BERRY (Jamaica, born 1924) spent his early years in a small Jamaican village but went to the UK in 1948. He is best known as a poet – his latest collection, *When I Dance* (Hamish Hamilton, 1988) won the *Signal Prize for Poetry* in 1989. His other poetry includes *Chain of Days* (OUP, 1985), and he has also edited important anthologies of black British writing, most notably *News for Babylon* (Chatto, 1984), and published collections of stories like *A Thief in the Village* (Hamish Hamilton, 1987) which won the US Library Award, the Coretta Luther King Honor Award, and the *Smarties Prize*.

NEIL BISSOONDATH(Trinidad, born 1955) emigrated to Canada in 1973. He worked as a teacher for a while but with the success of his collection of stories *Digging up the Mountains* (Penguin, 1986), from which his story 'Insecurity' is taken, he became a full-time writer. He published a much-praised novel, *A Casual Brutality* (Minerva), in 1988.

WAYNE BROWN (Trinidad, born 1944) won the Commonwealth Prize for his collection of poems *On the Coast*. He has written a major biography of the Jamaican sculptor Edna Manley, and edited a university edition of Derek Walcott's poetry. A second collection of poems, *Voyages*, and a collection of stories *The Child of the Sea* – from which 'Independence Day' is taken – are to be published in 1990 by Inprint Caribbean. He now lectures at the University of the West Indies and writes for the *Trinidad Express*.

HAZEL D. CAMPBELL (Jamaica) is a Creative Productions Consultant and an increasingly well-known Caribbean writer. With Savacou Co-operative she has published two collections of stories: *The Rag Doll* (1978) and *Woman's Tongue* (1985), from which 'The Thursday Wife' comes. In 1989, she published a new series of stories for UNESCO.

FAUSTIN CHARLES (Trinidad, born 1944) grew up in Trinidad but left to study in the UK in 1962. He made his reputation as a poet but has also written two novels, a book of short stories and a children's book. His most recent publications are the collection of poems *Days and Nights in the Magic Forest* (Bogle L'Overture, 1986) and his acclaimed novel *The Black Magic Man of Brixton* (Karnak House, 1985).

WILLI CHEN (Trinidad) is one of the first writers to emerge from the Chinese-West Indian community. He spent an itinerant childhood, travelling round Trinidad as his shopkeeper parents moved from district to district trying to establish themselves. Best known as a painter and sculptor, Willi Chen started writing quite late in life but gained immediate success with his plays, poems and stories. His stories have recently been collected in *King of the Carnival* (Hansib, 1988).

CYRIL DABYDEEN (Guyana, born 1945) made his name as a poet in Guyana, winning several prestigious prizes in the 1960s. He moved to Canada in 1970 and teaches at Algonquin College and University of Ottawa. His recent work includes the poetry collections *Islands Lovelier Than a Vision* (Peepal Tree Press, 1986), *To Monkey Jungle* (Third Eye Press, 1989) *Selected Poems* (Mosaic Press, 1990), a novel, *Dark Swirl* (Peepal Press, 1989), and a book of short stories – from which 'Mammita's Garden Cove' is taken – *Still Close to the Island* (Commoners' Publishing, Ottawa, 1980).

ZOILA ELLIS (Belize, born 1957) has always, except for periods of study at the University of the West Indies and Sussex University, lived in Belize, where she works as a lawyer. The story in this anthology, 'White Christmas an' Pink Jungle', is taken from her first collection *On Heroes, Lizards and Passions* (Cubola Productions, Belize, 1988).

LORNA GOODISON (Jamaica, born 1947) trained as a painter at the Jamaica School of Art and in New York. Best known as a poet of great power and presence – she has published three collections, *Tamarind Season* (Institute of Jamaica Publications, 1980), *I Am Becoming My Mother* (New Beacon, 1986) and *Heartease* (New Beacon, 1988) – she has been Writer-in-Residence at the University of the West Indies and at Radcliffe College, Massachusetts. Her story 'Bella Makes Life' is from *Baby Mother and the King of Swords* to be published by Longman in 1990.

CLYDE HOSEIN (Trinidad, born 1940) lived for a while in Britain but returned to Trinidad in 1963, where he worked as a journalist and broadcaster. In 1972 he emigrated to Canada and it was there that he wrote his first collection of stories, *The Killing of Nelson John* (London Magazine Editions, 1980).

AMRYL JOHNSON (Trinidad) spent her early childhood in Trinidad but emigrated to Britain when she was eleven. In recent years she has done much teaching of creative writing but has also spent more and more time back in the Caribbean. She is best known as a poet, her collection *Long Road to Nowhere* (Virago, 1985) winning wide acclaim. She has also published *Sequins for a Ragged Hem* (Virago, 1988), an autobiographical essay exploring the tensions of her sense of dual identity sparked off by one of her return journeys 'home'. A collection of short stories is due for publication soon.

JAMAICA KINCAID (Antigua) grew up in Antigua's capital, St John's, though she now lives in the USA. 'My Mother' is from her much-acclaimed collection of stories *At the Bottom of the River* (Farrar, Straus and Giroux, 1984).This was followed by a novel, *Annie John* (1985), and a brilliant critique of post-colonial 'realities' in the Caribbean, *A Small Place* (Farrar, Straus and Giroux, 1988).

JOHN ROBERT LEE (St Lucia, born 1948) is a librarian in St Lucia. Perhaps best known as a poet – he has published three collections, *Vocation* (1975), *Dread Season* (1978) *The Prodigal* (1983), *Possessions* (1984) and *Saint Lucian* (1988). He has also published his distinctive stories in many journals and anthologies.

EARL LOVELACE (Trinidad, born 1935) has always lived and worked in Trinidad, being at different times a teacher, an agricultural officer and a journalist. He is Writer-in-Residence at the University of the West Indies. He has published four novels, most recently the superb *The Wine of Astonishment* (Heinemann, 1982); a collection of plays, *Jestina's Calypso* (Heinemann, 1984); and the collection of stories that 'Shoemaker Arnold' is taken from, *A Brief Conversion* (Heinemann, 1988).

IAN McDONALD (Trinidad, born 1933) has lived in Guyana for most of his working life, where he is a director of the Guyana Sugar Corporation. A man of wide literary talents, he published a classic novel of Caribbean childhood, *The Hummingbird Tree*, in 1966. He recently brought out a much-admired collection of poems, *Mercy Ward* (Peterloo Press), and he edits the Guyanese cultural journal *Kyk-Over-Al*. He has also published plays and short stories and writes regular radio commentaries.

EARL McKENZIE (Jamaica, born 1943) teaches at Church Teachers' College in Jamaica. A collection of his stories, *A Boy Named Ossie*, will be published by Heinemann in 1991.

ROOPLALL MONAR (Guyana, born 1947) grew up on a sugar estate in Guyana and has worked as a teacher, an estate book-keeper, a journalist and a healer. 'Bahadur' is from his fine collection of stories *Backdam People*, (Peepal Tree Press, 1985). The same publisher brought out a collection of his poems, *Koker*, in 1987 and a novel, *Janjhat* (1989). A second collection of stories, *High House and Radio* is due mid-1990.

VELMA POLLARD (Jamaica, born 1937) is a lecturer in the School of Education, University of the West Indies in Kingston. She has published a collection of poems, *Crown Point* (Peepal Tree Press, 1988), and a volume of short stories, *Considering Women*, from which 'My Mother' is taken (Women's Press, 1989).

LAWRENCE SCOTT (Trinidad) resident London: teaches literature at a Sixth Form College. Winner of the Tom Gallon Award (1986). Published: *Trinidad & Tobago Review*, *Chelsea (N.Y.)*, *The Pen*, *Winter's Tales*. First novel and collection of stories to be published.

OLIVE SENIOR (Jamaica, born 1941) grew up in rural Jamaica and many of her stories reflect that experience. She has been editor of the *Jamaica Journal* for several years. In 1985 she published a collection of poems, *Talking of Trees* (Calabash Publications, Kingston), and a book of short stories, *Summer Lightning* (Longman, 1986), which won the Commonwealth Literature Prize. 'The Two Grandmothers', is published in *Arrival of the Snake Woman and other stories* (Longman, 1989).

JAN SHINEBOURNE (Guyana, born 1947) is a novelist and short story writer. She has published two novels, *Timepiece* (1986) and *The Last English Plantation* (1989), both from the excellent Peepal Tree Press. She presently lives in London.

Note: Where authors' dates of birth are known they have been included. Several writers declined to provide that information on the grounds that it was irrelevant.